America's Heartland

Best of the Best from

Mid-America

Cookbook

Selected Recipes from the
Favorite Cookbooks of
MISSOURI, ARKANSAS, and OKLAHOMA

LAKE OF THE OZARKS CVB

The Ozarks are a physiographic, geologic, and cultural highland region of the central United States. It covers much of the south half of Missouri and an extensive portion of northwest and north-central Arkansas. The region also extends westward into northeast Oklahoma. Recreational areas are abundant in the Ozarks due to its large number of rivers, lakes, forests, and wilderness areas.

Best of the Best from
Mid-America
Cookbook

Selected Recipes from the
Favorite Cookbooks of
MISSOURI, ARKANSAS, and OKLAHOMA

EDITED BY

Gwen McKee

AND

Barbara Moseley

QUAIL RIDGE PRESS

Preserving America's Food Heritage

América's Heartland

Library of Congress Cataloging-in-Publication Data

Best of the best from Mid-America cookbook : selected recipes from the favorite
 cookbooks of Missouri, Arkansas, and Oklahoma / edited by Gwen McKee
 and Barbara Moseley. — 1st ed.
     p. cm..— (Best of the best regional cookbook series)
  ISBN-13: 978-1-934193-36-5
  ISBN-10: 1-934193-36-4
     1. Cookery. 2. Cookery–Missouri. 3. Cookery–Arkansas. 4. Cookery-
 Oklahoma. I. McKee, Gwen. II. Moseley, Barbara.
     TX714.B445 2010
     641.5973–dc22

                                               2010019578

ISBN-13: 978-1-934193-36-5 • ISBN-10: 1-934193-36-4
Book design by Cyndi Clark
Cover photo by Greg Campbell • Illustrated by Tupper England

Printed in Canada
First edition, December 2010
On the cover: Lemon Chicken for the Grill, page 175

QUAIL RIDGE PRESS
P. O. Box 123 • Brandon, MS 39043
info@quailridge.com • www.quailridge.com

Contents

ARKANSAS DEPT. OF PARKS & TOURISM

The Ozark Folk Center, a living history state park located in scenic Mountain View, Arkansas, is dedicated to preserving Ozark cultural heritage and tradition. Self-reliance, ingenuity, and a strong work ethic, together with the joy of sharing stories, dance, and song, is presented to the public through live demonstrations and hands-on exhibits.

Quest for the Best Regional Cooking

The states that fall into the Mid-America region of our country, Oklahoma, Arkansas, and Missouri, are truly about as geographically centered as you can get. In a sense, they are border states, not of the country, but border states of regions within our country. Missouri is considered mid-west, Oklahoma leans west, and Arkansas is surely southern!

We traveled in all directions in these states, and found a great variety of hometown good cookin' everywhere we went. In this book you get a sampling of many types of cuisine. You can have Tortilla Wagonwheels, Red Beans and Rice, or a One Dish Pork Chop Meal. Breakfast can be as diversified as Butch's Rancher's Omelette, Orange Streusel Muffins, and Ham Red Eye Gravy . . . and don't be afraid to serve them all together. With desserts the likes of Missouri Upside Down Cake, Mammy's Strawberry Shortcake, or Aunt Susan's Red Earth Cake, you're going to find recipes that appeal to just about anybody's tastebuds.

Traveling to every state in the United States in search of the best cookbooks and recipes took Barbara and me the better part of 27 years. What started in our home state of Mississippi with one cookbook, grew to include our neighboring states, then as each one neared completion, we reached out farther and farther away from home to explore the cuisines of states far and wide. The experience has been one that has enabled us to bring home each new state's recipes to become ours forever.

But nothing seems so special and dear as when you share it with others who you know will enjoy it as much as you do. Our BEST OF THE BEST STATE COOKBOOKS feature chosen favorite recipes that we are proud to have brought from each state home to you, wherever you are. I wish we could introduce you to the many people we have met in every state who were proud of their cooking heritage and eager to show us just how good their recipes were, and are! Sometimes it was a particular local ingredient, or the way they kneaded the dough, or

browned the flour, or marinated the meat, or maybe a secret method they used to make something particularly unique to their way of cooking. It has truly been a delicious experience!

We are grateful to all the contributing cookbooks who have chosen favorite recipes from their cookbooks for this special regional BEST OF THE BEST cookbook. We are proud to include photos and facts and history along with the recipes that all take you to this beautiful region of our country where north meets south and east meets west. Take it from us, Mid-America serves it all up deliciously.

Gwen McKee

Gwen McKee and Barbara Moseley, editors of
BEST OF THE BEST STATE COOKBOOK SERIES

Beverages and Appetizers

WWW.WIKIPEDIA.ORG

For more than three decades, Route 66 was America's main east-west artery, pointing the nation toward all the promise that California seemed to hold. John Steinbeck dubbed it "The Mother Road." It has been immortalized in song and word. Route 66 is part of the American Dream and road tripping the ultimate expression of freedom. In Oklahoma, virtually all 400 miles of the route remain intact. The Oklahoma Route 66 Museum in Clinton is the home of special treasures collected from along the route.

Cranberry Tea

1 quart water
1 cup red hots

1 cup sugar
12–15 whole cloves

Boil together and set aside.

3 quarts water
1 small can frozen orange
  juice

2 quarts cranberry cocktail
1 small can frozen lemonade

Mix above ingredients together. Then mix with first mixture. Serve hot or cold.

Lavender and Lace (Missouri)

Holiday Cider

1 medium orange
1½ teaspoons whole cloves
1 gallon apple cider or
  juice

¾ cup cinnamon candies
  (red)
2 (3-inch) cinnamon sticks

Pour cider and candy into Dutch oven or large pot and place over medium heat. Cook slowly until candy is dissolved and mixture is well heated. Pour cider mixture into heat-proof punch bowl and add cloves, orange wedges, and cinnamon. Makes 1 gallon.

Southwest Cookin' (Arkansas)

Smoothie

1 cup ice
1 cup skim milk
½ cup frozen strawberries
½ banana

1 (3-ounce) scoop low-fat
  vanilla frozen yogurt
  (1 gram per 100 calories)

Combine all ingredients in blender for approximately 30 seconds. Serves 6.

Eat To Your Heart's Content! (Arkansas)

Orange Mint

It is my honest conviction that having this recipe should be a requirement, and that it should be issued when your social security number is given.

2½ cups water
2 cups sugar
Juice of 2 oranges and
grated rind of both

Juice of 6 lemons and grated
rind of 2
2 handfuls fresh mint leaves

Make a simple syrup of the sugar and water by boiling them together for 10 minutes. Add the juice of the fruits and the grated rind of the oranges and lemons. Pour this over the mint leaves, which have been well-washed. (I like to bruise a few of the leaves so that the flavor is more pronounced.) Cover tightly and let this brew for several hours. Strain through a sieve, then through one thickness of cheesecloth.

This makes one quart of rich juice, which may be kept in the refrigerator indefinitely.

To serve, fill tall glasses with finely powdered ice and pour ¼ cup (4 tablespoons) of this juice over the snow-like ice, then finish filling the glass with either ginger ale or cold water.

Long Lost Recipes of Aunt Susan (Oklahoma)

Hurricane Punch

1 large can Hawaiian Punch
1 (12-ounce) can frozen
orange juice
1 (6-ounce) can frozen
lemonade

¾ cup sugar
4 ounces rum per glass
Cherries
Orange slices

In large bowl, mix punch, orange juice, lemonade, and sugar. Fill 16-ounce glasses with crushed ice and add 4 ounces rum per glass. Fill glasses with punch. Garnish with cherries and orange slices. Serves 4-6.

Nibbles Cooks Cajun (Arkansas)

Vegetable Dip

This is very good with raw cauliflower plus any other raw vegetables.

1 cup mayonnaise or
  Miracle Whip
½ cup sour cream
¼ teaspoon salt
1 tablespoon chopped onion
1 tablespoon chopped parsley

2 tablespoons capers
½ teaspoon curry powder
1½ teaspoons lemon juice
1 tablespoon Worcestershire
1 tablespoon salad
  seasonings

Mix in blender. (Sometimes it is hard to find the capers, but it is good without them.)

A Collection of Recipes from the Best Cooks in the Midwest (Missouri)

Fun Veggies

Kids love them.

1 cup instant potato flakes
½ cup grated Parmesan
  cheese
½ teaspoon celery salt
¼ cup melted margarine or
  butter buds

¼ teaspoon garlic powder
Raw zucchini, green peppers,
  broccoli, cauliflower,
  mushrooms
2 eggs, or egg beaters

Combine first 5 ingredients. Dip vegetables in egg; coat with potato flakes mixture. Bake at 400° for 25 minutes. Serve with ranch-style dip.

Cooking A+ Recipes (Oklahoma)

Dilly Garden Dip

1½ cups low-fat cottage
  cheese
1 tablespoon lemon juice
2 tablespoons shredded
  carrot
1 tablespoon sliced green
  onions

1 tablespoon chopped fresh
  parsley
½ teaspoon fresh dill,
  or ½ teaspoon dill weed
Dash of pepper
1 tablespoon Beau Monde
  Seasoning

In a blender combine cottage cheese and lemon juice. Blend for 3–5 minutes at medium speed. Stir in remaining ingredients and refrigerate overnight. Serve with crackers or veggies. Makes 1½ cups.

Eat To Your Heart's Content! (Arkansas)

Spinach Dip

1 (16-ounce) carton (2%)
  low-fat cottage cheese
2 tablespoons skim milk
3 tablespoons lemon juice
1 (8-ounce) can water
  chestnuts, drained, chopped
  fine

1 package Knorr Vegetable
  Soup Mix
½ cup finely chopped onion
1 (10-ounce) package frozen
  spinach, thawed and well
  drained

Blend cottage cheese, milk, and lemon juice in blender until smooth. Add remaining ingredients and stir well. Serve with raw vegetables. Yields 3 cups (24 servings).

Take It to Heart (Arkansas)

Dairy Dip with Parmesan Potato Wedges

Crunchy, flavorful potatoes with a smooth rich dip.

2 cups cottage cheese
½ cup blue cheese, crumbled
½ cup sour cream
2 tablespoons lemon juice
1 teaspoon Worcestershire
2 tablespoons green onions, sliced

Blend all ingredients until almost smooth. Chill. Serve as a dip with Parmesan Potato Wedges. Makes 3 cups.

PARMESAN POTATO WEDGES:

2 cups puffed rice cereal, crushed
¼ cup grated Parmesan cheese
1 teaspoon salt
1 teaspoon paprika
6 baking potatoes
3 tablespoons butter or margarine, melted

Mix crushed puffed rice, Parmesan cheese, salt, and paprika. Scrub, dry, and cut potatoes into wedges. Dip each wedge into melted butter, then roll in rice coating. Place wedges on a buttered 15x10x1-inch pan and bake at 425° for 15 minutes. Makes 8 servings.

Home for the Holidays (Arkansas)

Chipped Beef Dip

2 (8-ounce) packages cream cheese, softened
1 (8-ounce) carton sour cream
1 teaspoon milk
1 banana pepper or 1 bell pepper, minced
½ cup finely chopped onion
2 (2½-ounce) packages smoked beef
½ jalapeño pepper, seeds removed, finely chopped

Cut beef in fine strips, then chop. Mix all ingredients together and pour into large pie plate. Bake at 350° for 45 minutes. Chopped nuts may be sprinkled on top. Serve hot. Best when served with nacho cheese tortilla chips.

The Farmer's Daughters (Arkansas)

Layered Dip

1 (8-ounce) carton sour cream
1 tablespoon taco seasoning
  mix (½ package)
1 (16-ounce) can refried beans
1 (6-ounce) carton avocado
  dip
1 (4½-ounce) can chopped
  ripe olives
2 large tomatoes, diced
1 onion or 1 bunch green
  onions
1 (4-ounce) can chopped
  green chiles
1½ cups (or more) shredded
  cheese

Combine sour cream and taco seasoning mix, then layer in 9x13-inch pan in order given. Needs to sit overnight or several hours. Remove from refrigerator about 30 minutes before serving. Serve with corn chips.

Thank Heaven for Home Made Cooks (Oklahoma)

Oklahoma Caviar Dip

2 (16-ounce) cans black-eyed
  peas, drained
1 (16-ounce) can white
  hominy, drained
2 medium tomatoes,
  chopped
3 green onions, chopped
2 jalapeño peppers, seeds
  removed, chopped
1¼ cups chopped onions
1 cup finely chopped parsley
1 clove garlic, minced
1 (8-ounce) bottle of Italian
  salad dressing

Combine peas, hominy, tomatoes, green onions, jalapeño peppers, onions, parsley, and garlic in bowl; mix well. Combine with salad dressing in serving bowl; mix well. Chill in refrigerator for 2 hours. Serve with large corn chips. May process half the pea mixture in blender for smoother consistency, if desired. Yields 12 servings.

The Pioneer Chef (Oklahoma)

Sooner Salsa

A quick and easy salsa!

**1 (16-ounce) can stewed
  tomatoes**
4 medium tomatoes, chopped
**3 small jalapeño peppers,
  seeded, chopped**

⅓ cup chopped onion
½ teaspoon salt
½ teaspoon cayenne pepper

Combine tomatoes, peppers, and onion in food processor and process until desired consistency. Add salt and cayenne pepper; process again to mix. Store in refrigerator.

Note: With jalapeños—keep as many or as few seeds as you wish; the more seeds, the hotter the salsa. Yields 4 cups.

Cafe Oklahoma (Oklahoma)

WIKIPEDIA.ORG

The site of the town of Kingfisher, Oklahoma, is located along the starting line of the famous Oklahoma 1889 Land Run. The town's Centennial Brick Wall near the county courthouse honors those settlers who made the run. The land run started at high noon on April 22, 1889, with an estimated 50,000 people lined up for their piece of the available two million acres. A number of the individuals who participated in the run entered early and hid out until the legal time of entry to lay quick claim to some of the most choice homesteads. These people came to be identified as "sooners." This led to hundreds of legal contests that arose and were decided first at local land offices and eventually by the U.S. Department of the Interior. The settlers who entered the territory at the legally appointed time were known as "boomers."

Roast Garlic Spread

2 heads whole garlic
4 sprigs fresh thyme
½ teaspoon fresh rosemary
2 cups grated Monterey Jack
  cheese

2–4 tablespoons olive oil
Coarse-ground black pepper
  to taste
Pink and green peppercorns
  for garnish

Preheat oven to 350°. Cut heads of garlic in half. Place 2 sprigs fresh thyme and ¼ teaspoon fresh rosemary between garlic halves. Wrap garlic in 2 thicknesses of aluminum foil and place in oven for 30 minutes. Remove from oven, unwrap, and let cool. Peel garlic.

Place grated cheese and herb-roasted garlic in a food processor and process briefly. Add ground pepper and 2 tablespoons olive oil. Process until smooth and creamy, adding more olive oil, if necessary. Garnish with pink and green peppercorns.

Serve in a crock or bowl alongside toasted French or sourdough bread or crackers. This spread is also excellent to brush on grilled lamb chops. Makes 2 cups.

Recipe by Californos
Kansas City Cuisine (Missouri)

Cheese and Bacon Spread

1 pound Hoffman's Super
  Sharp Soft Cheddar Cheese
16 slices crisp bacon,
  crumbled
1 teaspoon salt

12 green onions, chopped
  (include tops)
1 cup slivered almonds,
  toasted
2 cups mayonnaise

Grate cheese. Mix all ingredients in order given. Serve on Ritz Crackers or sesame Melba rounds. Keeps for days. Also good cooked in scrambled eggs.

Southern Accent (Arkansas)

Crabmeat Mold

I've been making this for more than a decade. No one ever seems to get tired of it. I like it best made with good, fresh crabmeat, but it's also tasty made with frozen snow crab (which has the advantages of not having to be picked over to remove shell), and with the less expensive imitation crab, available at most seafood counters and in some freezer cases. The original recipe used cream cheese and mayonnaise. I've changed it to the lower-fat Neufchatel cheese.

1½ cups crabmeat
  (canned, fresh or frozen)
½ can cream of
  mushroom soup
8 ounces Neufchatel cheese

1 envelope plain gelatin
2 tablespoons cold water
2 tablespoons minced onion
½ cup light salad dressing
½ cup chopped celery

Pick over the crabmeat, if necessary, to get rid of the shell bits. In a small saucepan put the soup and cheese, stirring over medium heat until they are mixed.

Soften the gelatin in 2 tablespoons cold water. Mix the gelatin, onion, dressing, celery, and crabmeat into the soup and cheese mixture. Pour into an oiled mold. Chill until set, at least 4 hours.

To serve, unmold on a bed of endive lettuce and serve with crackers. Makes about 3½ cups of spread.

Enjoying the Art of Southern Hospitality (Arkansas)

Missouri Crab Grass

If only real crab grass disappeared so quickly!

½ cup butter
½ cup chopped onion
1 (10-ounce) package frozen
  chopped spinach, cooked
  and drained

1 (7-ounce) can crabmeat,
  drained
¾ cup grated Parmesan
  cheese
Crackers

Sauté onion in butter. Stir in spinach, crabmeat, and cheese. Heat through. Serve in a chafing dish with crackers. Makes 3½ cups.

Sassafras! (Missouri)

Suzanne's Crab Appetizer

12 ounces cream cheese,
  softened
2 tablespoons Worcestershire
1 tablespoon lemon juice
2 tablespoons mayonnaise
1 small onion, grated

Dash of garlic salt
1 bottle Heinz Chili Sauce
1 (6½-ounce) can crab,
  drained
Parsley

Mix cream cheese, Worcestershire, lemon juice, mayonnaise, onion, and garlic salt; spread on shallow plate. Pour chili sauce over this mixture. Spread crab over chili sauce. Garnish with parsley. Serve with snack crackers.

Sooner Sampler (Oklahoma)

Salmon Party Log

1 (14¾-ounce) can Honey
  Boy Red Salmon
1 (8-ounce) package cream
  cheese, softened
1 tablespoon lemon juice
2 teaspoons grated onion
2 teaspoons horseradish

¼ teaspoon liquid smoke
  (optional)
¼ teaspoon salt
3 drops of bottled hot pepper
  sauce (optional)
⅓ cup chopped pecans
1 cup parsley flakes

Drain and flake salmon. If desired, remove skin and bones. Combine salmon, cream cheese, lemon juice, onion, horseradish, liquid smoke, salt, and hot pepper sauce. Mix well. Chill. Shape into log and roll in mixture of pecans and parsley flakes. Serve as a spread with crisp crackers. Makes 2½ cups.

Shattuck Community Cookbook (Oklahoma)

At Rogers State College in Claremore, Oklahoma, the Lynn Riggs Memorial honors the author of the 1931 play, *Green Grow the Lilacs* on which the musical "Oklahoma!" is based.

Spinach Cheese Squares

4 tablespoons butter
3 eggs
1 cup flour
1 cup milk
1 teaspoon salt
1 teaspoon baking powder

1 pound sharp cheese,
    grated
1 medium onion, grated
2 packages chopped, frozen
    spinach, thawed and well
    drained

Preheat oven to 350°. Melt butter in 9x13x2-inch pan in oven; remove. In mixing bowl, beat eggs, flour, milk, salt, and baking powder; mix well. Add grated cheese, onion, and drained spinach. (If you run the spinach through a food processor, it makes a better texture.) Pour into pan; bake for 35 minutes. Cool thoroughly; cut in squares. This freezes well.

The Bonneville House Presents (Arkansas)

Mushroom Squares

6 slices bread (trim crusts
    off and cut in quarters)
Butter
4 slices bacon, fried and
    crumbled
1 small can mushrooms,
    chopped and drained

2 tablespoons grated Swiss
    cheese
2 tablespoons mayonnaise
1 tablespoon parsley flakes
⅛ teaspoon rosemary leaves
Few grains of salt

Spread butter on bread and place, butter side down, on baking sheet. Top with small amount of other ingredients mixed together. Bake at 400° for 5 minutes.

Delicious Reading (Missouri)

Missouri Pâté

A well-spiced pâté is a convenient dish for a country picnic or a festive buffet table. Cornichons add an elegant touch to this mildly flavored regional version of a classic.

4 tablespoons unsalted
  butter
½ pound fresh mushrooms,
  chopped
1 shallot, minced
2 tablespoons bourbon
1 tablespoon cognac
8 ounces liverwurst

2 (8-ounce) packages cream
  cheese, softened
1 teaspoon chopped fresh dill
1 teaspoon chopped parsley
2 teaspoons Dijon mustard
Salt and freshly ground
  pepper to taste

Melt butter in a skillet. Sauté mushrooms and shallot until soft. Stir in bourbon and cognac; cool.

Place mushroom mixture and remaining ingredients in a food processor or blender; process until very smooth. Transfer to a crock or serving bowl. Refrigerate for at least 24 hours before serving. Garnish with sprigs of fresh dill. Serve with party rye and cornichons. Serves 12.

Note: Cornichon is French for "gherkin." These pickles are slightly less salty then the average pickled gherkin, a good substitute.

Past & Repast (Missouri)

Champignons Marine
(Marinated)

1 pound mushrooms
  (medium)
½ cup olive oil
½ cup red wine
1 teaspoon crushed oregano

½ teaspoon crushed basil
1 teaspoon capers
2 cloves garlic, crushed
2 teaspoons seasoned salt
1 teaspoon parsley

Mix everything but mushrooms together. Add mushrooms. Chill at least 24 hours. Serve with toothpicks. Serves 8–10.

Nibbles Ooo La La (Arkansas)

Tortillitas

1 (8-ounce) package cream
  cheese, softened
1 cup sour cream
5 green onions, chopped
1 (4-ounce) can chopped
  green chiles

1–2 teaspoons garlic salt
6–7 (12-inch) flour tortillas
Picante sauce

Combine all ingredients except tortillas and picante sauce. Mix until
smooth. Cover 1 tortilla with about 3–4 tablespoons of the mixture,
spreading to the edges. Place another tortilla on top of this and spread
with mixture. Continue layering until tortillas and mixture are used,
ending with a tortilla on top. Chill thoroughly and cut into squares.
Spear with a toothpick and serve with picante sauce. Can be made a
day in advance. Makes 35–40 tortillitas.

Gateways (Missouri)

Tortilla Wagonwheels

2 (8-ounce) packages cream
  cheese, softened
3 tablespoons sour cream
1 (4-ounce) can mild
  chopped green chiles,
  drained
1 cup finely diced bell
  pepper
3 tablespoons chopped
  pimento

4 green onions, finely
  chopped
4 slices bacon, cooked and
  crumbled (may substitute
  real bacon bits)
Seasoning salt and garlic to
  taste
6–8 large flour tortillas

Mix cream cheese and sour cream until smooth. Add remaining ingredients, except tortillas; combine well. Spread mixture ⅛ inch thick on
each flat tortilla. Tightly roll each tortilla, jellyroll style. Chill. Cut in
½-inch slices and serve. Yields 7–8 dozen.

Cafe Oklahoma (Oklahoma)

Pepper Jelly

1 cup ground bell pepper
2 tablespoons ground hot
  peppers
1½ cups cider vinegar

6½ cups sugar
1 (6-ounce) bottle liquid
  fruit pectin
Green food coloring

Mix everything except fruit pectin in saucepan and bring to a boil. Let boil for 5 minutes, remove from heat and add fruit pectin, stirring until mixture starts to jell. Pour into sterile jelly jars and seal. (This is good spooned over a brick of cream cheese and served with ginger snaps.)

The Farmer's Daughters (Arkansas)

Monterey Cubes

8 eggs
½ cup flour
1 teaspoon baking powder
¾ teaspoon salt
12 ounces shredded
  Monterey Jack cheese

12 ounces cottage cheese
2 (4-ounce) cans mild green
  chiles, chopped and
  drained

In a large bowl, beat eggs until light, 4–5 minutes. Mix flour, baking powder and salt. Add to eggs and mix well. Fold in cheeses and chiles. Turn into greased 9x13-inch baking dish and bake at 325° for 40 minutes. Cut into one-inch cubes and serve warm. Makes 4 dozen.

Pulaski Heights Baptist Church Cookbook (Arkansas)

Cucumber Sandwiches I

1 large cucumber
1 (8-ounce) package cream
  cheese, softened
½ cup mayonnaise
1 tablespoon fresh lemon
  juice

3 small green onions and
  tops, finely chopped
Tabasco, to taste
Garlic salt, to taste
Seasoned pepper, to taste

Peel, seed, and coarsely grate cucumber. Wring out excess cucumber juice in clean cup towel. Cream cheese with mayonnaise and lemon juice. Add cucumber, onions, and seasonings to taste. Serve on party rye slices. Also good for dips. Keep refrigerated.

Prairie Harvest (Arkansas)

Ranch Seasoned Bagel Chips

2 bagels
2 egg whites, slightly beaten
1 (1-ounce) package dry
  ranch dressing mix

Butter flavor nonstick
  cooking spray

Preheat oven to 400°. Stand a bagel on its edge and carefully slice ¼-inch slices horizontally. Each bagel should make 5–6 slices. Spray a large baking sheet with butter-flavor nonstick cooking spray. Using a pastry brush, paint both sides of each bagel slice lightly with egg white; do not soak. Place slices on baking sheet and sprinkle with dry ranch dressing mix. Spray lightly with nonstick cooking spray and bake at 400° for 4–5 minutes. Turn each slice and bake another 5–6 minutes or until golden brown. Allow to cool and store in airtight container. Try different kinds of seasonings using the same method. Makes 4 servings.

Other Suggested Seasonings: Molly McButter Sour Cream; Molly McButter Bacon Flavor; salt and dill weed; salt and garlic.

Fat Free & Ultra Lowfat Recipes (Oklahoma)

Log Cabin Cheddar Sticks

An original recipe from the kitchens of Silver Dollar City, these are a favorite of the Log Hewers. To serve, arrange the sticks as if assembling a miniature log cabin and serve around your favorite party dip.

¼ cup soft butter
1 cup grated Cheddar cheese
¼ cup milk
¼ teaspoon salt
Dash of Tabasco

Dash of paprika
Dash of cayenne
¾ cup sifted flour
1½ cups fine, soft bread
  crumbs

Soften butter to a creamy state and blend in cheese, milk, salt, Tabasco, paprika, and cayenne. Combine flour and bread crumbs and add to mixture. Divide mixture in half and refrigerate overnight.

   After it's chilled, roll out half of the dough at a time between 2 pieces of wax paper until very thin. Work quickly. Take a knife or pastry wheel and cut into strips about 5 inches long and 1 inch wide. Place strips on cookie sheet and top with coarse salt or grated Parmesan cheese. Bake at 350° for about 15 minutes or until golden brown. This will make about 40 sticks.

Silver Dollar City's Recipes (Missouri)

Glazed Barbequed Salami

1 (1-pound) log salami
1 bottle sweet and sour
  sauce

¼ cup barbeque sauce
1 tablespoon Dijon mustard

Peel and score the salami, making large X's. Combine the remaining ingredients to make a sauce. Bake in a 275° oven for 1½ hours, basting frequently with sauce. This can be made ahead.

Serve at room temperature and slice thinly. Surround with cocktail tomatoes, parsley, party rye, and dollar rolls. Place bowl of sauce or mustard on the side. Serves 8.

From Generation to Generation (Missouri)

Cranberry Meatballs

An excellent blend of ingredients.

2 pounds ground beef
1 cup cornflake crumbs
⅓ cup dried parsley flakes
2 eggs
2 tablespoons soy sauce

¼ teaspoon pepper
½ teaspoon garlic powder
⅓ cup ketchup
2 tablespoons chopped onion

In a large bowl mix ground beef, crumbs, parsley, eggs, soy sauce, pepper, garlic powder, ketchup, and onion. Blend well and form into small balls. Brown in oven at 400° for 15 minutes. Pour off grease.

SAUCE:
1 (16-ounce) can jellied
  cranberry sauce
1 (12-ounce) bottle chili
  sauce

2 tablespoons brown sugar
1 tablespoon lemon juice

While meatballs are baking, combine cranberry sauce, chili sauce, brown sugar, and lemon juice. Cover drained meatballs with Sauce and bake uncovered at 300° for 15 minutes. Serve in chafing dish. Makes 80–90 meatballs.

Finely Tuned Foods (Missouri)

Sweet and Sour Meatballs

MEATBALLS:

1 pound ground beef
1 egg, beaten
¼ cup finely chopped onion

1¼ cups bread crumbs
1 teaspoon pepper
1 tablespoon parsley flakes

Mix ingredients together and form into bite-size meatballs. Brown in large skillet. Drain and put in baking dish.

SAUCE:

1 (16-ounce) jar apricot
  preserves

¾ cup hot barbecue sauce

Mix apricot preserves and barbecue sauce and pour over meatballs. Bake at 350°, uncovered, for 30 minutes. Serve hot in chafing dish.

Cookin' Along the Cotton Belt (Arkansas)

Frosted Ham Ball

½ pound cooked ham,
  finely ground
⅓ cup white raisins
1 tablespoon grated onion
¼ teaspoon curry powder

¼ cup mayonnaise
1 (3-ounce) package cream
  cheese, softened
1 tablespoon milk
Chopped parsley

Mix ham, raisins, onion, curry powder, and mayonnaise. Chill. Shape into ball. Whip cream cheese with milk. Frost Ham Ball. Roll in parsley. Chill. Serve with crackers.

Nibbles Fa La La (Arkansas)

Sausage-Cheese Balls

1 pound bulk sausage
¼ cup chopped onion
16 ounces sweet sauerkraut,
  drained well
4 ounces cream cheese,
  softened

1 cup plus 2 tablespoons
  bread crumbs, divided
Parsley flakes
½ cup flour
2 eggs
¼ cup milk

SAUCE:
1 cup mayonnaise
1 teaspoon mustard

Tabasco, if desired

Cook sausage and onion; drain and cool. Combine sauerkraut, cream cheese, 2 tablespoons bread crumbs, and parsley flakes. Add sausage to this; mix and refrigerate for 1 hour. Shape into 1- to 1½-inch balls. Roll balls in mixture of flour and remaining 1 cup bread crumbs. Dip balls in mixture of eggs and milk. Then dip back in flour mixture. Deep-fry for 2–3 minutes. Serve with Sauce.

Watonga Cheese Festival Cookbook 17th Edition (Oklahoma)

Sausage-Onion Snacks

As quick as can be.

1 pound bulk pork sausage
1 large onion, chopped
2 cups biscuit baking mix
¾ cup milk
2 eggs

1 tablespoon caraway or
  poppy seed·
1½ cups dairy sour cream
¼ teaspoon salt
Paprika

Grease a 13x9x2-inch baking pan. Cook sausage and onion over medium heat until browned. Drain. Mix biscuit mix, milk, and 1 egg together. Spread in baking pan. Sprinkle with caraway seeds. Top with sausage mixture. Mix sour cream, salt, and remaining egg. Pour evenly over sausage. Sprinkle with paprika. Bake uncovered at 350° until set, 25–30 minutes. Cut into rectangles. Serve warm. Makes 32 rectangles.

Finely Tuned Foods (Missouri)

Stuffed Bread

5–6 submarine or other hard
   crusted rolls
½ pound liverwurst
2 (8-ounce) packages cream
   cheese
¼ cup beer

1 tablespoon dry mustard
¼ cup chopped watercress
   (or spinach)
¼ cup chopped onion
¼ cup chopped radish

Heat oven to 350°. Slice off ends of rolls and scoop out as much of the inside as possible. Crumble or cube this bread and toast lightly in oven. Cut liverwurst into small cubes. Beat cream cheese until smooth and soft. Mix beer, mustard, and cream cheese. Add watercress or spinach, onion, and radish, and mix well. Add liverwurst and toss lightly.

Cool toasted crumbs to room temperature and stir into cheese mixture. Pack stuffing into bread shells. Wrap and chill at least 4 hours or overnight. Slice thin. Makes beautiful hors d'oeuvres to take on a boat or picnic.

Kitchen Prescriptions (Missouri)

The Anheuser-Bush brewery in downtown St. Louis, Missouri, is the nation's largest brewery since 1957. In 1860, Eberhard Anheuser, a prosperous German-born soap manufacturer, became owner of a small struggling brewery. Adolphus Busch, Anheuser's son-in-law, became partner in 1869, and became president when Anheuser died in 1880. Busch was the first U.S. brewer to use pasteurization to keep beer fresh, the first to use artificial refrigeration and refrigerated railroad cars, and the first to bottle beer extensively. In 1876, Busch introduced America's first national beer brand: Budweiser. The Brew House, the Clydesdale Stable, and the main office building have been designated National Historic Landmarks. The company now operates 12 breweries in the United States and 15 in other countries.

Puppy Chow – Dog Food
(Crispy Cereal Snack)

1 stick margarine
1 small bag chocolate chips
1 cup peanut butter

1 box Crispix cereal
1 box powdered sugar

Melt together the margarine, chocolate chips, and peanut butter; add Crispix and stir. Pour warm mixture and powdered sugar into a brown paper bag, close tightly, and shake to coat. Turn out on foil or wax paper. Spread out and stir around a little to cool. Put in large plastic container with a lid and shake often. Keeps well. If you want to make a big hit, buy a large dog dish to serve it in.

Lavender and Lace (Missouri)

Bread and Breakfast

U.S. NATIONAL PARK SERVICE

The Gateway Arch in St. Louis is an integral part of the Jefferson National Expansion Memorial, and reflects Missouri's role in the westward expansion of the United States during the nineteenth century. The "Gateway to the West" stands 630 feet tall, making it the tallest monument in the United States.

Buttermilk Biscuits

2 cups self-rising flour
Pinch of baking soda

3 tablespoons oil
¾ cup buttermilk

Mix all this together. Dough should be soft and sticky. Scrape out on a floured board. Now get your hands covered in flour and knead all that mess around and over till you have dough that is not sticky. Pat out till it's about a half-inch thick. (That is more or less, just depends on how thick you like biscuits.)

Cut the biscuits out with a biscuit cutter. Now you can buy a nice biscuit cutter or use an old cookie cutter, or a water glass. I use a little canned-milk can that has had one end cut off so it leaves a nice slick cuttin' surface, and some holes punched in the other end to let the air out. After you cut the biscuits out, get a glass pie pan or a cake pan or a cookie sheet or whatever. Don't make much difference as long as the oil won't run off the edges, cause I want you to pour enough oil in the pan to cover the bottom, and then take them biscuits and sop the top in oil, turn it over on its bottom and set it down.

Cook em about 20 minutes in a oven that is close to 375°. Now keep watchin' em cause when they get the shade of brown you like, they'll be done.

Ever recipe you have ever read will tell you to serve biscuits wrapped in a napkin or such and then put in a basket. Tell you a little secret. Reach in that oven, take the pan out and put 1 biscuit on everybody's plate and stick the rest back in the oven. Course you know to turn that sucker off! When everybody has lapped up that biscuit, go get em another one.

Biscuits is good with anything, anytime, but if you want a real treat, set that bucket of molasses and the peanut butter jar on the table. Let each one mix up about half & half of syrup & peanut butter. Talk about good! After you have made these biscuits a time or two, you'll sure chunk rocks at canned biscuits.

Sunday Go To Eatin' Cook Book (Arkansas)

Bake Ahead
Butter Cheese Biscuits

2 cups flour
3 teaspoons baking powder
½ teaspoon salt

½ cup butter
½ cup grated Cheddar cheese
¾ cup milk

Combine dry ingredients. Cut in butter to consistency of cornmeal. Add cheese and mix lightly. Stir in milk. Turn onto floured board and roll to ½-inch thickness. Cut with a biscuit cutter and place on ungreased cookie sheet. Bake at 400° for about 15 minutes. Brush with melted butter after baking.

Biscuits may be stored in plastic bag until time to serve.

Slice, butter and toast lightly. Wonderful when piled high with chicken salad. Biscuits freeze beautifully.

Silver Dollar City's Recipes (Missouri)

Yeast Rolls

2 cups warm water
2 packages active dry yeast
1 tablespoon salt
½ cup sugar
2 eggs, beaten

6 tablespoons oil or ½ cup
    margarine, melted
5½ cups sifted all-purpose
    flour

Mix ingredients in a large mixing bowl in order given. Mix thoroughly. Let rise until double in bulk in a warm place, bowl covered. Punch down and cool in refrigerator until needed. Make out into rolls at least 2 hours before using. Grease fingers with oil, pinch off a piece of dough about the size of a walnut, and place 2 of these in each hole of a greased muffin tin. Let rise 2 hours. Bake in a 400° oven for 12 minutes or until brown. Makes 3 dozen rolls.

Favorite Recipes from Associated Women for Harding (Arkansas)

Caraway Crescent Rolls

A "quickie" for busy days!

1 cup Rice Krispies, crushed
1 teaspoon salt
2 tablespoons caraway seeds

1 (8-ounce) package crescent
 refrigerator rolls
½ cup milk

Mix crushed cereal with salt and caraway seeds. Remove rolls from container and cut each triangle in half to make 2 small triangles. Dip each piece of roll dough in milk, then in dry cereal mixture. Starting with narrow side, roll up dough and place on a cookie sheet. Bake rolls in preheated oven 450° for 10–12 minutes. Serve warm. Yields 16.

The Cook Book (Missouri)

Speedy Rolls and Bread

This recipe is from St. Mary's School Hot Lunch recipe book. These were baked during the 1950s, '60s, and '70s.

2 (1-ounce) cakes or 2
 packages dry yeast
1 pint water, lukewarm
½ cup sugar
¾ cup butter, shortening or
 oil, softened or melted

1¾ quarts flour
½ cup dry milk
1 tablespoon salt

Put yeast and lukewarm water in mixing bowl; add sugar. Let set until dissolved, then add melted butter. Add combined flour, dry milk, and salt, using dough hook (if by hand, knead well). Let dough rise once and knead before shaping. Shape into rolls or loaves and let rise double. Bake rolls at 425° for 7–12 minutes. Bake bread at 325° for 30–45 minutes.

Note: For cinnamon rolls, roll dough into a rectangle. Brush with melted butter. Sprinkle with sugar and cinnamon. Roll and slice. Let rise double. Bake and add a glaze.

Cooking A+ Recipes (Oklahoma)

 Lambert's Cafe in Sikeston, Missouri, is "Home of the Throwed Rolls." They literaly throw you a roll when you ask for one!

Italian French Bread

This is wonderful with spaghetti, lasagna, or any Italian dish. Also goes great with grilled steak or grilled chicken.

1 loaf French bread, split
  lengthwise
1 stick margarine, softened
½ cup real mayonnaise
  (Hellmann's)
4 or 5 green onions, finely
  chopped

1 small can of black olives,
  sliced
4–5 ounces shredded
  mozzarella cheese

Divide ingredients in half and layer on each half of the bread in the order given above. Close bread together and wrap in foil and place in refrigerator overnight. When ready to bake, unwrap and discard foil. Open up the 2 halves and place on a Pam-sprayed cookie sheet and bake at 350° for 15–20 minutes uncovered. Slice and serve immediately. Yields 6–8 servings.

Betty Is Still "Winking" at Cooking (Arkansas)

Cheese Popovers

Crisp and a lovely dark golden color, these popovers make a delightful change from the usual breads served with barbecue.

Light oil for coating pan
4 large eggs
1 cup milk
1 cup all-purpose flour

½ teaspoon salt
1 cup grated sharp Cheddar
  cheese (do not pack cheese
  into the cup)

Preheat oven to 450°. Brush muffin tin or popover cups with oil. Place the pan in the oven to get piping hot while mixing the batter. Combine all the ingredients in a blender. Blend on medium; stop and scrape down the sides of the blender jar. Blend again at high speed until the batter is well mixed. Remove pan from the oven, close the oven door, and pour batter into the cups, filling each about ⅔ full. Return to the oven and bake 20 minutes. Reduce heat to 350° and bake another 20 minutes. If the popovers seem to be browning too deeply, bake only 15 minutes. Makes 12.

Quick Breads, Soups & Stews (Oklahoma)

Fancy Bread Sticks

½ cup butter
½ teaspoon dill seed
1½ teaspoons parsley
   flakes
1 tablespoon onion flakes

2 tablespoons grated Parmesan
   cheese
1 can Pillsbury Crescent
   Dinner Rolls

Melt butter in pan. Stir in herbs and cheese. Let stand 30 minutes. Shape each crescent triangle into a roll and twist, forming a bread stick. Brush with herbed butter. Bake at 425° for 12–15 minutes.

In Good Taste (Arkansas)

Bacon Spoon Bread

¾ cup cornmeal
1½ cups cold water
2 cups shredded sharp
   Cheddar cheese
¼ cup soft butter or
   margarine
2 cloves garlic, crushed

½ teaspoon salt
1 cup milk
4 egg yolks, well beaten
½ pound bacon, crisp-cooked
   and drained
4 egg whites, stiffly beaten

Combine cornmeal and water; cook, stirring constantly, until the consistency of mush. Remove from heat; add cheese, butter, garlic and salt. Stir to melt cheese. Gradually add milk. Stir in egg yolks. Crumble bacon, reserving some for garnish if desired, and add to cornmeal mixture. Fold in egg whites. Pour into greased 2-quart soufflé dish or casserole. Bake in slow 325° oven about 65 minutes or until done.

Spoon into warm dishes; top with butter and serve with spoon. Serves 6.

Bacon Spoon Bread is a hearty main dish soufflé that makes a simple supper with a salad and fruit. It is also good for a breakfast party.

Feasts of Eden (Arkansas)

Bread Soufflé

4 slices white bread
Butter
½ pound hoop cheese
½ teaspoon salt
1 teaspoon dry mustard

4 eggs
2½ cups milk
3 jalapeño peppers, chopped,
    peeled and seeds removed
Seasoned salt

Cut off crusts of bread and butter each slice. Grate cheese and mix salt and mustard. Beat the eggs and add milk. Butter soufflé dish and place 2 slices of bread on bottom. Top with half of cheese mixture, half the peppers and sprinkle with seasoned salt. Repeat. Pour egg and milk mixture over all.

Prepare this dish 6 hours ahead of time or let it stand in refrigerator overnight. Bake at 300° for 1½ hours. Yields 5–6 servings.

In Good Taste (Arkansas)

Corn Pone

This method was used in the late 1800s. Cornbread made with water instead of milk was often called Adam's Ale Bread. This is similar to the bread made by the Indians for the early settlers which was also shaped by hand.

Take 3 cups of cornmeal and sprinkle over it 1 teaspoon salt. Pour over the meal 1½ cups of boiling water, or enough to make a real stiff dough. Have an 8x10-inch bread pan "simply swimming" in grease. Shape the dough into a flat loaf by using your hands and pressing fingers into the dough, leaving long ridges on the top. Bake in a hot oven until brown around the edges. Serve with lots of butter.

Grandma's Ozark Legacy (Missouri)

Broccoli Cornbread

2 sticks butter
1 teaspoon dried or fresh
  onion, (optional)
2 (8½-ounce) boxes corn
  muffin mix

4 eggs
1 cup cottage cheese
1 (10-ounce) box frozen
  chopped broccoli

Melt butter in 9x13-inch pan. Mix all ingredients together. Spoon mixture into pan with melted butter.

Bake according to instructions on corn muffin box. (May need to bake longer.)

The Never Ending Season (Missouri)

Company's Comin' Cornbread

Dedicated to the Arkansas Sesquicentennial of 1986.

2 tablespoons shortening
1 cup buttermilk or sweet
  milk
2 eggs
2 tablespoons honey
½ cup chopped onion
1 small jar pimentos,
  drained
1 (17-ounce) can whole-
  kernel corn, drained

1 (4-ounce) can chopped
  green chile peppers or
  about ½ cup pickled
  peppers, chopped
1 cup yellow cornmeal
1 cup white flour
1 teaspoon salt
1 teaspoon baking soda
1 cup grated cheese

Place a 10- or 12-inch cast-iron (or heavy weight) skillet in oven with the 2 tablespoons shortening while preheating oven to 350°. Stir together liquid ingredients and combine with dry, reserving the cheese to fold in as the last step. When oven is preheated and skillet sizzling hot, pour mixture in and bake for 1 hour.

Arkansas Celebration Cookbook (Arkansas)

Jalapeño Cornbread

"Muy caliente!" they say in Spanish. This dish is hot, hot, hot! But great, if you're an aficionado of Mexican cuisine or just like super spicy foods. Whether you're planning a fiesta or simply want something to wake up a plate of pinto beans, try this zesty cornbread.

3 cups yellow cornmeal
1 cup cream-style corn
1 teaspoon sugar
2 teaspoons salt
1 cup chopped onion
1½ teaspoons baking
  powder

1 cup vegetable oil
3 eggs
1¾ cups sweet milk
½ cup chopped jalapeño
  peppers
1⅓ cups grated cheese

Mix all and pour into a 9x13-inch ungreased pan and bake in a preheated 350° oven for one hour.

Note: If you're not familiar with the jalapeño pepper, be forewarned: These hot green peppers are not for people with timid taste buds. And don't be fooled by a can marked "mild" jalapeño peppers. Even the "mild" variety can make your eyes water.

Pow Wow Chow (Oklahoma)

Spicy Cornbread Muffins

1½ cups yellow cornmeal
1 teaspoon baking soda
1 teaspoon sugar
½ teaspoon salt
2 egg whites

¼ cup picante sauce
¼ cup vegetable oil
1 (8-ounce) carton plain
  non-fat yogurt
Vegetable cooking spray

Combine first 4 ingredients in a large bowl. Make a well in center of mixture. Combine egg whites and next 3 ingredients; add to dry ingredients, stirring just until moistened. Spoon into muffin pans coated with cooking spray, filling ⅔ full.

Bake at 425° for 18–30 minutes. Remove from pans. Yields 1 dozen.

The Pink Lady...in the Kitchen (Arkansas)

Flower Pot Bread

A fun way to present the "staff of life."

1 package (1 tablespoon) active dry yeast	**1 teaspoon salt**
½ cup warm water (114°–120°)	**1 (13-ounce) can evaporated milk**
⅛ teaspoon ginger	**2 tablespoons vegetable oil**
3 tablespoons sugar	**4–4½ cups unsifted flour**
	Butter, melted

Season a 6-inch clay flower pot before first use by greasing well and baking 30 minutes at 350°. Cool and repeat seasoning procedure. Set pot aside to cool while preparing dough.

In a large mixing bowl, dissolve yeast in warm water. Blend in ginger and 1 tablespoon of the sugar. Let stand in a warm place until bubbly, about 15 minutes. Stir in the remaining 2 tablespoons sugar, salt, evaporated milk, and oil. Mix at low speed. Add flour, 1 cup at a time; beat well after each addition. The dough should be stiff, but too sticky to knead. Place dough in lightly oiled pot. Let rise in warm place until dough is 1½ inches over top of pot, about 60 minutes.

Preheat oven to 350°. Bake 60 minutes. (For smaller loaves, use two 4-inch pots and bake 40-45 minutes.) Crust will be very brown. Brush top with melted butter. Let cool 5-10 minutes and loosen crust around edge. Store in flower pot for freshness. Makes 1 loaf.

Sassafras! (Missouri)

KCINSIDER.COM

Fourteen exhibits in the Hallmark Visitors Center in Kansas City, Missouri, tell visitors the story of this world-famous greeting-card company—from its humble beginnings in 1910 by founder "Mr. J.C." Hall to the creation of the world-famous Hallmark greeting cards and Hallmark Keepsake Ornaments to the acclaimed Hallmark Hall of Fame television series.

Little Boy Blueberry Orange Bread

2 tablespoons butter
¼ cup boiling water
½ cup plus 2 tablespoons
  orange juice, divided
4 teaspoons grated orange
  rind, divided
1 egg
1 cup sugar

2 cups sifted flour
1 teaspoon baking powder
¼ teaspoon baking soda
½ teaspoon salt
1 cup fresh or frozen
  blueberries
2 tablespoons honey

Melt butter in boiling water in small bowl. Add ½ cup juice, and 3 teaspoons rind. Beat egg with sugar until light and fluffy. Add dry ingredients alternately with orange liquid, beating until smooth. Fold in berries. Bake in greased 9x5x3-inch pan at 325° for 1 hour and 10 minutes. Turn out onto rack. Mix 2 tablespoons orange juice, 1 teaspoon rind and 2 tablespoons honey. Spoon over hot loaf. Let stand until cool. Or frost with:

ORANGE GLAZE:

1½ teaspoons butter flavoring
1½ teaspoons almond
  flavoring

1½ teaspoons vanilla flavoring
¼ cup orange juice
⅓ cup sugar

Mix ingredients and use as glaze on warm bread.

Recipes from Missouri . . . With Love (Missouri)

Spicy Pineapple Zucchini Bread

3 eggs
1 cup oil
2 cups sugar
2 teaspoons vanilla
3 cups flour (or ½ cup
  wheat germ and
  2½ cups flour)
1 teaspoon salt
2 teaspoons baking soda

½ teaspoon baking powder
1½ teaspoons cinnamon
¾ teaspoon nutmeg
2 cups grated zucchini (skin
  and all, about 2 medium)
1 cup well-drained crushed
  pineapple
1 cup walnuts
1 cup raisins (optional)

Beat eggs, oil and sugar until thick and foamy; add vanilla, wheat germ, flour, salt, baking soda and baking powder, cinnamon, and nutmeg. Mix until smooth. Stir in by hand the zucchini, pineapple, walnuts, and raisins. Divide into 2 greased and floured large loaf pans. Bake at 350° about 1 hour or until toothpick comes out clean. Let cool 10 minutes, then turn out onto wire rack.

Betty "Winks" at Cooking (Arkansas)

Southwest Missouri Blueberry Cream Cheese Muffins

1 cup Missouri blueberries
2 cups flour, divided
¾ cup sugar
1½ teaspoons baking
  powder
3 ounces cream cheese

2 teaspoons lemon juice
2 teaspoons vanilla
½ cup milk
¼ cup butter, melted
2 eggs
Pinch of salt

Toss blueberries with 2 tablespoons flour; set aside. Combine remaining dry ingredients; set aside. With blade in food processor, blend cheese, lemon juice, vanilla, milk, and butter. Add eggs; pulse 4–5 times. Add flour; pulse 6 times. Stir in blueberries by hand. Fill greased muffin cups ⅔ full. Bake at 400° for 18–20 minutes.

The Never Ending Season (Missouri)

Blueberry Oatmeal Muffins

¾ cup unsweetened, frozen
  blueberries
1 cup quick-cooking oats
1 cup buttermilk
1 cup flour
¼ cup sugar

1 tablespoon baking powder
¼ teaspoon salt
⅛ teaspoon cinnamon
¼ cup egg substitute
¼ cup polyunsaturated oil

Thaw, rinse and drain blueberries. Combine oats and buttermilk; let stand for 5 minutes. Combine flour, sugar, baking powder, salt, and cinnamon in large bowl. Make well in center. Combine oat mixture, egg substitute, and oil; stir well. Add to center of dry ingredients and stir just until moistened. Gently stir in blueberries.

Spray muffin pan with vegetable spray. Fill cups ⅔ full. Bake in preheated 425° oven for 20 minutes or until browned. Yields 16 muffins.

Take It to Heart (Arkansas)

Pumpkin Apple Streusel Muffins

2 cups sugar
2½ cups flour
2 teaspoons cinnamon
½ teaspoon ginger
2 eggs, slightly beaten
1 cup pumpkin
½ cup vegetable oil

2 cups peeled and diced
  apples
1 teaspoon baking soda
¼ teaspoon salt
¼ teaspoon cloves
¼ teaspoon nutmeg

Mix dry ingredients in large bowl. Combine eggs, pumpkin, and oil; add to dry ingredients. Mix only until moistened. Stir in apples. Spoon into greased or paper-lined muffin tins, filling ¾ full. Sprinkle with Streusel Topping. Bake at 350° for 35–40 minutes or until toothpick comes out clean.

STREUSEL TOPPING:
2 tablespoons flour
¼ cup sugar

½ teaspoon cinnamon
4 teaspoons butter

Combine dry ingredients; cut in butter until mixture is crumbly.

Apples, Apples, Apples (Missouri)

Tumbleweeds

Delicious high-fiber muffins. . . .

3 egg whites
½ cup water
½ cup vegetable oil
2 cups low-fat buttermilk
2½ cups flour
2½ teaspoons baking soda
½ teaspoon salt
2½ teaspoons cinnamon

2 cups bran cereal (not flakes)
1 cup quick-cooking oats
1 cup oat bran hot cereal, dry
1 cup Sugar Twin or sugar
   substitute
4 bananas, mashed (optional)
1 cup raisins (optional)

In a small bowl, combine egg whites, water, oil, and buttermilk. Set aside. In a large bowl, sift together flour, baking soda, salt, and cinnamon and then add remaining dry ingredients and stir to mix. Add buttermilk mixture to dry ingredients and stir, just until moistened. Stir in mashed bananas and raisins, if desired. Spray muffin tins with non-stick cooking spray or line with paper cups. Fill ⅔ full and bake at 400° for 15–20 minutes or until golden brown. Yields 2 dozen.

Note: This recipe doubles nicely and batter stores well in refrigerator (before adding bananas and raisins).

Stir Ups (Oklahoma)

The final resting place of the great Apache warrior, Geronimo (June 16, 1829–February 17, 1909) is at Fort Sill, Oklahoma, in the Apache Indian Prisoner of War Cemetery. Geronimo was a prominent Native American leader and medicine man of the Chiricahua Apache who fought against Mexico and the United States and their expansion into Apache tribal lands for several decades during the Apache Wars. In his old age, Geronimo became a celebrity. He appeared at fairs, including the 1904 World's Fair in St. Louis, Missouri, and sold souvenirs and photographs of himself. He rode in President Theodore Roosevelt's 1905 inaugural parade.

LIBRARY OF CONGRESS

Orange Streusel Muffins

The true essence of orange was elusive, but after eight experiments, I finally caught it in a muffin. This lovely muffin and its variations are delicious with a cup of hot tea.

2 cups all-purpose flour
½ teaspoon salt
2 teaspoons baking powder
¼ cup sugar
Grated rind of 1 large orange
2 large eggs

½ cup orange juice
1 tablespoon lemon juice
½ cup milk
¼ cup butter or margarine,
    melted

Preheat oven to 425°. Brush 12 (2½-inch) muffin cups with melted butter or coat with vegetable spray. Combine the flour, salt, baking powder, sugar, and orange rind in a mixing bowl, blending thoroughly. In a separate bowl beat the eggs, orange juice, and lemon juice together. Add to the dry ingredients with the milk and melted butter, stirring rapidly with a rubber spatula until just moistened. Fill each muffin cup ¾ full. Top each muffin with about one tablespoon of Streusel. Bake muffins 20 minutes until lightly golden.

STREUSEL:

½ cup cold butter
½ cup all-purpose flour

½ cup sugar
Grated rind of 1 large orange

Place all ingredients for the Streusel in a food processor and whirl until the butter is thoroughly cut into the dry ingredients. The remainder of the Streusel may be placed in a covered container and frozen for future use.

Quick Breads, Soups & Stews (Oklahoma)

The "Berry-Best" Muffins

1 cup butter, softened
2 cups sugar
4 eggs
2 teaspoons vanilla
4 cups flour
4 teaspoons baking powder

1 teaspoon salt
1 cup milk
4–5½ cups fresh or frozen
 blueberries, blackberries,
 raspberries, or cranberries

Cream butter and sugar in large mixing bowl. Add eggs (one at a time) and vanilla. Blend thoroughly. Combine flour, baking powder, and salt. Alternately add flour mixture and milk to first mixture (the batter will be very thick). Blend well. Fold in berries. Grease muffin tins. (Because batter will need to expand over the rim, it is best to grease or oil muffin tin beyond rims of cups. You may use paper liners, but top of tin should still be oiled to allow for overage.) So that muffins will take on a mushroom shape, heap batter above rim of muffin tins. This will produce a beautiful shape. Sprinkle generously with sugar and bake in preheated 425° oven for 10 minutes. After 10 minutes of baking, turn oven temperature down to 375° and bake an additional 15 minutes until muffins are done in center and a rich golden brown on top. Yields 16–18 muffins.

Stir Ups (Oklahoma)

Apple Biscuit Coffee Cake

2 tablespoons butter or margarine
2 cooking apples, peeled and sliced
¼ cup raisins
1 can refrigerated ready-to-bake biscuits

¼ cup brown sugar
½ teaspoon cinnamon
¼ cup light corn syrup
1 egg
¼ cup walnuts
1 tablespoon butter or margarine

Melt 2 tablespoons butter in bottom of 9-inch round cake pan. Arrange sliced apples over butter. Sprinkle raisins over apples. Cut each of the biscuits into fourths and place over apples.

Mix together brown sugar, cinnamon, corn syrup, and egg until well blended and sugar is dissolved. Pour over biscuits. Sprinkle walnuts over top. Dot with 1 tablespoon butter.

Bake at 350° for 35–45 minutes. Invert onto serving plate, spooning juices over top. Yields 6–8 servings.

From the Apple Orchard (Missouri)

Raspberry Cream Cheese Coffee Cake

1 (3-ounce) package cream cheese, softened
4 tablespoons softened butter

2 cups Bisquick
⅓ cup milk
½ cup raspberry preserves

GLAZE:
1 cup powdered sugar
1½ tablespoons milk

½ teaspoon vanilla

Cut cream cheese and butter into Bisquick until crumbly. Blend in milk. Turn onto floured surface and knead 8–10 times. Place on wax paper and roll to 12x8-inch rectangle. Turn onto greased jellyroll pan and remove paper. Spread preserves down center of dough. Make two ½-inch cuts at 1-inch intervals along both long edges of rectangle. Fold strips over filling, sealing sides with fingers to prevent preserves from leaking out. Bake at 425° for 12–15 minutes. Combine ingredients for Glaze and drizzle over coffee cake. Makes 8 servings.

Come Grow with Us (Oklahoma)

Cream Cheese Braid

PASTRY:

1 cup sour cream	2 packages dry yeast
½ cup sugar	½ cup warm water
1 teaspoon salt	2 eggs, beaten
½ cup margarine, melted	4 cups flour

Heat sour cream over low heat. Stir in sugar, salt, and margarine. Cool to lukewarm. Dissolve yeast in warm water. Combine sour cream mixture, yeast mixture, eggs, and flour. Mix this well. Cover and refrigerate overnight.

FILLING:

16 ounces cream cheese, softened	1 egg, beaten
	⅛ teaspoon salt
¾ cup sugar	2 teaspoons vanilla

GLAZE:

4 tablespoons milk	2 teaspoons vanilla

The next day combine cream cheese and sugar. Then add egg, salt, and vanilla. Divide dough into fourths. Roll one of the fourths into a 12x8-inch rectangle. Spread ¼ of the cream cheese Filling over this dough. Roll up jellyroll style, pinching the edges to seal it. Place seam side down on a greased baking sheet and make slits ⅔ of the way down at 2-inch intervals to resemble braids. Cover and let rise till double (approximately 1 hour). Bake at 375° for 12–15 minutes. Pour Glaze over braid while warm.

Sooner Sampler (Oklahoma)

Apricot Nibble Bread

2 (3-ounce) packages cream
  cheese, softened
⅓ cup sugar
1 tablespoon flour
1 egg
1 tablespoon grated orange
  rind
1 cup dried apricots
1½ cups warm water

2 cups flour
1 cup sugar
2 teaspoons baking powder
1 teaspoon salt
¼ teaspoon baking soda
¾ cup chopped pecans
1 egg
¼ cup vegetable shortening
½ cup orange juice

Cream together cream cheese, sugar, flour, egg, and grated orange rind and set aside. Mix dried apricots and warm water; let stand 5 minutes, drain well (reserve water), cut into small pieces, and set aside.

    Combine flour, sugar, baking powder, salt, baking soda, pecans, egg, and vegetable shortening. Mix together with orange juice and 1 cup water drained from apricots. Stir apricots into flour mixture. Turn ⅔ of batter into greased and floured 9x5-inch bread pan. Spoon cream cheese filling on top of batter, then add ⅓ of batter on top of cream cheese. Bake 65 minutes at 350°. May be baked in 8x10-inch pan.

Old and New (Oklahoma)

Marge's Marshmallow Puffs

¼ cup sugar
1 teaspoon cinnamon
16 marshmallows

¼ cup margarine, melted
2 cans crescent rolls,
  separated

LIGHT GLAZE:
2 cups powdered sugar
1 tablespoon melted
  margarine

Milk to make glazing
  consistency
1 cup chopped nuts

Combine sugar and cinnamon. Dip marshmallows, one at a time, into the melted margarine, then into the sugar mixture, and roll into one crescent roll. Seal all seams very securely. Dip each roll into the melted margarine, and put in muffin tin. Bake at 375° for 10–15 minutes. Remove from tins as soon as set enough and put on racks to cool. When cool, dip tops in Light Glaze and then in nuts. These freeze well.

Breakfast Ozark Style (Missouri)

Apple Pancake

You can whip up this pancake in no time with a blender or food processor. The first time I made it everyone in my family stood around the kitchen sampling and making suggestions for toppings. We had votes for maple syrup, whipped cream, cold applesauce, and light molasses. I chose vanilla ice cream. Then we tried it in soup bowls with cold milk poured over it. My sainted magnolias, but it's good all those ways!

2–3 apples	**3 tablespoons granulated**
¼ cup butter	**sugar**
Ground cinnamon	**½ teaspoon vanilla extract**
2 eggs, beaten	**2 cups self-rising flour**
1⅓ cups milk	**Ground nutmeg (optional)**

Preheat oven to 450°. Peel, core, and slice the apples. Melt the butter in a 10- or 12-inch iron skillet, swirling it around so the sides are completely coated. Cover the bottom of the pan with the apples. Sprinkle them heavily with cinnamon.

In the blender or food processor, blend the eggs, milk, sugar, and vanilla. Add the flour and blend again until the mixture is smooth. Pour the batter over the apples. Grate a small amount of nutmeg over the batter if you wish.

Bake 15–20 minutes, until the batter is cooked through and the pancake begins to come away from the sides of the pan. Turn the pancake out onto a serving plate carefully, using a spatula to coax all the apples loose from the bottom of the pan if necessary. Serve hot with any topping that appeals to you. May be baked ahead and reheated in the microwave oven. Makes 6 servings.

Enjoying the Art of Southern Hospitality (Arkansas)

Almond Crusted Oven Pancakes

Oven pancakes make a spectacular breakfast and for all their puffed glory they are amazingly easy to prepare. Its concave center can be filled with fresh fruits or simply sprinkled with sugar and lemon juice. The pancake in its various forms will bring exclamations of admiration for your prowess in the kitchen.

3 large eggs
½ cup milk
½ cup all-purpose flour
½ teaspoon salt
1 teaspoon sugar

Pinch of nutmeg (optional)
2 tablespoons butter
½ cup blanched slivered
**   almonds**

Preheat oven to 425°. Select a round skillet or a quiche pan. Combine eggs, milk, flour, salt, and sugar and whirl in a blender or beat with a wire whip. If using a blender, scrape down its sides to be certain all the flour is in the batter, and whirl again until creamy. If you are baking the pancake in a skillet, place it over a burner, add butter and almonds and sauté the almonds for 2 minutes. If a quiche pan is used, place in the oven with the butter until melted, add the almonds and let cook about 2–3 minutes. Carefully pour in the batter and bake 20 minutes. The pancake will rise with the sides encrusted with almonds. Serve filled with fresh fruit if desired, or with cooked apples on the side. Serves 4 amply.

Quick Breads, Soups & Stews (Oklahoma)

WIKIPEDIA.ORG

Guthrie is one of America's most charming time capsules. It was Oklahoma's territorial capital for 20 years. When the capital was moved to Oklahoma City in 1910, Guthrie was thrust into a 75-year sleep. Today there are 400 city blocks of vintage architecture on the National Register of Historic Places, making it one of the nation's largest living museums.

Crisp Buttery Waffles

Heat your well-seasoned waffle iron.

2 cups sifted flour   **½ teaspoon salt**
4 teaspoons baking powder   **2 tablespoons sugar**

Sift these ingredients into a large mixing bowl, preferably one with a pouring spout.

2 eggs, separated   **8 tablespoons butter, melted (or**
1¾ cups milk   **half butter, half shortening)**

When you separate the eggs, place the yolks in one bowl and the whites in a clean non-plastic bowl. Beat the whites until they stand in stiff peaks. The volume will be greater if the eggs are room temperature when you beat them. Set this bowl aside. You can use the same beater to beat the yolks until they are thickened and lemon-colored. Add the milk and melted butter. Mix the liquid ingredients into the bowl of dry, sifted ingredients. Lightly fold the stiff egg whites through the batter. Do not overmix.

Bake the waffles in your heated waffle iron. Pour the batter into the center of the iron, but do not fill it too full. Close and do not open again until the steam stops pouring out of the sides of the iron. Serve the waffles on a heated plate, unstacked. When finished, let the waffle iron stand open to cool.

Have you tried sprinkling broken pecans over the batter after you pour it in the iron? Drained blueberries can be added the same way. Crumbled broiled bacon makes a delicious waffle to serve under creamed chicken. How about that for Sunday night suppers? Bake as usual. Serves 4–6.

Spiced with Wit (Oklahoma)

Ham and Eggs 4th of July

8 frozen Pepperidge Farm
  Patty Shells
2 ounces mushrooms, sliced
2 tablespoons butter
2 tablespoons flour
⅛ teaspoon thyme
1 cup milk

⅓ can condensed cream of
  chicken soup
1 cup cubed ham
4 eggs, slightly beaten
¼ teaspoon salt
¼ cup milk
Parsley sprigs

Prepare the patty shells according to the directions on the package. Brown the mushrooms in the butter and stir in the flour and the thyme. Add the milk and cream of chicken soup. Stir until smooth. Add the ham. Heat, stirring occasionally.

    Gently scramble the eggs with the salt and milk. Put the eggs into hot patty shells and top with the ham mixture. Garnish with sprigs of parsley. Serves 6.

Bouquet Garni (Missouri)

Cheese and Eggs Olé

The green chiles add distinction to an easy and tasty brunch dish. Serve with bowls of salsa, guacamole, sour cream, and a huge basket of crispy tortilla chips.

1 dozen eggs, beaten
½ cup flour
1 teaspoon baking powder
1 pound Monterey Jack
  cheese, shredded

½ cup butter, melted
2 (4-ounce) cans green
  chiles, diced
1 pint cottage cheese

Preheat oven to 350°. Combine all ingredients. Pour into a buttered 9x13-inch baking dish. Bake 35 minutes or until done. Serve immediately. Serves 8–10.

Past & Repast (Missouri)

Impossible Bacon Quiche

12 slices bacon, cooked and
  crumbled
1 cup shredded natural Swiss
  cheese, about 4 ounces
⅓ cup chopped onion

2 cups milk
1 cup Bisquick baking mix
4 eggs
¼ teaspoon salt
⅛ teaspoon pepper

Preheat oven to 400°. Lightly grease a 10-inch pie plate. Sprinkle bacon, cheese, and onion in the pie plate. Beat milk, Bisquick, eggs, salt, and pepper in a medium-size bowl with electric mixer until smooth, about I minute. Pour into pie plate.

Bake in hot oven for 35 minutes or until top is golden brown and knife inserted halfway between center and edge comes out clean. Let stand 5 minutes before cutting. Garnish with tomato slices and bacon strips, if you wish. Refrigerate any leftovers.

Covered Bridge Neighbors Cookbook (Missouri)

Scrapple

This scrapple is a long-time favorite.

1½ pounds bulk pork
  sausage
4 cups water
1 teaspoon salt

½ teaspoon sage
1 cup cornmeal
1 cup cold water

Crumble pork sausage in a frying pan; add 4 cups water, and heat to boiling. Reduce heat, cook for 20 minutes. Then drain meat, reserving 3 cups stock. Add salt and sage to stock. Bring to boiling. Combine cornmeal and 1 cup cold water. Gradually add to stock, stirring constantly. Cover and cook over low heat for 10 minutes. Stir occasionally. Then add sausage, stir it all together and pour into loaf pan. Refrigerate overnight. Next morning slice and fry until set. Serve with syrup, if desired.

Grandma's Ozark Legacy (Missouri)

Karen's Breakfast Scramble

This is one of the easiest and tastiest buffet dishes I know of. Make a little more than you think you'll need, because people always come back for more. For each diner, allow:

Butter
1 medium-size red boiled
    potato, skin on, sliced
½ medium onion, sliced
¼ cup chopped cooked
    ham or corned beef

1 egg, beaten
¼ cup cottage cheese
2 tablespoons dry Pepperidge
    Farm Poultry Stuffing
Salt and pepper
Sliced tomatoes or oranges

In a heavy skillet melt enough butter to cover the bottom of the pan generously. Over medium heat, sauté the potato and onion until the onion begins to soften. Stir in the cooked meat. When all these ingredients are hot, pour in the beaten egg and cook until the egg is barely set. Remove from the heat. The egg will continue to cook for several minutes. Stir in the cottage cheese and dry stuffing, and salt and pepper to taste. Move to a warm platter and season to taste. Garnish with tomatoes or oranges if tomatoes are out of season. For buffet service, use an electric warming tray.

    To prepare ahead, have all ingredients ready and refrigerated so that all you have to do is scramble them together to serve. Makes 1 serving. Multiply ingredients for each additional diner.

Enjoying the Art of Southern Hospitality (Arkansas)

ARKANSASEDC.COM

One of many grist mills in Arkansas, The Old Mill in North Little Rock is featured in an opening scene of the movie classic "Gone With the Wind." It is believed to be the only remaining structure from that film.

Baked Eggs in Herbed Cheese Sauce

HERBED CHEESE SAUCE:

6 tablespoons butter
6 tablespoons flour
¼ teaspoon oregano
½ teaspoon savory

⅛ teaspoon cayenne pepper
Dash of Worcestershire
3 cups hot milk
3 cups grated Cheddar cheese

Melt butter in a saucepan and whisk in the flour, stirring rapidly. Add the oregano, savory, cayenne, and Worcestershire. Whisk thoroughly and let bubble 1 minute to give the herbs a chance to meld into the roux. Remove from the burner and add the hot milk all at once. Stir quickly with the whisk until smooth. Return to burner and continue cooking until thick and smooth. Add the cheese and blend until melted. For the baked eggs, this will be more sauce than needed, but the remainder can be used over broccoli or cauliflower or may be frozen for future use.

BAKED EGGS:

6 large eggs
½ cup bread crumbs
½ teaspoon dried basil

1 tablespoon chopped parsley
2 tablespoons butter

Preheat oven to 350°. Brush a glass baking dish or a round attractive pottery plate with melted butter. Pour one-half the hot herbed cheese sauce in dish. Break the 6 eggs, one at a time, into a saucer and slip each into the cheese sauce. Spoon a little sauce over each egg. Combine the bread crumbs, basil, parsley, and butter.

Sprinkle the crumb mixture over the eggs. Place the baking dish in shallow pan of hot water and cover loosely with aluminum foil. Bake the eggs 25–30 minutes. If you are concerned about how done the eggs are, take a spatula and lift one of the eggs. If not done, bake a few more minutes. Serve each egg atop toast or a Holland Rusk.

Mary's Recipe Box (Oklahoma)

Butch's Rancher's Omelette

6 slices bacon, diced
2 tablespoons finely chopped
  onion
1 cup grated raw potato
6 eggs, slightly beaten

½ teaspoon salt
⅛ teaspoon white pepper
Dash of hot sauce
2 tablespoons minced fresh
  parsley

Fry bacon until crisp. Drain and set aside, reserving 2 tablespoons drippings in skillet. Sauté onion until soft in reserved drippings. Add potato and cook until light brown. Pour eggs into skillet. Add salt, pepper, and hot sauce. Cook over low heat, lifting up eggs with spatula to let uncooked egg mixture flow underneath. When firm, sprinkle with crumbled bacon and parsley. Fold omelette in half. Serve immediately. Serves 4–6.

Submitted by Butch McCain, Oklahoma City television personality.
The Oklahoma Celebrity Cookbook (Oklahoma)

Cheese Grits Casserole

1½ cups grits (quick
  cooking)
1½ teaspoons salt
6 cups boiling water
3 tablespoons Cheez Whiz
1 pound Velveeta cheese,
  grated
1 stick margarine

4 eggs, beaten
2 tablespoons chopped onion
Dash of celery salt
¼ teaspoon thyme
Dash of garlic salt
1 tablespoon Worcestershire
1 teaspoon paprika
1 tablespoon chopped parsley

Add grits to salted, boiling water and cook until done. (You may need to add more hot water if the grits get too thick before the grains are soft.) Then add cheese and margarine. When melted, add beaten eggs, one at a time, and beat well. Add onion, seasonings, and Worcestershire. Cook for 2 minutes. Pour into a greased 9x13-inch baking dish and bake, covered, for 40 minutes at 350° (longer if needed). Sprinkle paprika and parsley on top.

Dine with the Angels (Oklahoma)

Peach Butter

(Spicy)

10 cups chopped ripe peaches	**1 teaspoon nutmeg**
2½–3 cups water	**1 teaspoon powdered cloves**
2 teaspoons cinnamon	**4 cups honey**

Cook peeled, cut peaches and water over low heat until smooth and turning brown, 4–5 hours. Stir occasionally to prevent sticking. Add spices and honey. Cool butter and press through a sieve. Pour into sterilized canning jars. Close tightly.

Heavenly Delights (Missouri)

Show Me Preserves

An unusual taste combination of Missouri's backyard produce—strawberries and black walnuts.

3 pints fresh strawberries, hulled, or 1 quart frozen unsweetened strawberries	**½ cup fresh lemon juice**
	2 tablespoons Kirsch or curaçao
3 cups sugar	**¾ cup black walnut pieces**

Combine strawberries, sugar, lemon juice, and Kirsch in a large, heavy saucepan. Cook over low heat 5 minutes or until sugar dissolves. Increase the heat and boil 30 minutes, stirring frequently. Remove from heat and stir in walnuts. Pour immediately into hot sterilized ½-pint jars, leaving ½-inch head space. Seal jars and process in boiling water bath 10 minutes. Makes eight ½-pint jars.

Sassafras! (Missouri)

Missouri's "Show-me" nickname has been around for a long time, but it gained fame in 1899 when Congressman Willard Vandiver of Cape Girardeau County said in a Philadelphia speech: "Gentlemen, frothy eloquence neither convinces nor satisfies me. I'm from Missouri; you've got to show me."

World's Best Pimento Cheese

We had never liked pimento cheese until we ate it at Papa Robin's, a now-defunct restaurant in Jasper, Arkansas. Our re-creation of their marvelous pimento cheese:

4 tablespoons mayonnaise
1 (3-ounce) package cream
  cheese, softened
3 cloves garlic
Handful fresh parsley
Several vigorous shots of
  Pickapepper and Tabasco

1 cup chopped pecans
1 small jar diced pimentos
  and all juice
12 ounces extra sharp
  Cheddar cheese

Purée till smooth in processor the mayonnaise, cream cheese, garlic, parsley and sauces. Turn into a bowl. Now, in food processor, process just till coarsely chopped, 1 cup pecans; add pecans and pimentos, with juice, to mayonnaise mixture. Now grate in food processor 12 ounces extra sharp Cheddar cheese. Turn into bowl with remaining ingredients. Stir well to combine. Let stand, refrigerated, at least 1 hour. Even better the next day.

The Dairy Hollow House Cookbook (Arkansas)

Turkey Cranberry Sandwiches

6 ounces smoked turkey
  breast, thinly sliced
4 slices low-fat cheese
  (Swiss, mozzarella,
  Cheddar)

8 tomato slices
4 lettuce leaves
8 slices whole-wheat bread

DRESSING:
½ cup whole berry
  cranberry sauce
1 tablespoon Kraft Free
  Nonfat Miracle Whip

⅓ cup diced celery
1 tablespoon lemon juice

Mix together Dressing ingredients and set aside. Assemble sandwiches, dividing turkey and cheese evenly among the 4 sandwiches. Spread bread with Dressing and serve.

Eat to Your Heart's Content, Too! (Arkansas)

Lentil Walnut Burgers

This delightful, meatless cheeseburger is a popular item on the daily menu of the Station restaurant in Fayetteville, Arkansas. The owners were kind enough to let me share the recipe, presented here with a few "low-cholesterol" substitutions.

½ pound lentils
½ cup chopped walnuts
2 cups bread crumbs
4 egg whites
1 cup chopped onion
¼ cup ketchup
¼ teaspoon ground cloves

½ teaspoon salt
½ teaspoon pepper
4 slices or ½ cup shredded
   imitation mozzarella cheese
Cooking spray
1 tablespoon olive oil

Cook lentils until tender. Drain and cool. Chop lightly roasted walnuts. Lightly toast bread crumbs. Mix all ingredients and mash into a slightly lumpy paste. Portion into 3-ounce patties and cook in a sprayed skillet to which you have added 1 tablespoon olive oil. (Some people prefer crisp patties.) Top each patty with cheese and serve on bun with traditional garnish. Serves 4.

Cooking to Your Heart's Content (Arkansas)

Stromboli

2 loaves white frozen
   unbaked bread
1 can mushrooms, drained
1 green bell pepper, chopped

1 tablespoon butter
1 package pepperoni
1 package Canadian bacon
1 package Provolone cheese

Let bread thaw and rise for 4 hours. Punch bread down flat. Sauté mushrooms and pepper in butter. Layer all ingredients in center of bread loaves. Cut sides into strips and fold strips over the top. Bake at 350° for 30 minutes or until done.

Seasoned with Love (Oklahoma)

Soups, Chilis, and Stews

COURTESY OF ARKANSAS DEPT. OF PARKS & TOURISM

The first federally protected area in the nation's history, Hot Springs National Park, Arkansas, features thermal waters, rich history, and beautiful architecture. The heart of the park, Bathhouse Row, offers a unique glimpse into the health spa craze of the late 19th and early 20th centuries. They played host to many famous faces during that time, including Franklin Delano Roosevelt, Babe Ruth, and Al Capone.

Wild Rice Soup

This is a must to try! It's our four-star choice!

½ cup wild rice, uncooked
9 slices thick bacon
1 medium onion, chopped
2 cups whole milk
2 cups half-and-half

2 cans potato soup (undiluted)
2 cups (8-ounces) shredded
 American cheese
Parsley (optional)

Cook wild rice 20 minutes. Drain. Add fresh water and cook 20 minutes more. Drain. Add fresh water again and cook 20 minutes or until rice is fluffy (makes 3 cups).

Dice bacon. Cook until crisp. Drain on paper towels. Sauté onion in bacon grease. Drain. Combine all ingredients in a heavy saucepan and cook over low heat until cheese melts. Garnish with parsley, if desired. Serves 6–8.

Finely Tuned Foods (Missouri)

Gail's Cheesy Broccoli Soup

¾ cup chopped onion
2 tablespoons margarine
6 cups water
6 chicken bouillon cubes
8 ounces fine egg noodles
1 teaspoon salt

2 (10-ounce) packages frozen
 chopped broccoli
½ teaspoon garlic powder
6 cups milk
1 pound Velveeta cheese, cubed
1 teaspoon pepper

Sauté onion in margarine. In large pot, put 6 cups water and bouillon cubes. Bring to a boil. Add noodles and salt. Cook for 3–4 minutes until noodles are tender. Remove from heat and stop boiling. Add onion, broccoli, and garlic powder.

Cook for 3 minutes more and remove from heat again. Add milk, cheese, and pepper. Stir until cheese melts. Makes 4 quarts or approximately 12 servings. Can be made ahead and frozen for 1 month.

USO's Salute to the Troops Cookbook (Missouri)

Cheesy Broccoli Soup

½ (10-ounce) package
  frozen chopped broccoli
½ cup thinly sliced carrot
½ cup water
1 teaspoon instant chicken
  bouillon granules
1 cup milk
½ cup shredded American
  cheese (2 ounces)

½ cup chopped cooked
  chicken or finely chopped
  fully cooked ham
⅛ teaspoon pepper
¼ cup water
2 tablespoons all-purpose
  flour

In a 1-quart casserole, combine the frozen chopped broccoli, thinly sliced carrot, the ½ cup water, and instant chicken bouillon granules. Micro-cook, covered, on 100% power for 5–7 minutes or until the vegetables are tender, stirring once.

To the vegetables in the 1-quart casserole, stir in the milk, shredded American cheese, chopped chicken or finely chopped ham, and pepper. In a small bowl stir together the ¼ cup water and flour; stir into the vegetable/cheese mixture in the casserole. Micro-cook, uncovered, on 100% power about 5 minutes or until the mixture is thickened and bubbly, stirring every minute. Micro-cook, uncovered, on 100% power for 30 seconds more. Makes 2 servings.

Around the Bend (Arkansas)

Country Potato Soup

3 cups raw potatoes, diced
½ cup diced celery
½ cup diced onion
2 chicken bouillon cubes
1½ cups water

2 cups milk, divided
1 (8-ounce) carton sour cream
2 tablespoons flour
1 teaspoon chives (optional)
Bacon, crumbled

Cook potatoes, celery, onion, and bouillon cubes in water about 20 minutes in large saucepan. Add 1 cup milk and heat. In medium bowl mix sour cream, flour, chives, and remaining 1 cup milk. Slowly add to heated mixture. Cook, stirring until thickened. Serve hot, topped with crumbled bacon and fresh bread.

Pulaski Heights Baptist Church Cookbook (Arkansas)

Herbed Black Bean Soup with Smoked Chicken

¼ cup (½ stick) unsalted butter
1 cup peeled, diced broccoli stems
½ cup chopped carrot
½ cup chopped onion
½ cup chopped celery
1 tablespoon dried thyme, crumbled
1 teaspoon Cajun seasoning
1 tablespoon dried oregano
1 tablespoon dried basil, crumbled
½ cup dry white wine
4 cups chicken stock or canned broth
2 cups broccoli florets
1 (16-ounce) can black beans, rinsed and drained
8 ounces smoked chicken, shredded and chopped
1 tablespoon Worcestershire
½ teaspoon hot pepper sauce
2 cups heavy cream
Salt and freshly ground pepper, to taste

In a sauté pan, melt butter over medium heat. Add broccoli stems, carrot, onion, and celery and sauté for 5 minutes. Add thyme, Cajun seasoning, oregano, and basil and sauté for 5 minutes more. Pour in wine and bring mixture to a boil. Add stock and cook until liquid is reduced by half, stirring occasionally (approximately 12 minutes).

Stir broccoli florets, beans, chicken, Worcestershire, and hot pepper sauce into soup and simmer for 5 minutes, stirring occasionally. Add cream and simmer for 5 minutes more. Season with salt and pepper and serve. Serves 6.

Note: A smoky, spicy soup that's even better when prepared a day in advance. Garnish with cilantro, broccoli florets, pimento, curled carrots, or homemade croutons.

Above & Beyond Parsley (Missouri)

Ozark Bean Soup

1 package Ozark (mixed)
  beans (2 cups)
1 (48-ounce) can V–8 juice
1 onion, sliced
1 cup each: carrots and
  celery, sliced
1 green bell pepper, diced
3 cups water
¼ cup crushed garlic
1 tablespoon basil, thyme,
  and oregano
2 tablespoons Worcestershire
¼ pound Italian sausage

Combine all of the above ingredients in a large pot and cook for several hours until beans are tender. Serve with Mexican cornbread for a great low-fat meal. Serves 8–10.

Eat to Your Heart's Content! (Arkansas)

8 Bean Soup

½ cup pinto beans
½ cup split peas
½ cup small red beans
½ cup black turtle beans
½ cup red kidney beans
½ cup Great Northern beans
½ cup lentils
½ cup black-eyed peas

HERBS:
¾ tablespoon basil
¾ tablespoon chili powder
¾ tablespoon thyme
¾ tablespoon dried onions
½ tablespoon tarragon
½ tablespoon rosemary
¼ tablespoon black pepper

Pour dry beans in a large bowl and mix thoroughly. Soak the beans overnight in water. Pour off this water and rinse beans. Place the beans in a slow cooker and cover with water. Add Herbs and cook on low heat until tender.

The Homeplace Cookbook (Oklahoma)

Chuck Wagon Bean Hot Pot

1 pound Western dry beans
½ cup butter
1 large onion
1 teaspoon chili powder
1 teaspoon paprika
1 tablespoon red pepper

1 teaspoon salt
1 can tomato sauce
1 can tomatoes
1 teaspoon garlic
1 cup water
1 pound ground beef

Cook Western dry beans for 2½ hours after soaking in hot water for 1 hour. Cook butter, onion, chili powder, paprika, red pepper, salt, tomato sauce, tomatoes, garlic and water in saucepan. Cook beef alone and then drain off grease. Mix beans, tomato mixture and beef together. Let cook for 1 hour.

Oklahoma Cookin' (Oklahoma)

Chicken Soup

1 whole chicken
4 yellow onions
1 bulb garlic
5 stalks celery, chopped
1 bottle dry white wine

2 cups diced carrots
2 cups diced zucchini
1 pound thin pasta
2 cups diced celery
1 pound sliced mushrooms

Cover first 4 ingredients with water and the bottle of wine. Simmer for 60 minutes. Strain broth and dice or shred chicken. Add rest of ingredients to strained broth; simmer 30 minutes. Add chicken; warm and serve. Serves 8.

The Bonneville House Presents (Arkansas)

Spicy Chicken Tomato Pasta Soup

Those who love pungent full-meal soups with cornbread sticks or muffins will be warmed to their cockles when served this soup before a roaring fire in the mid-winter.

6 cups canned or homemade
    chicken broth
1 cup chopped onion
1 cup diced zucchini
½ cup diced carrot
1 cup diced celery
1 bay leaf
¼ teaspoon thyme
1 large garlic clove, peeled
    and minced
¼ cup finely chopped
    parsley
Grindings of black pepper

3 sprigs fresh basil or 1 sprig
    dried basil
1 (1-pound 12-ounce) can
    crushed tomatoes with purée
Approximately ½ cup Ro-Tel
    brand tomatoes and green
    chiles (½ of a 10-ounce can)
1 cup elbow macaroni or tiny
    pasta
2 cups chopped cooked
    chicken
Salt to taste

Measure the chicken broth into a soup kettle, bring to a boil, and add the onion, zucchini, carrot, celery, bay leaf, thyme, garlic, parsley, pepper, and basil. Bring to a simmer and cook 15 minutes uncovered until vegetables are tender. Add the crushed tomatoes, Ro-Tel tomatoes and green chiles, and pasta. (If a spicier soup is desired, add the remaining half can of Ro-Tel tomatoes and green chiles.) Bring to a boil, lower to simmer, and cook gently 20 minutes until the pasta is tender. Add the chicken and simmer until thoroughly heated. If the soup becomes too thick after the pasta is added, add 1–2 cups additional chicken broth to suit your own taste. Adjust for salt. Serves 10–12.

Quick Breads, Soups & Stews (Oklahoma)

Crab and Mushroom Soup

The easiest way to make this outstandingly good soup is in a metal double boiler with a top that can be set directly on the burner. A food processor is helpful for chopping the celery and parsley fine and slicing the mushrooms. Do not put the onion in a food processor because it makes the flavor strong and bitter.

3 tablespoons butter
2 cups finely chopped celery
½ cup finely chopped
  parsley
1 small onion, minced by
  hand

3 tablespoons flour
1 cup chicken stock
1 cup sliced mushrooms
1 cup crabmeat
¼ cup Sauterne cooking wine
2 cups milk

Melt the butter in the top of the double boiler over direct heat. Stir in the celery, parsley, and onion. Cook and stir over medium heat until the vegetables are soft and translucent but not brown.

Stir in the flour and cook a few minutes more until the flour begins to be golden. Whisk in the chicken stock, beating until all lumps are gone from the flour. Set the mixture over hot water in the double boiler and steam for about one hour, until the celery is tender.

Stir in the mushrooms, crabmeat, and wine. The recipe may be prepared ahead to this point.

At serving time, add the milk and reheat the soup until it is piping hot. Do not let it cook further once the milk has been added. Makes 6–8 servings.

Enjoying the Art of Southern Hospitality (Arkansas)

America's only national park located in a city, Hot Springs, Arkansas, has been famous for its healing waters from thermal springs for over a century. The "Valley of the Vapors" has long been a destination for tourists from around the world, beginning with the Spanish explorer, Hernando DeSoto, who discovered the famous hot springs.

Taco Soup

2 pounds hamburger
1 large onion, finely chopped
2–3 cloves garlic, minced
1 small can chopped green
  chiles
3 cans diced tomatoes
1 can corn
1 can red kidney beans

1 can pinto beans
1 can black-eyed peas
1 package Old El Paso Taco
  Seasoning
1 package Hidden Valley
  Original Ranch Dressing Mix
2 cups water

Brown hamburger with onion and garlic; drain. Add remaining ingredients and bring to boil; simmer at least 2 hours.

100 Years of Cooking (Oklahoma)

Creamy Carrot Soup

Children love this soup because of the natural sweetness of the carrots.

1 small onion, coarsely
  chopped
6 carrots, scrubbed, coarsely
  chopped
1 white potato, coarsely
  chopped, or 1 (16-ounce) can
  white beans, drained

1½ cups vegetable or
  nonfat chicken broth
½ cup skim milk or
  evaporated skim milk

Place the onion, carrots, potato, and broth in a saucepan and bring to a boil. Simmer, covered, until vegetables are tender. Place in a blender and purée until smooth, adding milk until the desired consistency.

Note: This recipe will work for most all favorite vegetables. It's a quick and easy way to have a delicious, healthy soup.

Healthy America (Oklahoma)

Red Pepper Bisque

One of our favorite starters.

1 cup unsalted butter
2 tablespoons vegetable oil
4 cups chopped leeks
6 large red peppers, sliced
3 cups chicken broth

Salt
6 cups buttermilk
White pepper to taste
Chives or lemon slices and
  caviar

Melt butter and oil in a large saucepan. Add leeks and red peppers. Reduce heat and cook, covered, until vegetables are soft. Add chicken broth and salt to taste. Simmer, partially covered, over low heat for 30 minutes or until vegetables are very soft.

Blend mixture in a food processor until smooth. Strain into a large bowl. Stir in buttermilk and white pepper to taste. Chill. Garnish with chives or a thin slice of lemon with a small scoop of caviar in the middle. Serves 10–12. For single servings, dole the soup into green pepper shells.

Gateways (Missouri)

Bisque Crevettes

(Shrimp Bisque)

½ cup chopped green
  onions
2 tablespoons chopped parsley
½ cup butter
2 tablespoons flour
1 cup milk
1 teaspoon salt

½ teaspoon white pepper
⅛ teaspoon cayenne
1½ cups half-and-half
2 cups boiled shrimp,
  cut in pieces
2 tablespoons vermouth

Sauté onions and parsley in 4 tablespoons butter. In separate skillet, melt the remaining butter and add flour. Mix like a roux. Add milk and cook until thickened. Add salt, pepper, and cayenne. Add onions and parsley and half-and-half. Bring to a boil, stirring constantly. Reduce heat. Add shrimp and simmer 5 minutes. Add vermouth. Serves 4.

Nibbles Ooo La La (Arkansas)

Chicken Vegetable Gumbo

A low-fat recipe.

1 cup coarsely chopped onion
1 cup sliced fresh mushrooms
½ cup sliced celery
½ cup chopped green pepper
2 cloves garlic, minced
2 (14½-ounce) cans chopped
  tomatoes, undrained
1 (10½-ounce) can chicken
  broth
1 teaspoon chicken-flavored
  bouillon granules

½ cup dry sherry
1 teaspoon dried Italian
  seasoning
¼ teaspoon pepper
2 cups cubed cooked chicken
  breasts
⅔ pound fresh okra (tipped,
  stemmed, and sliced), or
1 (10-ounce) package frozen
  sliced okra

Coat large Dutch oven with cooking spray. Over medium heat cook onion, mushrooms, celery, green pepper, and garlic 5 minutes. Add tomatoes, chicken broth, bouillon granules, sherry, Italian seasoning, and pepper. Bring to a boil, cover, and simmer 1 hour or until vegetables are tender. About ½ hour before done, add cubed chicken and okra. Finish cooking. Preparation time: 1½ hours. Makes 2 quarts.

Cooking A+ Recipes (Oklahoma)

Ham and Potato Chowder

¼ cup butter, melted
1 medium onion, minced
¾ cup diced ham
½ cup chopped celery
1½ cups finely diced raw
  potatoes

¼ cup flour
1½ teaspoons salt
¼ teaspoon pepper
4 cups milk

In large saucepan, melt butter and sauté onion, ham, and celery. Add potatoes and cook 10 minutes longer. Remove from heat and add flour, salt, and pepper. Mix well. Add milk and return to heat. Warm slowly; do not let boil. If not served immediately and soup thickens, add warm water to thin to desired consistency. Serves 4–6.

Silver Dollar City's Recipes (Missouri)

Potato Bacon Chowder

8 slices bacon, cut up
1 cup chopped onion
4 cups cubed potatoes
1 cup water
1 can cream of chicken soup

1 cup sour cream
1¾ cups milk
½ teaspoon salt
Dash of pepper

Fry bacon until crisp. Remove bacon and sauté onion in drippings. Remove onion and drain on paper towel. Cook potatoes in the 1 cup water; add soup, onion, bacon (save some to crumble on top), sour cream, and milk, plus seasonings. Simmer, but do not boil. Serves 6.

Stir Ups (Oklahoma)

Herbed Corn Chowder

1 medium onion, diced
1 medium green bell pepper, diced
2 (1-pound) cans creamed corn
2 cans cream of potato soup

2 cans skim milk
1 tablespoon fresh parsley
1 tablespoon fresh chives
1 tablespoon fresh dill or thyme

Sauté onion and green pepper in skillet sprayed with cooking spray. Add corn, potato soup and milk and stir until smooth.

While chowder is warming, add chopped parsley, chopped chives, and either the dill or thyme. Serves 6.

Eat to Your Heart's Content! (Arkansas)

Jack's Chili con Carne

3½ pounds top round
   steak, cut into ½-inch
   cubes
5 tablespoons vegetable oil
2 cups coarsely chopped
   onions
4 cloves garlic, minced
4 tablespoons chili powder
1½ teaspoons oregano
1½ teaspoons cumin
1 teaspoon crushed red
   pepper

2 cups beef broth
1 (19-ounce) can whole
   tomatoes with juice
1 (6-ounce) can tomato paste
1 tablespoon salt
1 teaspoon sugar
3 (16-ounce) cans kidney or
   chili beans
1–2 tablespoons yellow cornmeal

Pat the meat dry with paper towels. Heat 3 tablespoons of the oil in a large, heavy Dutch oven. When hot, add the meat. Sear until all pieces are lightly browned, 3–4 minutes. Drain fat and transfer to a bowl. Set aside. Add remaining 2 tablespoons oil to the Dutch oven and sauté onion and garlic until onion is wilted but not browned. Stir in chili powder, oregano, cumin, and red pepper. Add broth, canned tomatoes with juice, tomato paste, salt, and sugar, mixing well and breaking up tomatoes. Add seared meat. Cover and simmer 40–50 minutes. Add beans and heat through. Thicken with cornmeal to desired consistency. Serves 4–6.

This recipe was contributed by Missouri U.S. Senator John C. Danforth.

Sassafras! (Missouri)

Hot 'n' Spicy Chunky Beef Chili

2¼ pounds lean boneless
   beef chuck, cut into ¾-inch
   pieces
1 cup coarsely chopped onion
2 cloves garlic, minced
2 tablespoons vegetable oil
1 teaspoon salt
1 (28-ounce) can plum
   tomatoes, broken up
1 cup water
1 (6-ounce) can tomato paste

3 tablespoons chili powder
1 teaspoon dried oregano
   leaves
1 teaspoon crushed red
   pepper pods
1 cup chopped green bell
   pepper
6 tablespoons each: shredded
   Cheddar cheese and sliced
   green onions

Brown beef (half at a time) with onion and garlic in oil in large frying pan or Dutch oven. Pour off drippings. Sprinkle salt over beef. Add tomatoes, water, tomato paste, chili powder, oregano, and crushed red pepper. Cover tightly and simmer 1½ hours or until beef is tender. Add green pepper and continue cooking uncovered, 30 minutes. Sprinkle each serving with cheese and green onion slices. Serves 8 (1½ cups each).

Submitted by Reba McEntire, singer, songwriter, entertainer and Oklahoman.
The Oklahoma Celebrity Cookbook (Oklahoma)

WIKIPEDIA.ORG

One of the greatest athletes the world has ever known was an Indian from Oklahoma. Jim Thorpe (May 28, 1888–March 28, 1953) was born on a farm near Prague to parents who were part Sac and Fox and Pottawatomie. Thorpe became an international sports hero at the 1912 Olympics in Stockholm, Sweden, where he won the pentathlon and decathlon. Thorpe also starred in football and baseball, and a 1950 Associated Press poll of the nation's sportswriters picked him as the greatest athlete of the first half of the twentieth century.

Terry's White Chili

Terry Davis is a full blood Cherokee Indian, an expert on chili, and the fine chef of Mary's Bread Basket in Tulsa. Terry's avocation is following chili contests in Arkansas, Texas, New Mexico, Colorado and Kansas. His cooking apparel is a handsome apron with Seminole patchwork in red and green and a big bright red pepper below the patchwork—and he wins those chili cookoffs!

6 cups chicken broth
3 cups navy beans (small white beans)
2 teaspoons cumin
1 teaspoon oregano
8 ounces canned green chiles, chopped
1 clove garlic, peeled and minced
1 cup chopped onion
½ teaspoon white pepper
½ teaspoon ground cloves
1 pound cooked chicken, cut in pieces
Salt to taste

Combine in a soup kettle the chicken broth, beans, cumin, oregano, chiles, garlic, onion, white pepper, and cloves. Place over medium heat and bring to a boil, then lower heat and simmer until the beans are tender, 1½–2 hours. When the beans are tender, add the chicken, bring to a simmer, and salt to taste. Simmer 10–15 minutes to allow ingredients to meld. Serves 10.

Quick Breads, Soups & Stews (Oklahoma)

Ed's Bachelor Chili

5 pounds ground beef
1 large onion, chopped
3 (31-ounce) cans
   chili beans
6 (16-ounce) cans stewed
   tomatoes
2 (16-ounce) cans whole
   potatoes, quartered
1 (8-ounce) can tomato sauce
1 (16-ounce) jar mild taco
   sauce
1 (8-ounce) jar hot taco
   sauce

1 (heaping) tablespoon
   Grey Poupon (mustard)
½ teaspoon cayenne pepper
1 teaspoon chili powder
Generous sprinkle of dill
   weed, garlic powder, and
   coarse ground pepper
2 small Hershey bars
1 large green bell pepper,
   chopped

Sauté meat; drain. Add remaining ingredients, except Hershey bars and green pepper. Cover and simmer 1 hour and 50 minutes. Add chocolate and green pepper; simmer an additional hour. Yields 12–14 servings.

Sing for Your Supper (Missouri)

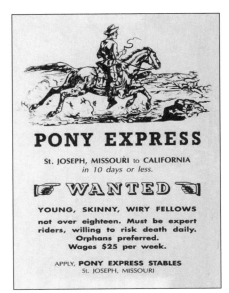

PONY EXPRESS
St. JOSEPH, MISSOURI to CALIFORNIA
in 10 days or less.

☞ WANTED ☜

YOUNG, SKINNY, WIRY FELLOWS
not over eighteen. Must be expert
riders, willing to risk death daily.
Orphans preferred.
Wages $25 per week.

APPLY, PONY EXPRESS STABLES
St. JOSEPH, MISSOURI

The Pony Express was a system of mail delivery by continuous horse and rider relays between St. Joseph, Missouri, and Sacramento, California (April 1860–October 1861). The 1,800-mile route had 157 stations and required about 10 days to cover. Each rider generally rode 75 to 100 miles. In the era before the telegraph, the Pony Express was the thread that tied East to West. Shown here is the ad recruiting riders. Buffalo Bill Cody, perhaps its most renown rider, signed up at age 14 and later re-enacted the rides in his Wild West shows. The Pony Express stables in St. Joseph, Missouri, now houses the Pony Express Museum.

Indian Corn Stew

2 tablespoons vegetable oil
1 medium onion, chopped
3 cloves garlic, minced
3–4 skinless, boneless
 chicken breasts, cut in
 bite-size pieces
1 (4-ounce) can diced mild
 green chiles
1 (16-ounce) can tomatoes,
 chopped, with liquid

1 cup water
1 (16-ounce) package frozen
 corn, or 2 cups fresh grated
 corn
¼ teaspoon salt (optional)
½ teaspoon cumin
1 teaspoon chili powder
2 medium ripe tomatoes, diced
1 bell pepper, diced

In a Dutch oven or large soup pot, over medium-high heat, sauté in oil the onion and garlic until onion is transparent. Add the chicken and brown, stirring frequently for about 5 minutes.

Add green chiles, canned tomatoes, water, corn and spices. Simmer 5 minutes. Add chopped tomatoes and bell pepper and simmer 20 minutes. Yields 6–8 servings.

Serve with warm buttered tortillas.

STEAMING CORN TORTILLAS:
1 dozen corn tortillas

Wet a clean dish towel and ring out excess water until cloth is damp. Remove tortillas from their package and place them on the damp towel on a baking sheet. Fold the towel over the tortillas and tuck in all sides.

Place in the preheated 350° oven for 10 minutes.

Eating Healthy in the Fast Lane (Arkansas)

Lentil Stew

This hearty stew is so colorful and special that we serve it every Christmas Eve.

2 tablespoons olive oil
3 red bell peppers, cut in
 ¼-inch crescent shapes
2 cloves garlic, minced
1 large onion, chopped
 coarse
1 medium potato, cut in
 large chunks
1 large carrot, cut in
 ¼-inch rounds

1 stalk celery, sliced chunky
1 (14½-ounce) can whole
 tomatoes
1¾ cups brown lentils, rinsed
 and drained
4 cups water
1 teaspoon dried basil
1 teaspoon dried thyme
2 tablespoons red wine vinegar

In a 4-quart soup pot over medium-high flame, heat oil and add all ingredients (except red wine vinegar) in the order listed. Bring to boil over high heat. Cover and reduce to simmer.

Simmer 40 minutes or until lentils are tender. Stir occasionally to prevent sticking. Just before serving, stir in vinegar. Yields 6–8 servings.

Variation: Add preservative-free turkey Italian sausage, sliced in ¼-inch rounds.

Eating Healthy in the Fast Lane (Arkansas)

Salads

COURTESY OF OKLAHOMA TOURISM

Talimena Skyline Drive winds through the Ouachita National Forest providing fifty-four miles of amazing vistas and excellent photo opportunities. It is the only scenic byway located in Mid-America, stretching from Talihina, Oklahoma, to Mena, Arkansas. Its name comes from the combination of both towns.

St. Louis Favorite Salad

1 head romaine lettuce, torn
  into pieces
1 head iceberg lettuce, torn
  into pieces
1 (10-ounce) jar artichoke
  hearts, drained and cut into
  pieces
1 (4-ounce) jar pimentos
Red onion slices
¼ cup grated Parmesan
  cheese
½ cup oil
⅓ cup white vinegar
Hearts of palm (optional)

Wash and tear lettuces into bite-size pieces. Cut artichoke hearts and pimentos into pieces. Combine with thinly sliced red onion in a large salad bowl. Add cheese. In a separate container, combine vinegar and oil. Just before serving, add hearts of palm, if desired; pour oil mixture over salad and toss until well coated. Serves 10–12.

From Generation to Generation (Missouri)

Caesar Salad

1 clove garlic
6 anchovy fillets
2 eggs, coddled* 1–1½
  minutes
½ cup olive oil (fresh
  press or virgin, be sure to
  use very delicate oil)
Juice of 1 large lemon
2–3 heads young romaine
  lettuce, washed, dried and
  torn
½ cup freshly grated
  Parmesan cheese
2 cups croutons, plain
Fresh-ground pepper to taste

Crush the garlic in a wooden bowl with the back of a wooden spoon and rub around the bowl, keeping the garlic in one piece. Stir in anchovy fillets and rub around bowl. Remove remaining garlic, but leave anchovy pieces in the bowl. Add the eggs and beat well. Add the oil and lemon juice, beating the entire time. Add the lettuce and Parmesan cheese; toss. Add the croutons, toss again and serve. Grind pepper to taste over each serving. Serves 8–10.

*Cook in water just below the boiling point.

The Bonneville House Presents (Arkansas)

Greek Salad

1 head lettuce
3 tomatoes
1 onion, thinly sliced
1 green bell pepper, chopped
1 cup black olives, halved
1 cucumber, sliced

½ cup olive oil
¼ cup red wine vinegar
½ teaspoon oregano
Salt and pepper
Feta cheese, crumbled

Combine all vegetables and chill. When ready to serve, beat oil and vinegar until smooth. Pour over salad. Add oregano, salt and pepper. Then add crumbled cheese. Toss. Serve at once. Serves 8.

Arkansas Favorites Cookbook (Arkansas)

Greek Salad

DRESSING:
½ cup olive oil (or ¼ cup olive oil and ¼ cup vegetable oil)
2–3 tablespoons red wine vinegar
4–6 anchovy fillets, rinsed and chopped

1 teaspoon Dijon mustard
¼ teaspoon salt
⅛ teaspoon pepper
1 cup (4 ounces) feta cheese, crumbled
1 tablespoon capers, drained

Prepare day before so that all seasonings blend well. Combine all ingredients together in jar with a lid. Shake and refrigerate.

SALAD:
1 medium tomato, cut into small wedges
1 medium cucumber, thinly sliced
1 medium onion, sliced

1 medium-size head romaine lettuce
1 medium-size head iceberg lettuce

Place in a large bowl first the tomato, cucumber, and onion. Break up lettuces on top. When ready to serve, pour Dressing over, toss and serve. Yields 4–6 servings.

The Art of Hellenic Cuisine (Missouri)

Spinach Salad

One of my favorites! A secret is in the onions. Mild, meaty Texas 1015, or sweet purple onions make a difference.

DRESSING:

2 slices bacon
3 tablespoons vegetable oil
½ onion, chopped
½ teaspoon cornstarch
½ cup cider or wine vinegar
2 tablespoons raspberry
** vinegar (or other vinegar)**

¼ teaspoon salt
¼–½ cup sugar, depending
** on your taste (a sugar-free**
** sweetener may be substituted**
** if added just after cooking)**

Fry bacon until crisp; remove and drain on paper towel. Retain the grease. Over low heat, add oil, and sauté onion until translucent. Add cornstarch. Stir until cornstarch is absorbed. Add vinegars, stir, and heat until boiling. Add salt and sugar. Remove from heat. Stir until sugar dissolves.

1 bunch (about a pound)
** stemmed spinach**
½ onion, chopped or sliced
** thin**
Few sprigs of cilantro,
** chopped (optional)**

½ cup sliced almonds or
** chopped pecans, toasted**
** (275° for 15 minutes)**
1 (8-ounce) can Mandarin
** oranges, drained**
½ cup sliced mushrooms

Wash and drain spinach thoroughly. Add chopped onions, cilantro, toasted nuts, Mandarin oranges, mushrooms, crumbled bacon (from Dressing). Toss thoroughly. Warm Dressing almost to boiling and pour over salad mix. Serves 2-4.

When a Man's Fancy Turns to Cooking (Oklahoma)

Sensational Spinach Salad

1 pound spinach, torn into
 pieces
1 cup sliced mushrooms
½ cup pitted ripe olives
½ cup coarsely chopped
 walnuts
⅓ cup bacon bits
¾ cup Wish-Bone Creamy
 Italian Dressing
3 hard-cooked eggs, sliced
½ cup seasoned croutons

In large bowl, combine spinach, mushrooms, olives, walnuts and bacon. Just before serving, toss with creamy Italian dressing; top with eggs and croutons. Makes about 6 servings.

Around the Bend (Arkansas)

Marinated Vegetable Salad

1 (16-ounce) can English peas
1 (16-ounce) can French
 green beans
1 (12-ounce) can shoepeg
 corn
1 small can or jar pimentos
½–1 cup chopped celery
½–1 cup chopped onions
½ cup chopped green bell
 pepper
1 cup sugar
Pepper to taste
½ teaspoon salt
½ cup vegetable oil
¾ cup vinegar

Drain all vegetables and put in a large bowl. Mix sugar, pepper, salt, oil and vinegar. Bring to a boil. Pour over the vegetables while hot. Let set at least 24 hours in a tightly sealed bowl. Better several days old. Will keep in refrigerator a long time; stir once in a while.

Southwest Cookin' (Arkansas)

Tomato Salad

6 medium-to-large tomatoes
2 large bell peppers
1 large onion

2 tablespoons sugar
Salt and pepper
2 tablespoons vinegar

Dice vegetables. Mix together and sprinkle with sugar, salt and pepper. Add vinegar and stir. This will make its own juice from the vinegar. Let set several hours and stir at intervals before serving.

The Farmer's Daughters (Arkansas)

Summer Tomato Salad with Brie

5 medium garden fresh
  tomatoes, cut into chunks,
  save juice
½ pound Brie cheese, rind
  removed, torn into pieces
½ cup fresh basil, snipped
  into strips with scissors

3 large garlic cloves, minced
⅓ cup olive oil
½ teaspoon salt
½ pound fresh pasta,
  linguini, shells, etc.
½ cup freshly grated
  Parmesan cheese

Combine tomatoes and juice, Brie, basil, garlic, olive oil, and salt. Leave at room temperature at least 2 hours. Cook pasta as directed on package. Drain and immediately toss with tomato mixture. Brie should melt. Mix. Sprinkle with Parmesan. Add more salt to taste. Serve at room temperature. Serves 6–8.

Note: Freeze Brie for 20 minutes to remove the rind easily.

Gourmet Our Way (Oklahoma)

Trees and Raisins

An unusual, make-ahead broccoli salad.

1 large head broccoli, cut
 into small flowerets
10–12 strips bacon, fried
 crisp and crumbled
½ cup raisins

¼ cup chopped red onion
1 cup mayonnaise
½ cup sugar
2 tablespoons vinegar

Combine broccoli, bacon, raisins, and onion in a large bowl. Blend together mayonnaise, sugar, and vinegar. Pour over broccoli mixture. Stir to coat well. Cover and marinate at least 1 hour. Serves 6.

Sassafras! (Missouri)

Carrot Raisin Salad

3 cups grated raw carrots
 (about 5 or 6)
1 cup seedless raisins
1 tablespoon honey
6 tablespoons mayonnaise

¼ cup milk
1 tablespoon fresh lemon juice
¼ teaspoon salt
¼ teaspoon nutmeg

Toss carrots lightly with raisins. Blend remaining ingredients and stir into carrot mixture. Chill at least 30 minutes before serving. Makes 6–8 servings.

The Wonderful World of Honey (Arkansas)

Eureka Springs, Arkansas, named for the 63 springs found there, is a charming village etched into the mountainside. It has been called "Little Switzerland of America," "The Stairstep Town," and "The Town That Water Built." A real getaway from the hustle and bustle—there are no traffic lights. "Eureka" means "I have found it."

Herman's Slaw

This is the original slaw served at Herman's Fish Market—a favorite of many in the 1930s and '40s.

1 (4-pound) head cabbage
2 medium onions
½ cup plus 2 tablespoons
  sugar, divided
1 cup cider vinegar

1 teaspoon dry mustard
2 teaspoons salt
1 teaspoon celery seed
1 clove garlic, minced
½–¾ cup oil

Shred cabbage and onions. Cover with the ½ cup sugar. Set aside. Boil vinegar, 2 tablespoons sugar, mustard, salt, and celery seed; pour over cabbage while hot. (Add grated carrots or diced pimentos for color.) Add garlic and oil. Let set 24 hours; serve cold. It's quite tart, so add sugar "to taste." Will keep in refrigerator for weeks.

Four Generations of Johnson Family Favorites (Oklahoma)

Cabbage Slaw

By all means, try this new slant on slaw!

1 head cabbage, chopped
8 green onions, chopped
2 (3-ounce) packages
  uncooked Ramen noodles
2–3 tablespoons butter or
  margarine
½ cup sesame seeds

½ cup slivered almonds
4 tablespoons sugar
1 cup vegetable oil
1 teaspoon freshly ground
  pepper
2 teaspoons salt
6 tablespoons rice vinegar

Toss cabbage, onions, and noodles (broken) together. Do not add seasoning packet to noodles. In a small skillet, melt butter and stir in sesame seeds and almonds. Sauté until lightly browned. Toss with the cabbage mixture.

Combine sugar, oil, pepper, salt, and rice vinegar in a blender. Mix well. Pour dressing over cabbage mixture and toss. Chill, stirring frequently. Can be made 2 or 3 days in advance. Serves 12.

Gateways (Missouri)

Red Potato Salad with Caraway Seeds

This potato salad is lighter than most with a refreshing flavor.

3 pounds small red potatoes unpeeled
¼ cup tarragon vinegar
2 tablespoons sugar
¼ teaspoon paprika
Salt and freshly ground pepper to taste
⅓ cup chopped green bell pepper
¼ cup chopped green onions
1 teaspoon caraway seeds, crushed
¼ teaspoon celery seed
½ cup sour cream
½ cup mayonnaise
Large Boston lettuce leaves
Chopped fresh chives (optional)

Boil potatoes until tender. Drain and pat dry. Cool slightly. Cut into ½-inch slices.

Combine vinegar, sugar, paprika, salt, and pepper in a large bowl. Stir in warm potatoes. Marinate 45 minutes. Gently stir in green pepper, onions, caraway and celery seeds. Combine sour cream and mayonnaise and mix into salad. Cover and chill overnight.

When ready to serve, line a serving bowl with lettuce leaves. Sprinkle fresh chives over salad, if desired. Doubles easily. Serves 6.

Gateways (Missouri)

Hot Baked Potato Salad

1 onion, chopped
¼ cup diced bell pepper
¾ cup oil
1 tablespoon flour
1 teaspoon sugar
¼ teaspoon paprika
½ teaspoon dry mustard
1 teaspoon salt
½ teaspoon seasoned salt
½ cup water
¼ cup vinegar
6 cups cubed cooked potatoes
1 pimento, chopped
Grated cheese

Cook onion and bell pepper in oil until tender. Remove from heat. Add flour, sugar, paprika, mustard, salt, seasoned salt, water, and vinegar. Cook until thickened. Add potatoes and pimento. Pour into 9x9-inch casserole. Arrange grated cheese on top and a few pieces of pimento for color. Bake long enough to melt cheese at 350°.

Cooking on the Road (Missouri)

Shoepeg Salad

1 can shoepeg corn
1 can Le Sueur peas
1 can green beans
1 (4-ounce) jar diced pimentos
1 bunch green onions, chopped
1 small green bell pepper,
  chopped
1 teaspoon salt
1½ teaspoons pepper
½ cup vinegar
½ cup oil
½ cup sugar

Drain corn, peas, green beans, and pimentos. Place drained vegetables in large bowl and add chopped green onions, chopped green pepper, salt and pepper. Mix together well.

In small pan place vinegar, oil, and sugar. Boil together and pour over vegetables. Mix well. Let set in refrigerator for 24 hours.

Thank Heaven for Home Made Cooks (Oklahoma)

Creamy Cornbread Salad

1 (6-ounce) package corn-
  bread mix
½ cup chopped green onions
½ cup chopped green bell
  pepper
½ cup chopped tomatoes
4 ounces ham slices,
  chopped

4 ounces cream cheese,
  softened
¼ cup Miracle Whip
¼ cup creamy cucumber
  ranch salad dressing
½ teaspoon salt
2 tablespoons dry mustard

Prepare and bake cornbread using package directions. Cool; crumble into large bowl. Add green onions, green pepper, tomatoes, and ham; toss well. Blend cream cheese, salad dressing, cucumber salad dressing, salt, and mustard in small bowl. Pour over cornbread mixture; mix well.

Watonga Cheese Festival Cookbook 17th Edition (Oklahoma)

Pasta Salad

1 (16-ounce) bag of your
  favorite pasta (elbow
  macaroni, curly pasta, or
  any fun shape variety pasta)
2 cucumbers, peeled and
  chopped
1 green bell pepper, chopped
1 red bell pepper, chopped
1 (2¼-ounce) can black
  olives, chopped and drained

1 onion, chopped
1 (16-ounce) can tuna (packed
  in water), drained
¼ teaspoon crushed basil
¼ teaspoon crushed tarragon
¼ teaspoon crushed thyme
¼ teaspoon crushed dill
1 large bottle zesty Italian
  salad dressing

Boil pasta, then drain water. Let cool; does not need to be cold. Prepare other ingredients while pasta is boiling. When pasta is cooled, add all other ingredients and serve.

The Homeplace Cookbook (Oklahoma)

Ham-Pecan-Blue Cheese Pasta Salad

Grab a glass of white wine and pleasurize your palate with this tasty salad.

1 (12-ounce) package bow tie
  pasta
4 ounces cooked ham, cut
  into strips
1 cup coarsely chopped
  pecans
1 (4-ounce) package blue
  cheese
⅓ cup chopped fresh parsley

2 tablespoons fresh rosemary
  or 2 teaspoons dried
  rosemary
1 clove garlic, minced
½ teaspoon coarsely ground
  pepper
¼ cup olive oil
⅓ cup grated Parmesan
  cheese

Cook pasta according to directions. Drain. Rinse with cold water and drain. Combine pasta and remaining ingredients, except Parmesan cheese, tossing well. Sprinkle with Parmesan cheese. Serve immediately or chill if desired. Serves 6.

Cooking A+ Recipes (Oklahoma)

Chicken and Pasta-Stuffed Tomatoes

1 cup uncooked 4-color rotini
1 (7-ounce) can chicken white
  meat, drained
½ cup plain lowfat yogurt
½ cup shredded cucumber
¼ cup shredded carrot

2 tablespoons reduced-calorie
  mayonnaise
¼ teaspoon dill weed
¼ teaspoon salt
⅛ teaspoon pepper
4 medium tomatoes

Cook pasta using package directions; drain. Combine chicken, yogurt, cucumber, carrot, mayonnaise, dill weed, salt and pepper in medium bowl. Add pasta; toss to mix well. Remove a ½-inch section of core from each tomato with sharp knife; invert tomatoes on work surface. Cut each tomato into 6 wedges, cutting to, but not through bottom. Place on serving plates; spread wedges gently. Fill with chicken mixture. Yields 4 servings.

The Pioneer Chef (Oklahoma)

Broiled Chicken Salad

2 cups diced cooked chicken
Salt and pepper to taste
1 cup diced celery
¼ cup French dressing
½ cup Miracle Whip
⅓ cup sour cream
¼ cup toasted slivered
  almonds
2 cups crushed potato chips
1 cup grated Cheddar cheese

Salt and pepper the cooked chicken lightly. (Almost all the other ingredients are already salted!) Marinate with the celery in the French dressing 1 hour. Combine salad dressing and sour cream. Drain chicken and celery. Add almonds and sour cream mixture; place salad in a large shallow broiler-proof pan. Mix potato chips and cheese and cover the top of salad with the mixture. Put under broiler only till cheese melts (you don't want to heat the salad). Serves 4.

Clabber Creek Farm Cook Book (Arkansas)

Chinese Chicken Salad

1 medium head lettuce,
  torn into bite-size pieces
2 green onions, chopped (or
  purple onion rings)
2 tablespoons toasted
  almonds
2 tablespoons toasted
  sesame seeds
4 or 5 broiled chicken
  breasts, taken off the
  bones in small pieces
Won ton skins, cut into thin
  strips and fried until
  golden brown

DRESSING:
2 teaspoons salt
1 teaspoon black pepper
4 tablespoons sugar
2 teaspoons Ac'cent
½ cup oil
6 tablespoons salad wine
  vinegar

Mix salad ingredients together, adding Dressing just before serving.

Asbury United Methodist Church Cook Book (Arkansas)

Mooney's Grilled Teriyaki Chicken Salad

4 large chicken breasts
Celery

Mayonnaise
Lemon pepper to taste

MARINADE:
4–6 cloves garlic, sliced
½ cup soy sauce
¼ cup sake or dry sherry

2 tablespoons sugar
2 teaspoons dry mustard

Clean chicken breasts thoroughly. In a glass dish, combine Marinade ingredients. Add chicken to this mixture and refrigerate 4–6 hours, turning several times.

Grill over medium coals for approximately 35–45 minutes. (It's okay if skin becomes blackened, but don't allow chicken to overcook and become dry.)

Remove chicken from heat and allow to cool. Skin and debone the breasts, then coarsely chop the meat. In a bowl, combine chopped chicken, celery, mayonnaise, and lemon pepper.

Serve on lettuce plate with sliced tomatoes and hardtack or good-quality wheat crackers. Garnish with lemon wedge and fresh dill weed. Serves 4.

The Passion of Barbeque (Missouri)

Katy Trail State Park
Missouri Department of Natural Resources

The Katy Trail State park stretches for more than 200 miles across Missouri, from St. Charles to Sedalia and beyond. The compacted limestone surface of the former route of the Missouri-Kansas-Texas Railroad, better known as the "Katy" (hence the park's name), is ideal for hiking and bicycling along the scenic route that follows the Missouri River. The nickname "Katy" comes from the phonetic pronunciation of K-T in the railroad's abbreviated name, MKT.

Chicken Salad
with Cranberry Dressing

4 cups cooked and cubed
   chicken
1 cup chopped celery
2 cups seedless green or red
   grapes

½ teaspoon salt
½ teaspoon pepper
½ cup mayonnaise
½ cup sour cream
½ cup sliced almonds, toasted

CRANBERRY DRESSING:
½ cup jellied cranberry
   sauce
¾ cup vegetable oil
¼ cup wine vinegar
1 teaspoon salt

1 teaspoon sugar
½ teaspoon paprika
¼ teaspoon dry mustard
Dash of pepper

Combine salad ingredients. Whip cranberry sauce and other Dressing
ingredients. Pour over salad. Serves 4.

Gourmet Our Way (Oklahoma)

Cashew Shrimp Salad

Shrimp salad with a touch of the Orient.

1 (10-ounce) package
   tiny frozen peas
1 pound shrimp, steamed,
   peeled, deveined and
   chopped into bite-size
   pieces
2 cups chopped celery
1 cup mayonnaise

1 tablespoon fresh lemon
   juice
1 teaspoon curry powder
Garlic salt to taste
1 cup unsalted cashews
1 (5-ounce) can chow mein
   noodles

Combine the first 7 ingredients in a large bowl and toss well. Cover
and chill at least 30 minutes. Add cashews and noodles and toss again.
Serve on lettuce leaves. Serves 6.

Gateways (Missouri)

Tangy Apricot Salad Mold

1 cup orange juice
1 (6-ounce) or 2 (3-ounce)
   packages apricot Jell-O
2 (16-ounce) cans apricot
   halves, drained
2 cups buttermilk

1 (15¼-ounce) can crushed
   pineapple, drained
1 cup broken pecan pieces
1 (6-ounce) bottle green
   maraschino cherries

Heat orange juice in saucepan until hot. Add Jell-O to hot orange juice. Stir until dissolved. Set aside. Cut 1 can drained apricot halves into fourths. Reserve second can of apricots for garnish. Add to orange juice/Jell-O mixture. Stir in buttermilk. Fold in drained crushed pineapple and nuts. Pour into oiled mold and chill until firm.

To serve, unmold on bed of lettuce, surrounded with second can of drained apricot halves and green cherries placed in center of each apricot half. Serve with Cream Cheese Dressing.

Preparation time: 12 minutes. Makes 10 individual molds or 1 (½-quart) mold.

CREAM CHEESE DRESSING:

1 (3-ounce) package cream
   cheese, softened
½ cup mayonnaise (no
   substitutes)

1 tablespoon milk
Salt to taste
1 teaspoon bottled lemon
   juice (optional)

Mix cream cheese, mayonnaise, and milk together until well blended. Add dash of salt and lemon juice. Beat by hand until light and fluffy. Refrigerate until ready to serve. Preparation time: 6 minutes. Makes 1 cup.

Rush Hour Superchef! (Missouri)

Clamato Aspic Salad

Artichokes in a zesty aspic... Terrific!

1 (3-ounce) package lemon
  gelatin
1½ cups Clamato juice
1 teaspoon lemon juice
Salt and pepper to taste
1 (7-ounce) can artichoke
  hearts, drained, cut in half

½ cup finely chopped green
  bell pepper
½ cup finely chopped avocado
1 head Boston lettuce

Dissolve gelatin in heated Clamato juice. Add lemon juice. salt, and pepper. Cool slightly. Grease a 6-cup muffin pan. Place 1 tablespoon gelatin mixture in each cup. Place half an artichoke heart in each cup. Chill until firm. Chill remaining mixture until partially thickened. Add green pepper and avocado. Fill muffin cups with this mixture; chill thoroughly. Unmold on cups made from Boston lettuce.

Finely Tuned Foods (Missouri)

Red Hot Jell-O Salad

¼ cup cinnamon red hots
½ cup water
3 ounces cherry Jell-O
1 cup boiling water

2 cups peeled and chopped
  apples
½ cup chopped celery
½ cup chopped pecans

Soak red hots in water overnight. Dissolve Jell-O in boiling water. Add red hot liquid. Chill until partially set. Stir in apples, celery, and chopped nuts. Chill until firm. Serves 6.

Company's Coming (Missouri)

Apricot Soufflé Ring
with Chicken Salad

SOUFFLÉ RING:

1 cup apricot juice (from
   can of apricots)
1 cup apricot nectar
6 ounces lemon Jell-O

2 cups heavy cream, whipped
Paprika for garnish
Fresh mint leaves for garnish

Bring apricot juice and apricot nectar to a boil. Add Jell-O and stir until dissolved. Chill until mixture is consistency of honey. (Check after 45 minutes.) Fold into whipped cream and chill in 6-cup ring mold.

CHICKEN SALAD:

1 large onion, sliced
4 stalks celery with leaves,
   sliced
Salt and pepper
4 whole chicken breasts
8 hard-boiled eggs, chopped

3–4 stalks celery, chopped
½ cup white grapes (optional)
¼ cup chopped pecans
   (optional)
¾ cup mayonnaise

Place onion, celery, salt, and pepper in large kettle of water. Bring to boil and add chicken breasts. Simmer 1 hour, or until tender. Remove breasts and chill.

Skin and bone chicken and cut into cubes. Add eggs, celery, grapes, and nuts. Add only enough mayonnaise to mix thoroughly, but not to saturate.

Dip soufflé ring very quickly in hot water and unmold on round serving platter. Mound chicken salad in center of ring. Dust with paprika and garnish with fresh mint leaves. Serves 8–10.

Company's Coming (Missouri)

Spiced Peach-Mandarin Salad

1 package lemon Jell-O
1 package orange Jell-O
1 can Mandarin oranges,
  drained

1 (16-ounce) can spiced
  peaches, drained, pitted,
  and mashed

Prepare Jell-Os according to directions, using the juice from both fruits for the required liquid, plus water to make the correct amount. Add the mashed peaches and Mandarin oranges when partially thickened, and pour into oiled molds or into long pan. Chill until firm; unmold on salad greens or cut into squares and serve on lettuce.

Perfectly Delicious (Arkansas)

Raspberry Salad 1

Delicious! This makes a beautiful lavender-colored salad.

1 (3-ounce) package cream
  cheese, mashed
1 package black raspberry
  Jell-O, dissolved in 1 cup
  hot water
1 small can crushed
  pineapple, without juice

1 can fruit cocktail, juice
  and all
Some chopped nuts and
  miniature marshmallows
1 pint whipping cream, whipped

Add cream cheese to warm Jell-O. Add remaining ingredients except whipping cream. Refrigerate until it starts congealing, and then add whipped cream. Let it congeal in refrigerator.

Perfectly Delicious (Arkansas)

Mom's Blueberry Salad

2 packages grape Jell-O
2 cups boiling water

1 can crushed pineapple
1 can blueberry pie filling

TOPPING:

1 (8-ounce) package cream
  cheese, softened
½ cup sugar
½ pint sour cream

Few drops lemon juice
½ cup chopped nuts
1 teaspoon vanilla

Add grape Jell-O to boiling water and dissolve. Add crushed pineapple (do not drain) and blueberry pie filling. Mix well and let congeal in a 9x13-inch dish. Blend first 4 ingredients of Topping and add nuts and vanilla. Spread over gelatin and return to the refrigerator, covered.

Note: This makes a big salad, and is so rich it could be served as a dessert.

Sisters Two and Family Too (Oklahoma)

Avocado Mousse

1 (¼-ounce) envelope
  unflavored gelatin
½ cup cold water
½ cup boiling water
4 avocados, mashed

1 tablespoon lemon juice
½ teaspoon onion juice
1 teaspoon salt
½ cup cream, whipped
½ cup mayonnaise

Soak gelatin in cold water; dissolve in boiling water. Let cool.

Mash avocado and add lemon juice, onion juice, and salt. Whip cream stiff and fold in mayonnaise. Add dissolved gelatin. Combine with avocado mixture. Pour into individual molds and chill. Yields 6 servings.

In Good Taste (Arkansas)

Horseradish Yogurt Salad

1 small (3-ounce) package
  lemon gelatin
1 cup very hot water
1 cup (8-ounce container)
  lemon-flavored yogurt
½ cup mayonnaise

1 small can crushed
  pineapple
1 cup cottage cheese
1½ tablespoons (or more)
  prepared horseradish

Mix gelatin and hot water. Cool and add remaining ingredients. Mold. Keeps well. Good with chicken or pork.

Talk About Good (Missouri)

Honey-Mustard Dressing

1 cup mayonnaise
4 tablespoons prepared
  mustard
4 tablespoons vinegar
4 tablespoons honey
3 sprigs parsley, chopped

¼ medium onion, finely
  chopped
Pinch of salt
½ teaspoon sugar
1 cup vegetable oil

Combine all ingredients, except oil. Add oil slowly, beating it in constantly. Refrigerate in covered jar. Keeps well for several weeks.

Victorian Sampler (Arkansas)

The natural beauty that characterizes Missouri is more than skin deep. Missouri, the Cave State, has more than 5,000 caves providing plenty of challenges for daring spelunkers. More than 20 caves have safely guided tours: on foot, from your seat in a Jeep-drawn tram, or in a boat on an underground lake.

Ranch Dressing

Cowboys were never known for their love of fresh greens. Some clever cookie invented this sensational dressing made with those cowboy favorites, buttermilk and mayonnaise (both used with a heavy hand in modern ranch cooking), and cowboys have been asking for seconds of salad ever since.

¾ cup mayonnaise
¼ cup buttermilk
⅓ cup minced celery with
  leaves
2 tablespoons chopped fresh
  parsley
1 tablespoon grated onion
  (1 small onion)

1 clove garlic, crushed through
  a press
¼ teaspoon dried thyme
¼ teaspoon celery seed
¼ teaspoon salt
⅛ teaspoon freshly ground
  pepper

In a medium bowl, combine all the ingredients. Cover and refrigerate until ready to use, up to 5 days. Makes about 1½ cups.

Variation: Cucumber Ranch Dressing: Peel a medium cucumber. Cut in half lengthwise and scoop out the seeds with the tip of a spoon. Grate on the large holes of a cheese grater. A handful at a time, squeeze out the excess liquid from the grated cucumber. Stir the grated cucumber into the prepared ranch dressing.

National Cowboy Hall of Fame Chuck Wagon Cookbook (Oklahoma)

Vegetables

ANDREW BALET

Cardiff Hill and the nearby town of Hannibal, Missouri, are immortalized in Mark Twain's book, *The Adventures of Tom Sawyer*. Twain (Samuel Clemens) spent his boyhood years here along the banks of the Mississippi River. He has been called "the father of American literature."

Creole Asparagus

⅓ cup butter
½ cup flour
Salt and pepper to taste
2 cans asparagus
Milk

1 tablespoon chopped green
  bell pepper
4 hard-cooked eggs, sliced
⅓ cup buttered bread crumbs
½ cup grated cheese

Heat oven to 450°. Melt butter. Stir in flour, salt and pepper. Drain and reserve liquid from asparagus. Add milk to asparagus liquid to make 2 cups. Add to flour mixture. Cook, stirring constantly, until thick. Layer asparagus, green pepper, eggs, and sauce in 1½-quart casserole. Sprinkle bread crumbs and cheese on top. Bake about 30 minutes. Yields 4–6 servings.

Sing for Your Supper (Missouri)

Escalloped Asparagus

1 can asparagus
4 hard-boiled eggs, sliced
White Sauce

Butter
Grated cheese

Layer ½ asparagus, sliced eggs, and remaining asparagus. Cover with White Sauce then dots of butter and grated cheese. Bake 1–2 hours at 325°.

WHITE SAUCE:
3 tablespoons butter
⅓ cup flour

Milk
Salt and pepper, to taste

Brown butter, add flour, stir. Add milk to make a medium thickened sauce. Add salt and pepper to taste.

Here's What's Cookin' at Zion (Oklahoma)

Broccoli Balls

2 pounds fresh broccoli or 3
  (10-ounce) packages frozen
  broccoli
1 (12-ounce) carton small-
  curd cottage cheese
⅓ cup plus ½ cup grated
  Parmesan cheese, divided

⅓ cup fine bread crumbs
½ teaspoon salt
2 eggs, beaten
⅓ cup flour
¼ cup margarine

Cook broccoli in a small amount of water just until tender; drain and chop. Combine broccoli, cottage cheese, ⅓ cup Parmesan cheese, bread crumbs, salt, and eggs. Mix well. Shape into 8 balls; refrigerate overnight.

Roll balls in flour and place in a buttered 9x13-inch baking dish. Dot with margarine. Bake at 400° for 10 minutes. Sprinkle with ½ cup Parmesan cheese and bake 5 minutes longer. Makes 8 generous servings.

United Methodist Cookbook 1993 (Oklahoma)

Broccoli Swiss Bake

Nice colors!

1½ cups summer squash
  (½-inch pieces)
3 cups chopped fresh broccoli
½ cup butter or margarine
1 egg, beaten
½ cup shredded Swiss
  cheese

¼ cup milk
¼ teaspoon dry mustard
1 teaspoon salt
Pepper and cayenne to taste
½ cup grated Parmesan cheese
2 tablespoons toasted sesame
  seeds

Steam squash and broccoli so they are crisp-tender. Layer in casserole. Melt butter and mix with egg, Swiss cheese, milk, and seasonings. Pour over broccoli and squash. Top with Parmesan cheese and sesame seeds. Bake 20 minutes at 350°. Serve immediately.

With Hands & Heart Cookbook (Missouri)

Broccoli-Corn Bake

1 (16-ounce) can cream-style
  corn
1 (10-ounce) package frozen
  chopped broccoli, thawed
  and well drained
1 egg, beaten
½ cup coarsely crumbled
  Ritz Crackers (12)

2 tablespoons melted butter
2 teaspoons dehydrated onion
Salt and freshly ground pepper
1 tablespoon butter, melted
¼ cup coarsely crumbled
  Ritz Crackers (5)

Preheat oven to 350°. Combine first 6 ingredients in a large bowl and mix thoroughly. Spoon into lightly greased 1-quart baking dish and season with salt and pepper. Combine butter and Ritz Crackers. Mix thoroughly. Sprinkle this mixture over top of casserole. Bake uncovered until golden brown, about 30 minutes.

Gourmet: The Quick and Easy Way (Oklahoma)

Jalapeño Corn Pudding

Some corn puddings are wimpy, tenderfoot food, but not this one. If you can find them, Kent suggests adding 1 cup drained canned cactus (nopales) pieces.

2 (16-ounce) cans cream-style
  corn
2 cups (8 ounces) shredded
  sharp Cheddar cheese,
  divided
½ cup yellow cornmeal

½ cup vegetable oil
2 large eggs, beaten
2 tablespoons canned chopped
  green chiles, drained
2 cloves garlic, minced
½ teaspoon salt

Preheat the oven to 350°. Lightly butter a 12x7-inch baking dish. In a medium bowl, whisk corn, 1 cup cheese, cornmeal, oil, eggs, chiles, garlic, and salt. Spread the batter in the baking dish, then sprinkle with the remaining 1 cup cheese.

    Bake until the center feels set when pressed gently with a finger, about 1 hour. Let stand 5 minutes before serving. Makes 4–6 servings.

National Cowboy Hall of Fame Chuck Wagon Cookbook (Oklahoma)

Fried Corn

Select 12 ears of corn at the perfect stage. Husk the corn and remove silk by brushing back and forth with a soft brush or cloth. Cut from the cob with a very sharp knife. Cut only half the depth of the kernel. Use the back of the knife to scrape out the remaining pulp and juice. Should yield 5 cups of corn. Heat ½ cup of butter, sizzling hot in heavy skillet. Add corn and enough water to give consistency of thin gravy. Season with salt and pepper, stirring constantly. Cook 5 minutes. Reduce heat to simmering. Cover tightly and cook about 20 minutes longer. The corn will be thick. Serve hot. Very good with fried chicken.

Oklahoma Cookin' (Oklahoma)

Company Corn

¼–½ pound bacon, fried
   crisp and crumbled
2 tablespoons chopped onion
2 tablespoons bacon drippings
2 tablespoons butter
4 tablespoons flour
1 cup dairy sour cream
2 (16-ounce) cans whole-kernel
   corn, drain 1 can

Fry bacon in a large skillet; set aside. Sauté onion in bacon drippings and butter until tender. Add flour and mix well. Stir in sour cream. Mix in corn and cook over low heat until mixture begins to thicken. Stir in bacon, saving some to use as garnish. Pour into a serving dish and garnish with reserved bacon; serve immediately. Serves 8.

Sassafras! (Missouri)

ATALOA LODGE MUSEUM COLLECTION

Ataloa Lodge Museum in Muskogee, Oklahoma, houses one of the best collections of privately owned traditional and contemporary Native American art in the United States. One of the unique attractions at Ataloa Lodge is the 500 Stone Fireplace made of rocks from around the world, with at least one stone from each of the United States, and a fossilized dinosaur egg.

Spicy Corn

1 (8-ounce) package cream
  cheese
2 tablespoons butter or
  margarine
1/4 cup milk
3 cans white shoepeg corn

1 small can chopped green
  chiles
Cayenne pepper to taste
Pepper to taste
Salt to taste
Garlic powder to taste

Melt cream cheese and butter in milk in saucepan. Add corn, green chiles, peppers, salt, and garlic powder; mix well. Cook on top of stove until bubbly.

Cooking for Good Measure (Arkansas)

Hominy Casserole

1 medium onion, chopped
1 stalk celery
Butter
2 cans yellow hominy (drain
  1/2 juice off)

1 (8-ounce) carton sour cream
1/4 cup pimento
1 cup grated cheese (American)

Sauté onion and celery in butter. Combine all ingredients and pour in buttered casserole dish. Bake in slow oven until bubbling (20–30 minutes).

Seems Like I Done It This A-Way III (Oklahoma)

Harvard Beets

2 teaspoons cornstarch
2 teaspoons flour
1/2 cup sugar
1/4 teaspoon salt
Dash of cinnamon

A bit of grated orange peel
1 (16-ounce) can sliced beets,
  drained, reserve 1/2 cup juice
2 tablespoons melted margarine

Mix dry ingredients. Add liquid from beets and margarine and cook over low heat about 10 minutes. Pour over beets and let stand one-half hour before serving.

Cookin' Along the Cotton Belt (Arkansas)

Tangy Green Beans

4 slices bacon, cut into
  ½-inch pieces
½ cup chopped onion
2 (16-ounce) cans whole
  green beans, drained

¾ cup water
3 tablespoons white vinegar
1 beef-flavored bouillon cube
¼ teaspoon pepper

Cook bacon in a large skillet until lightly browned. Stir in onion and cook until tender. Add beans and remaining ingredients; cook until thoroughly heated.

St. Ambrose "On the Hill" Cookbook (Missouri)

Green Bean Casserole

2 (9-ounce) packages frozen
  green beans
1 (10¾-ounce) can cream
  of mushroom soup
½ cup milk
1 teaspoon soy sauce

Dash of pepper
½ cup sliced pitted ripe olives,
  divided
1 (2.8-ounce) can French fried
  onions, divided

Place beans in medium micro-safe bowl. Cover. Microwave on HIGH 9 minutes or until tender. Drain. In 1½-quart micro-safe casserole, stir soup until smooth. Add milk, soy sauce, and pepper; stir until well blended. Stir in beans, half of the olives and half of the onions. Cover; microwave on HIGH 7 minutes or until hot and bubbling, stirring once during cooking. Let stand, covered, 5 minutes. Sprinkle with remaining olives and onions. Makes 6 servings.

Around the Bend (Arkansas)

K.C. Masterpiece Barbequed Baked Beans

2 (16-ounce) cans pork and
  beans, drained
1 ounce golden raisins
½ cup brown sugar
1 tart apple (such as
  Jonathan), peeled, cored,
  and chopped

1 medium onion, chopped
¾ cup K.C. Masterpiece
  Original Sauce
3 strips uncooked bacon, cut
  in half (or substitute 2
  tablespoons butter or
  margarine)

Preheat oven to 350°. Mix all ingredients except bacon in a 2-quart baking dish. Top with uncooked bacon (or butter). Bake uncovered for 1 hour.

Kansas City BBQ (Missouri)

Southwestern Pinto Beans

1 (16-ounce) package pinto
  beans
½ pound bacon, cut up
2 cups chopped onions
3 garlic cloves, minced
2 (8-ounce) cans tomato sauce

2–3 tablespoons chili powder
½ teaspoon oregano leaves
½ teaspoon salt
½ teaspoon pepper
⅛ teaspoon cumin

Rinse beans well. Soak overnight in 6 cups water; do not drain.

Simmer beans, covered, for 3–3½ hours until tender. In large skillet, cook bacon, onions, and garlic over medium heat until bacon is crisp. Do not drain. Add bacon mixture, tomato sauce, chili powder, oregano, salt, pepper, and cumin to beans; stir well. Simmer, uncovered, an additional 20–30 minutes. These are good as a main dish. They can also be used as a burrito filling, or can be served over cooked white rice and topped with your favorite shredded cheese.

Oklahoma Cookin' (Oklahoma)

Cotton Eyed Joe's Baked Beans

On the south edge of Claremore, Oklahoma, just across the railroad track from Route 66, is Cotton Eyed Joe's, a serious barbecue stop.

2 (16-ounce) cans pork and
  beans
⅛ teaspoon salt
3½ tablespoons brown sugar
2 tablespoons Worcestershire

¼ cup barbecue sauce
1 teaspoon powdered mustard
3 drops liquid smoke
1 teaspoon powdered onion

Combine all ingredients in a large casserole dish and bake at 300° for one hour. Makes 10 servings.

The Route 66 Cookbook (Oklahoma)

Sweet and Tangy Beans

Not every good bean recipe starts with dried beans. In this one, canned pintos get dressed up with barbecue sauce, apples, and raisins. They make a perfect pairing with baked ham.

3 strips bacon
1 medium apple, peeled,
  cored, and cut into ½-inch
  pieces
1 medium onion, finely
  chopped

1 cup golden raisins
1 cup prepared barbecue sauce
¾ cup packed light brown
  sugar
3 (16-ounce) cans pinto
  beans, drained

Preheat the oven to 350°. Rub the inside of a 2-quart round flame-proof casserole with one of the bacon strips to lightly grease, and place the bacon strip in the bottom of the casserole. Cut the remaining 2 bacon strips into 1-inch pieces.

In a large bowl, stir the apple, onion, raisins, barbecue sauce, and sugar until well combined. Stir in the beans. Transfer to the prepared casserole. Top with the bacon pieces.

Cover and bake for 30 minutes. Uncover and continue baking until bubbling throughout and the bacon is browned, about 30 more minutes. Serve the beans hot. Makes 4–6 servings.

National Cowboy Hall of Fame Chuck Wagon Cookbook (Oklahoma)

Baked Onions

6 medium onions, peeled
    and sliced in half
6 slices bacon (optional)
¼ cup tomato juice or
    ketchup
2 tablespoons brown sugar

½ teaspoons salt
¼ teaspoon pepper
¼ teaspoon paprika
½ teaspoon dill or celery seed
Chopped parsley

Place cut onions in greased casserole, 10x6x2-inches. Fry bacon crisp and crumble. Combine tomato juice, brown sugar, and spices. Pour over onions and cover. Bake about 1 hour at 350°. Baste occasionally. Good with frozen broccoli or green beans, also roast chicken and rice.

Talk About Good (Missouri)

Onion Fries

¾ cup self-rising flour
½ teaspoon baking powder
1 tablespoon cornmeal
½ cup nonfat dry milk

2 teaspoons sugar
½ teaspoon salt
2½ cups chopped onions

Combine all ingredients except onions. Add cold water a little at a time until you have a very thick batter. Add onions and mix: well. Make small half-dollar size patties by dripping from spoon into hot shallow oil and flattening slightly with back of spoon. Brown on both sides.

The Farmer's Daughters (Arkansas)

Stuffed Baked Onions
(Ultra Lowfat)

4 large sweet onions
2 stalks celery, chopped fine
3½ cups boxed stuffing mix
  (should contain only 1 gram
  fat per serving for mix only)
Salt to taste

Black pepper to taste
1 egg white, slightly beaten
4 tablespoons lite sour cream
2 cups chicken broth (use
  canned and remove fat from
  top)

Preheat oven to 350°. Remove centers of onion, leaving outside shell to stand alone after center is removed. To remove centers, cut top and bottom from onion and carefully remove several inside layers from the onion, starting with the center and working out. Save enough of the onion centers to provide ½ cup chopped onion to mix with stuffing.

Brown remaining chopped onion and celery in skillet sprayed with nonstick cooking spray. Set aside to cool slightly. In large bowl combine stuffing mix, browned onion and celery, salt, pepper, and egg white. Fill each onion with stuffing mix.

In small bowl stir lite sour cream until creamy. Gradually add chicken broth and stir until all chicken broth is added. Place stuffed onions in baking dish sprayed with nonstick cooking spray. Pour a small amount of cream sauce over each stuffed onion and pour the rest of the sauce in the bottom of the baking dish. Bake uncovered at 350° for 35-40 minutes or until onions are tender. Serve as a side dish with meat if desired. Makes 4 servings.

Fat Free & Ultra Lowfat Recipes (Oklahoma)

Mushroom Pie

Excellent when served with steak or roast beef.

1 (9-inch) unbaked pie shell
2 tablespoons minced shallots
  or whites of green onions
4 tablespoons butter
1 pound mushrooms, thinly
  sliced
1½ teaspoons salt

1 teaspoon lemon juice
4 eggs
1 cup heavy cream
⅛ teaspoon pepper
⅛ teaspoon nutmeg
½ cup grated Swiss cheese

Prebake pie shell 8–10 minutes in 450° oven. In skillet, sauté shallots in butter and add mushrooms, salt, and lemon juice. Cover, and simmer 10 minutes. Uncover, increase heat, and cook rapidly until liquid has evaporated, stirring occasionally.

Beat eggs with cream, pepper, and nutmeg. Combine with mushrooms. Pour into partially cooked pie shell and sprinkle grated cheese over top. Dot with butter and bake in preheated 350° oven for about 35 minutes until puffed and slightly firm when you jiggle the pan. Serves 6–8.

The Cook Book (Missouri)

Molly's Landing Marinated Mushrooms

At the west edge of the twin bridges in Verdigris is Molly's Landing, an upscale restaurant with an unexpected twist.

1½ cups vegetable oil
½ teaspoon dry mustard
1½ cups vinegar
1½ tablespoons minced
  fresh garlic

3 tablespoons sugar
2 teaspoons Worcestershire
1 tablespoon salt
1 pound fresh mushrooms,
  cleaned

Combine all ingredients except mushrooms. Pour mixture over mushrooms and marinate for 24 hours in the refrigerator. Makes 5–6 servings.

The Route 66 Cookbook (Oklahoma)

Spanakopita
(Spinach Pie)

1 bunch green onions,
  chopped
1½–2 pounds fresh spinach
½ pound feta cheese,
  crumbled
½ pound cottage cheese,
  large curd

Salt and white pepper to taste
5–6 eggs
½ pound filo dough (or
  more, if preferred)
3–4 sticks butter, melted

In a small pot, sauté the green onions in a little butter and set aside. Rinse, chop, and drain the spinach and place in a large mixing bowl. Add the sautéed green onions, the feta and cottage cheeses, and the salt and pepper. Then slowly fold the beaten eggs into the spinach mixture and set aside. Butter a 9x13-inch baking pan, and one at a time, layer about 7 filo sheets in the bottom of the pan, brushing each one with melted butter. Spread the spinach mixture evenly over the pastry sheets. Top with about 7 more individually buttered filo sheets, and be certain to thoroughly butter the last filo sheet. Refrigerate the pita an hour or two, and then score into squares with the tip of a sharp knife. Do not cut all the way down through the pita. Bake the pita in a pre-heated 350° oven about 1 hour or until a light golden color.

After baking place on a wire rack to cool and cut into squares before serving. Do not cover the pita while cooling because it will get soggy.

Note: May substitute 3 (10-ounce) packages of frozen chopped spinach for the fresh spinach. Be sure the frozen spinach is completely thawed and well drained before adding to the other ingredients.

If time does not permit refrigeration before baking and scoring the pita, it may be baked immediately after preparation. It will be a little more difficult to score, but this should be done before baking.

Adventures in Greek Cooking (Missouri)

Spinach Madeleine

2 (10-ounce) packages
  frozen chopped spinach
4 tablespoons butter
2 tablespoons flour
2 tablespoons chopped
  onion
½ cup evaporated milk
½ cup vegetable liquor

½ teaspoon black pepper
¾ teaspoon celery salt
Salt to taste
¾ teaspoon garlic salt
1 teaspoon Worcestershire
Red pepper to taste
1½ cups shredded pepper Jack
  cheese

Cook spinach according to directions on package. Drain and reserve liquor. Melt butter in saucepan over low heat. Add flour, stirring until blended and smooth, but not brown.

Add onion and cook until soft but not brown. Add liquid slowly, stirring constantly to avoid lumps. Cook until smooth and thick. Continue stirring. Add seasonings and cheese which has been cut into small pieces. Stir until melted. Combine with cooked spinach.
This may be served immediately or put into a casserole and topped with buttered bread crumbs. The flavor is improved if the latter is done and kept in refrigerator overnight and then reheated. This may also be frozen. Serves 4–6.

In Good Taste (Arkansas)

ARKANSAS DEPARTMENT OF PARKS & TOURISM

Arkansas Highway 7 has been named "one of the ten most scenic highways in America," and "one of the most fun-to-drive highways in America" by leading magazine and travel writers. It is the state's first state-designated scenic byway, traversing the north-south length of the state from Harrison, Arkansas, to the Louisiana state line, offering spectacular views as it passes through the Ozark and Ouachita mountains. There are unique places to stay, camp, shop, and stop along this scenic picture-postcard route.

Spinach Bake

2 (10-ounce) packages
  frozen chopped spinach
¼ teaspoon pepper
½ teaspoon nutmeg

1 cup fresh mushrooms, sliced
2 tablespoons Butter Buds
2 ounces Cheddar/mozzarella
  cheese mixture

TOPPING:
¾ cup plain nonfat yogurt
1 tablespoon horseradish

2 teaspoons Dijon mustard
Paprika

Spray skillet with cooking spray and add frozen spinach; cook until defrosted. Add pepper and nutmeg and stir. Meanwhile, sauté mushrooms in Butter Buds. Add cheese and cook until melted. Combine with spinach mixture. Pour into casserole sprayed with cooking spray. Combine Topping ingredients, except paprika. Spread over spinach. Sprinkle with paprika and bake at 350° until brown. Serves 8.

Note: If you prefer a topping not quite so tangy, reduce amount of horseradish to 1 teaspoon.

Eat to Your Heart's Content, Too! (Arkansas)

Marvell Squash

Even people who don't like squash like this dish!

3 pounds squash, sliced
1 medium onion, chopped
½ stick butter
2 tablespoons flour

1 (13-ounce) can evaporated
  milk
½ pound American cheese
Potato chips, crumbled

Cook squash and onion in salted water until tender. Drain, and put into buttered 2-quart casserole. In saucepan melt butter. Add the flour, then gradually add milk. Stir in cheese and simmer until melted. Pour sauce over squash; sprinkle potato chips on top. Bake at 350° for 30 minutes.

High Cotton Cookin' (Arkansas)

Skillet Squash

Medium onion, sliced thinly
  and separated into rings
2 teaspoons margarine
2 cups thinly sliced zucchini
½ teaspoon sea salt
Dash of coarsely ground pepper
1 medium tomato, cut in
  wedges
1 cup sliced fresh mushrooms

Sauté onion slices in margarine until tender-crisp. Add squash and cook covered for 6 minutes, stirring occasionally. Add remaining ingredients and continue cooking about 4 minutes. Squash should be tender-crisp. Remove with slotted spoon. Serves 6.

A Great Taste of Arkansas (Arkansas)

Elegante Squash

2 (8-ounce) packages squash,
  cooked and drained
½ cup chopped onion
½ cup chopped green bell
  pepper
½ cup margarine
½ cup mayonnaise
1 cup sliced water chestnuts
½ cup shredded cheese
1 egg
1 tablespoon sugar
½ cup bread crumbs

Cook squash; drain and set aside. Sauté onion and green pepper in margarine until clear. Add squash, mayonnaise, chestnuts, and cheese. Beat egg with sugar; spread over vegetables in casserole. Cover with bread crumbs and bake at 350° until bubbly, about 30 minutes. Good!

Country Cooking (Oklahoma)

Zucchini Casserole

Different, with zip!

8 slices Pepperidge Farm
  Bread, trimmed
¼ cup butter (scant)
1 (1-pound) can whole corn,
  drained
2 cups thinly sliced zucchini
1 (4-ounce) can green chiles,
  seeded and chopped

½ pound Monterey Jack
  cheese, shredded (2 cups)
½ cup shredded sharp Cheddar
  cheese
4 eggs
2 cups milk
1 teaspoon salt
⅛ teaspoon pepper

Butter the bread and put in a 9x13-inch flat casserole, buttered side down. Cover bread with layered corn, zucchini, chiles, and both cheeses. Mix eggs, milk, salt, and pepper together. Pour over the vegetables. Let set 4 hours. Bake at 375° for 25 minutes. Let rest 10 minutes before serving. Easy. Do ahead. Serves 8.

With Hands & Heart Cookbook (Missouri)

Eggplant-Zucchini Parmigiana

1 medium eggplant, cut in
  12 (¼-inch) slices, peeled
1 tablespoon mayonnaise or
  sandwich spread
¼ cup Italian bread crumbs
1 cup low-fat cottage cheese
1 egg, slightly beaten

¼ teaspoon garlic salt
1 (8-ounce) can tomato sauce
2 tablespoons grated Parmesan
1 cup grated mozzarella
2 small zucchini, cut in
  ⅛-inch slices

Put peeled eggplant on cookie sheet. Spread with mayonnaise and crumbs. Bake in preheated 475° oven for 10 minutes.

Remove and turn oven to 375°. Mix cottage cheese, egg, and garlic salt. Layer all of eggplant, half of cottage cheese mixture, half of tomato sauce, half of Parmesan and mozzarella cheese. Top with zucchini and then layer the last half of the remaining ingredients. Bake uncovered at 375° for 30 minutes. Let stand for 5 minutes before cutting. Serves 6–8.

Cookin' in the Spa (Arkansas)

Basil Tomato Tart

Great to serve when your garden is bountiful with fresh tomatoes and basil.

1 unbaked 9-inch pie crust
1½ cups shredded mozzarella
   cheese, divided
6 Roma or 4 medium
   tomatoes
1 cup loosely packed fresh
   basil leaves

4 cloves garlic, minced
½ cup mayonnaise
¼ cup freshly grated
   Parmesan cheese
⅓ teaspoon ground white
   pepper
Fresh basil leaves (optional)

Place pie crust in quiche dish or glass pie plate. Flute edges and prick bottom and sides. Bake in preheated 475° oven 8–10 minutes until light brown. Sprinkle with ½ cup of the mozzarella cheese. Cool on a wire rack.

Cut tomatoes into wedges; drain on paper towels. Arrange tomato wedges atop melted cheese in the baked pie shell. In a food processor combine basil and garlic and chop coarsely. Sprinkle over tomatoes.
In medium mixing bowl combine remaining mozzarella cheese, mayonnaise, Parmesan, and pepper. Spoon cheese mixture over basil mixture, spreading evenly to cover the top. Bake in 375° oven 35–40 minutes or until golden and bubbly. Serve warm. If desired, sprinkle with basil leaves. Serves 6.

Gourmet Our Way (Oklahoma)

Okra-Tomato Supreme

A really delicious okra recipe--a meal in itself.

1½ cups fresh okra (cut
  in ½-inch pieces)
½ cup chopped onion
½ cup chopped green bell
  pepper
2 tablespoons oil

1 tablespoon sugar
1 teaspoon flour
¾ teaspoon salt
1 pint–1 quart cooked
  tomatoes

Cook okra gently in small amount of water until tender. Drain well and pour cold water over to rinse. Cook onion and green pepper in oil until tender, not brown. Blend sugar, flour, and salt and stir in tomatoes and okra. Heat until hot through. Stir as little as possible to prevent breaking okra.

Note: A variation of this recipe can be made by adding hamburger, browned and drained. Add onions, peppers, and tomatoes. Place thick raw slices of okra on top and let simmer and steam until okra is tender.

Treasured Recipes Book II (Missouri)

Dilled Okra

3 pounds young okra, uncut
6 cloves garlic, divided
6 large heads and stems dill
6 small red chile peppers

3 teaspoons mustard seed
1 quart water
1 pint vinegar
½ cup salt

Pack scrubbed okra into 6 hot, sterilized pint jars with one clove garlic, one head and stem dill, one red pepper, and ½ teaspoon mustard seed for each jar. Make brine of water, vinegar, and salt; heat to boiling. Pour into jars; seal at once. Let stand 3–4 weeks. Makes 6 pints.

Around the Bend (Arkansas)

Garden Goulash

This is an original recipe that my family loved, and since we raised a large vegetable garden, I had all the vegetables on hand. I often add other vegetables as well, such as eggplant and summer squash.

5 cups sliced okra
Meal, flour, and salt
1 small onion, chopped
⅛ cup chopped green bell
  pepper

1 cup whole-kernel corn
1 small jalapeño pepper
  (seeded), chopped
2–3 fresh tomatoes

Toss the okra in a mixture of cornmeal, flour, and salt. Brown slightly in oil. Don't overbrown. Then add remaining ingredients except tomatoes. Simmer slowly until done. Do not stir frequently. When done, peel and cut fresh tomatoes into chunks; place atop mixture. Simmer until tomatoes are slightly soft.

Recipes and Remembrances (Oklahoma)

Cottage-Fried Potatoes

¼ cup shortening or oil
6 cups potatoes, chopped

1 teaspoon salt
⅛ teaspoon pepper

Heat shortening or oil in a 10- or 12-inch pan with a tight fitting lid. Add potatoes when fat is hot enough to simmer gently around a piece of potato. Season with salt and pepper.

Cover tightly and fry gently until potatoes are brown, turning them occasionally as they cook. Remove cover for last few minutes of cooking time to crisp potatoes. Makes 6–8 servings.

Hint: For variety, add a medium onion, finely chopped, to the potatoes when browned on one side.

Home for the Holidays (Arkansas)

Latkes

3 cups potatoes, unpeeled,
    scrubbed and cut into
    chunks
1 egg
1 small onion, quartered

2 tablespoons flour
1 tablespoon soft butter
½ teaspoon sugar
½ teaspoon salt
Dash of pepper

Blend three-fourths of potatoes in a food processor, using steel knife. Add rest of ingredients. Using shredder, process rest of potatoes, mix well. Pour by spoonfuls onto hot well-greased griddle. Turn when edges are brown.

Gourmet Garden (Missouri)

Potato Puffs

4½ cups diced potatoes
2 teaspoons salt, divided
1½ cups water
6 tablespoons butter

1½ cups all-purpose flour
6 eggs
Oil

Boil potatoes in water to which 1 teaspoon salt has been added. Cook until potatoes are soft. Drain well; mash with potato ricer. Do not add the usual butter or milk.

In a saucepan, heat 1½ cups water, remaining teaspoon salt, and the butter until water boils and butter melts. Reduce heat. Add flour all at once and stir until batter is firm and leaves sides of pan. Remove from heat. Turn batter into bowl of electric mixer. Add eggs, one by one, beating well after each addition. Add potatoes and mix until well blended. Heat 1-inch oil in electric skillet to 370°. Drop potato mixture by teaspoons into hot oil. Fry until puffed and golden brown. Drain on paper toweling. Sprinkle with salt.

Puffs may be made ahead of time by frying only to a light brown. Place in a single layer on cookie sheet and place in freezer. At serving time, bake in preheated 450° oven, uncovered, 8–10 minutes, or until medium brown. Sprinkle with salt. Serves 8–12. Recipe may be halved.

Talk About Good (Missouri)

Spicy Potatoes

3 pounds potatoes, unpeeled
3 tablespoons oil
¾ teaspoon salt
½ teaspoon dried oregano
½ teaspoon paprika

¼ teaspoon crushed garlic
¼ teaspoon freshly ground
  pepper
¼ cup grated Parmesan
  cheese

Preheat oven to 450°. Grease a cookie sheet. Wash potatoes and cut each into 8 or 10 wedges; drain. Put them in a bowl and toss lightly with oil. Combine remaining ingredients. Sprinkle half of the cheese mixture over potatoes and toss. Add remaining cheese and toss. Place potatoes on the cookie sheets in a single layer and bake 25–30 minutes, flipping potatoes if necessary. Leftovers can be reheated. Easy. Can do ahead. Serves 6.

Cooking in Clover II (Missouri)

Creamy Grilled Potatoes

5 medium potatoes, peeled
  and thinly sliced
1 medium onion, sliced
8 tablespoons butter or
  margarine
⅓ cup shredded Cheddar
  cheese

2 tablespoons minced parsley
2 tablespoons Worcestershire
Salt and pepper to taste
⅓ cup chicken broth
2 tablespoons bacon bits

Place sliced potatoes and onion on 22x18-inch piece of heavy-duty foil. Dot with butter. Sprinkle with cheese, parsley, Worcestershire, salt, and pepper. Fold up foil around potatoes; add chicken broth. Sprinkle with bacon bits. Seal edges tightly. Grill packet on covered grill over medium-hot Kingsford briquets about 35 minutes or until potatoes are tender. Serves 6.

The Never Ending Season (Missouri)

Cowboy Potato and Vegetable Bake

The best way to get cowboys to eat their vegetables is to mix them with plenty of potatoes. No one at the dinner table will turn up their noses at this casserole.

½ cup (1 stick) unsalted
  butter, melted
4 medium baking potatoes
  (about 2½ pounds), peeled
  and sliced ⅛ inch thick
3 medium carrots, sliced ¼
  inch thick
2 medium zucchini, scrubbed
  and sliced ½ inch thick
4 ounces fresh mushrooms,
  sliced ¼ inch thick

1 medium onion, chopped
1 medium green bell pepper,
  seeded and chopped into
  ½-inch pieces
1 teaspoon salt
¼ teaspoon freshly ground
  pepper
½ cup (4 ounces) shredded
  sharp Cheddar cheese

Preheat the oven to 400°. Brush the inside of a 9x13-inch baking dish with some of the melted butter.

    Add the vegetables, drizzle with the remaining melted butter, sprinkle with the salt and pepper, and toss well. Bake, stirring occasionally, until the potatoes are tender, about 1 hour. During the last 15 minutes, sprinkle with the cheese. Makes 6–8 servings.

National Cowboy Hall of Fame Chuck Wagon Cookbook (Oklahoma)

Red Potato Strips

1 stick margarine, softened
1 package dry onion soup
Black pepper

5–6 red potatoes, scrubbed
  and quartered

Mix margarine and soup together and spread on peppered potatoes. Put potatoes into a Pam-sprayed casserole and seal with foil. Bake at 350° for 1 hour or until tender. Remove foil and bake another 10 minutes. Yields 10–12 servings.

Betty Is Still "Winking" at Cooking (Arkansas)

Laredo Potato

So many people love this dish! It's quick to fix, it's very tasty, very low in fat, and it's filled with energy.

1 medium potato
¼ cup chili hot beans
½ tomato, chopped
2 tablespoons chopped green
　onion

½ ounce (⅓ cup) shredded
　low-moisture, part-skim
　mozzarella cheese
Salsa

Bake potato in microwave 4 minutes, or till done; split and mash a bit. Top with the beans. Heat in microwave. Top with tomato, onion, and cheese. Now add salsa for great Mexican flavor. Makes 1 serving.

15 Minute, Lowfat Meals (Oklahoma)

Sweet Potatoes and Apples

This is a good "fix ahead" dish to serve with pork or fowl. When your oven is going, bake 3 or 4 sweet potatoes or pierce and cook in the microwave, then peel, cube and refrigerate a day or two until ready to use. For 4 servings:

2 tablespoons margarine
4 apples, peeled and cubed
¼ cup minced onion
2 tablespoons brown sugar,
　firmly packed

2 teaspoons lemon juice
¼ teaspoon cinnamon
Dash of allspice
3 or 4 sweet potatoes, cooked,
　cut in cubes

Heat margarine in skillet; add apples and onion. Cook 4 or 5 minutes until apples are soft. Stir in sugar, juice, and seasonings, stirring until sugar is melted; add sweet potatoes and cook until thoroughly heated.

Apples, Apples, Apples (Missouri)

Lo-Cal Carrots

4 cups sliced carrots
1 cup water
1 (15-ounce) can unsweetened
  pineapple tidbits, undrained

2 tablespoons cornstarch
½ teaspoon ginger

In a small saucepan cook carrots in water until crisp-tender; carrots may be steamed. Combine pineapple, cornstarch, and ginger in a small bowl; mix well; add to carrots. Cook over low heat, stirring constantly, until mixture thickens.

Celebration (Arkansas)

Company Carrots

1 pound carrots, thinly sliced
¼ cup golden raisins
¼ cup butter
3 tablespoons honey

1 tablespoon lemon juice
¼ teaspoon ground ginger
¼ cup sliced, unpeeled almonds

Preheat oven to 300°. Cook carrots, covered, in ½-inch boiling water for 8 minutes; drain. Place carrots in a 1-quart baking dish. Stir in raisins, butter, honey, lemon juice, and ginger. Bake, covered, for 30 minutes, stirring occasionally. Watch. Don't let burn. Sprinkle with almonds before serving. Serves 4.

Gourmet: The Quick and Easy Way (Oklahoma)

Since 1968 more than seven million people from all over the world have enjoyed *The Great Passion Play*, a premier outdoor religious drama performed on a multilevel staging area from May to November in Eureka Springs, Arkansas.

Vegetable Patties

These make a wonderful entrée, or a great substitute for a burger on a whole-wheat bun!

1 small onion, quartered
2 stems broccoli or 1 large
  zucchini
¼ cup skim or evaporated
  skim milk
1 (16-ounce) can green beans,
  drained

1 (15-ounce) can white beans,
  well drained
½ cup whole-wheat flour
½ cup whole-wheat bread
  crumbs
Olive or safflower oil

Steam onion and broccoli together for 5–6 minutes, or until broccoli is tender. Place in a food processor bowl. Add milk and both beans. Process until smooth. Place mixture in a large bowl. Stir in flour and bread crumbs. "Dough" should be soft but not runny. Add more bread crumbs if necessary.

Heat 1 teaspoon of oil over medium heat in a large skillet. Form a patty the size of a burger and place it in the skillet. Reduce heat to medium-low. Cook approximately 4 minutes on each side; cook longer over higher heat if a crisper patty is preferred. Patties should be golden brown. Serves 4–6.

Note: To make whole-wheat bread crumbs, simply dry out whole-wheat bread heels overnight, or bake in a 200° oven. Crumble using a food processor. Store in the refrigerator.

Healthy America (Oklahoma)

WIKIPEDIA.ORG

E.W. Marland amassed a large oil empire, founding the Marland Oil Company (now Conoco, Inc.) in Ponca City, Oklahoma. He later served as a U.S. Congressman and as the state's tenth governor, beginning in 1934. His breathtakingly beautiful 43,000-square-foot mansion, known as the "Palace on the Prairie," was modeled after the Davanzatti Palace in Florence, Italy. It is open to the public.

Swiss Vegetable Medley

1 (16-ounce) bag frozen
  broccoli, carrots, and
  cauliflower combination,
  thawed and drained
1 (10¾-ounce) can
  condensed cream of
  mushroom soup
1 cup shredded Swiss cheese,
  divided
⅓ cup sour cream
¼ teaspoon ground black
  pepper
1 (2.8-ounce) can Durkee
  French fried onions, divided

Combine vegetables, soup, ½ cup cheese, sour cream, pepper, and ½ can fried onions. Pour into a 1-quart casserole. Bake, covered at 350° for 30 minutes. Remove from oven and top with remaining cheese and onions. Bake uncovered 5 minutes longer.

Luncheon Favorites (Missouri)

Curried Fruit

1 (1-pound) can pear halves,
  drained
1 (1-pound) can pineapple
  tidbits, drained
12 maraschino cherries
1 (1-pound) can peaches,
  drained
1 (1-pound) can apricots,
  drained
¾ cup brown sugar
3 teaspoons curry powder
⅓ cup liquidized Butter Buds
⅔ cup almonds (optional)

Drain fruit and mix together in casserole dish. Combine sugar, curry powder, and Butter Buds; pour over the fruit mixture. Bake at 325° for 1 hour. Refrigerate overnight. If desired, sprinkle almonds on top. Reheat at 350° before serving. Serves 6–8.

Cooking to Your Heart's Content (Arkansas)

Baked Apricots

2 large cans peeled apricots
1–1½ boxes light brown
** sugar**

1 box Ritz Crackers
Butter—lots of it

Drain apricots well. In a greased baking dish, put a layer of apricots. Cover this with brown sugar, then a layer of crumbled Ritz Crackers. Dot with lumps of butter. Repeat layers to top of dish. Bake slowly at 300° for about one hour.

Dixie Cook Book V (Arkansas)

Chili Sauce

3 quarts ripe tomatoes,
** chopped**
6 green bell peppers, chopped
4 large onions, chopped

4 tablespoons sugar
4 tablespoons salt
2 tablespoons cinnamon
3 coffee cups vinegar (scant)

Combine chopped vegetables with other ingredients. Boil slowly 1½ hours and pour into sterilized jars; seal while hot.

Perfectly Delicious (Arkansas)

Pasta, Rice, Etc.

COURTESY OF ARKANSAS DEPT. OF PARKS & TOURISM

Arkansas is the largest rice-producing state, accounting for approximately 48 percent of U.S. rice production. Missouri is the sixth-largest rice-producing state. These states produce medium- and long-grain varieties. Stuttgart, Arkansas-based Riceland Foods Inc. is the world's largest rice miller and marketer of rice and rice products.

Homemade Noodles

½–1 cup flour
1 egg and 1 egg yolk
½ teaspoon salt
¼ cup water

1 drop of yellow food coloring
(place on toothpick to
keep from getting too much)

Place ½ cup flour in bowl. Add beaten egg and yolk, salt, water and food color; mix. Add more flour, as needed, to make a very thick dough. Fold over or knead just enough to hold shape on top of well floured board. Too much kneading makes noodles tough. Roll out to ⅛ inch thick. Let stand for an hour or two. Cut into strips. Cook in simmering broth for about 20 minutes or until tender. Do not remove lid during cooking time.

Mother would roll out the batter all over the table where it would dry until it would be cut into strips. The boys liked to eat the batter raw, so many times we would find holes along the edges.

Kohler Family Kookbook (Missouri)

LIBRARY OF CONGRESS

Hannibal, Missouri, is the setting for many favorite stories and novels by Samuel Langhorne Clemens (November 30, 1835–April 21, 1910), who spent most of his childhood there. Clemens wrote under the pen name Mark Twain. Clemens used different pen names before deciding on Mark Twain. He signed humorous and imaginative sketches Josh until 1863. Additionally, he used the pen name Thomas Jefferson Snodgrass for a series of humorous letters. He maintained that his primary pen name came from his years working on Mississippi riverboats, where two fathoms, a depth indicating safe water for passage of boat, was measured on the sounding line. A fathom is a maritime unit of depth, equivalent to two yards; *twain* is a term for "two." The riverboatman's cry was mark twain or, more fully, by the mark twain, meaning "according to the mark [on the line], [the depth is] two [fathoms]," that is, "there are 12 feet of water under the boat and it is safe to pass."

Pasta Primavera

½ cup unsalted butter
1 medium onion, minced
1 large clove garlic, minced
1 pound thin asparagus,
   tough ends trimmed, cut
   into ¼-inch slices
½ pound mushrooms,
   thinly sliced
6 ounces cauliflower,
   broken into florets
1 medium zucchini, cut
   into ¼-inch slices
1 small carrot, halved
   lengthwise, cut into
   ⅛-inch diagonal slices
1 cup heavy cream

½ cup chicken broth
2 tablespoons chopped fresh
   basil
1 cup frozen small peas,
   thawed
2 ounces prosciutto or
   cooked ham, chopped
5 green onions, chopped
Salt and freshly ground
   pepper to taste
1 pound fettuccine or linguini,
   cooked al dente, thoroughly
   drained
1 cup freshly grated Parmesan
   cheese

Heat large skillet over medium-high heat. Add butter, onion, and garlic, and sauté until onion is softened, about 2 minutes. Add asparagus, mushrooms, cauliflower, zucchini, and carrot, and stir-fry for 2 minutes. Remove vegetables and set aside.

Increase heat to high. Add cream, broth, and basil, and boil until liquid is reduced, about 3 minutes. Stir in peas, ham, and green onion, and cook 1 minute more. Season with salt and pepper to taste. Add pasta and cheese, tossing until thoroughly combined and pasta is heated through. Turn onto large platter and garnish with reserved vegetables. Serves 4–6.

Cooking for Applause (Missouri)

Manicotti

¾ pound ricotta cheese
6 ounces mozzarella cheese, grated, divided
2 tablespoons grated Parmesan cheese
2 tablespoons granulated sugar
1 egg, lightly beaten
6–8 manicotti noodles (uncooked)
Salt and pepper to taste
1 (32-ounce) jar of your favorite spaghetti sauce

Combine all ingredients except noodles and sauce and 2 tablespoons mozzarella cheese. Mix well. Fill uncooked manicotti using a teaspoon or a small rounded knife. Pour a generous amount of spaghetti sauce in the bottom of a greased 9x13-inch pan. Arrange filled manicotti in a single layer side by side. Cover baking dish with foil, crimping edges to seal tightly. Place in a preheated 400° oven for 40 minutes. After 40 minutes, remove foil, and add a little more sauce over manicotti. Sprinkle with grated mozzarella and Parmesan cheese. Allow to bake an additional 5–10 minutes with foil removed. Serves 4.

From Generation to Generation (Missouri)

Fettuccine with Fresh Tomatoes and Brie

A perfect merger.

2 tablespoons olive oil
4 large tomatoes, peeled, seeded, and chopped
1 clove garlic, crushed
1 bunch fresh basil, trimmed
Salt and freshly ground pepper to taste
6 ounces Brie cheese, rimmed and cubed
1 pound fettuccine

Heat olive oil and quickly sauté tomatoes, garlic, basil, salt, and pepper. Add Brie and cook until mixture is creamy, stirring constantly. Cook fettuccine according to package directions and drain. Pour sauce over fettuccine and toss. Serve immediately. Egg or spinach fettuccine may be used. Fresh is best. Serves 4-6.

Note: The word basil is derived from the Greek word for king, basileias. It was once used to make royal perfumes and medicines. Today, basil is one of the most popular herbs used with over 50 varieties available.

Gateways (Missouri)

Fast Fettuccine

SAUCE:

⅔ cup water or dry white
  wine
¼ cup butter, softened
2 tablespoons dried parsley
1 teaspoon crumbled dried
  basil

½ teaspoon oregano
1 (8-ounce) package cream
  cheese, softened
1 teaspoon Italian herbs
Salt and pepper to taste

Combine the water (or dry white wine), butter, parsley, basil, and oregano. Cook over low heat. Blend in the cream cheese, stirring constantly. Season this mixture with the Italian herbs. Salt and pepper to taste. Keep warm, but do not burn.

FETTUCCINE:

1 (10-ounce) package
  fettuccine, cooked and
  drained
¼ cup butter

1 garlic clove, smashed
¾ cup grated Romano cheese,
  divided

Cook the pasta according to package directions and drain. Set it aside. Melt ¼ cup butter in small skillet over low heat. Add the garlic and cook about 1–2 minutes. Do not burn. Pour this garlic butter over the warm pasta and toss gently. Sprinkle with ½ of the Romano cheese and toss again. Transfer this mixture to a serving platter and spoon the cream sauce over the top; sprinkle with the remaining cheese. Serve immediately.

Gourmet: The Quick and Easy Way (Oklahoma)

Crêpes Cannelloni

2 tablespoons vegetable oil
¾ cup minced onion
1 garlic clove, minced
1½ pounds ground chuck
1 cup chopped, drained,
  cooked spinach
1 egg, lightly beaten
¼ cup grated Parmesan cheese
Salt and freshly ground pepper
  to taste

4 tablespoons butter
4 tablespoons flour
2 cups milk
½ cup prepared spaghetti sauce
14 Basic Crêpes (page 177)
1 (6-ounce) package sliced
  mozzarella cheese, cut into
  1½x5-inch pieces

Heat oil in large skillet. Sauté onion and garlic over medium heat until translucent but not brown. Add beef and brown, stirring frequently; drain.

Combine meat with spinach, egg, and Parmesan cheese. Season with salt and pepper; taste and adjust seasonings. Reserve ¼ cup mixture for cream sauce.

Make the sauce by melting butter in a saucepan over medium heat; whisk in flour. Add milk, stirring constantly, until thickened and smooth. Stir in reserved meat mixture; simmer 5 minutes; season with salt and pepper to taste. Spread spaghetti sauce on bottom of greased 9x13-inch baking dish. Spread 2 tablespoons meat filling on each crêpe and roll. Place crêpe, seam side down, on spaghetti sauce. Spoon cream sauce over crêpes and top each with a slice of mozzarella cheese. Bake, uncovered, at 350° for 30 minutes or until thoroughly heated. Serves 7 or 8.

Victorian Sampler (Arkansas)

Mexican Lasagna

1 pound lean ground beef
1 (16-ounce) can refried beans
2 teaspoons oregano
1 teaspoon cumin
¾ teaspoon garlic powder
12 lasagna noodles
2½ cups water
2½ cups picante sauce

2 cups sour cream
¾ cup finely sliced green
  onions
1 (2-ounce) can sliced black
  olives, drained
1 cup shredded Monterey
  Jack cheese

Combine ground beef, beans, oregano, cumin, and garlic powder in bowl; mix well. Layer ⅓ of the uncooked lasagna noodles and ½ of the ground beef mixture in nonstick 9x13-inch baking pan. Repeat layers, ending with noodles. Pour mixture of water and picante sauce over top. Bake, covered, at 350° for 1½ hours or until noodles are tender. Spoon mixture of sour cream, green onions, and olives over top. Sprinkle with cheese. Bake for 5 minutes or until cheese melts. Yields 12 servings.

Discover Oklahoma Cookin' (Oklahoma)

The Pioneer Woman Museum in Ponca City, Oklahoma, preserves the legacy of women who have made significant contributions to the history of Oklahoma and the nation. The world-famous thirty-foot-tall bronze statue commemorating the heroic character of the women who braved dangers and hardships to settle in Oklahoma is featured.

Calzones

FILLING:

1 pound ground turkey breast
   or chicken breast
½ cup chopped onion
½ teaspoon oregano
½ teaspoon caraway seeds
⅓ cup fat-free Italian salad
   dressing
¼ teaspoon salt
1 cup 1% cottage cheese

Brown meat and onion in large skillet sprayed with nonstick cooking spray. Add oregano, caraway seeds, fat-free Italian dressing, and salt. Stir and cook until meat is done. Remove from heat and add cottage cheese.

CRUST:

6 egg roll wrappers
2 egg whites, slightly beaten
½ cup shredded fat-free cheese

Dip one side of the egg roll wrapper in egg white. The egg white side should be the outside. Place ½ cup filling in the center of the wrapper and add about 1 tablespoon fat-free cheese. Fold each corner of the wrapper to the center and form a sort of package. Place on baking sheet sprayed with nonstick cooking spray and bake at 375° for 20–25 minutes or until golden brown. Makes 6 servings.

Fat Free & Ultra Lowfat Recipes (Oklahoma)

Smoke-House Spaghetti

¼ pound bacon, cut in
  1-inch pieces
1 medium onion, chopped
1 pound ground beef
2 (8-ounce) cans tomato
  sauce or tomato soup
Salt to taste
⅛ teaspoon pepper
½ teaspoon oregano

½ teaspoon garlic salt
1 (4-ounce) can mushrooms
¾ pound spaghetti
¼ pound shredded provolone
  cheese or mozzarella
  (about 1 cup)
¼ pound shredded Cheddar
  cheese (about 1 cup)

Sauté bacon in skillet; add onion and ground beef. Brown. Stir in tomato sauce, salt, pepper, oregano, garlic salt, and mushrooms. Simmer 15 minutes.

Break spaghetti in half and cook until done, then stir into sauce. Place half the mixture in a 2-quart baking dish. Top with half of the cheeses. Repeat layers. Bake in a 375° oven 20–25 minutes. Serves 6–8. Will freeze.

Wanda's Favorite Recipes Book (Missouri)

Spaghetti Casserole

2 pounds ground beef
2 onions, chopped
½ bell pepper, chopped
2 cloves garlic, chopped
1 tablespoon oregano
Salt and pepper to taste
1 (10½-ounce) can
  Campbell's tomato soup
1 (8-ounce) can tomato sauce

1 (12-ounce) package
  vermicelli spaghetti
1 (8-ounce) package American
  cheese slices, torn in pieces
1 (2-ounce) bottle stuffed green
  olives, sliced
1 (10½-ounce) can cream of
  mushroom soup

Brown together beef, onions, pepper, and garlic. Drain liquid; add oregano, salt, pepper, tomato soup, and tomato sauce. Simmer 30 minutes. Cook vermicelli according to package directions. Grease a 3-quart casserole. Layer spaghetti, spaghetti sauce, cheese, and green olives. Repeat layers until bowl is full. Pour mushroom soup over the top. Cook in oven at 350° for 30 minutes. May be refrigerated or frozen before cooking.

In Good Taste (Arkansas)

Chicken Tetrazzini

Delicious served with a tossed green salad and sliced French bread or bread sticks.

8 chicken breasts
4 cups water
1 (12-ounce) package
  spaghetti
2 teaspoons Worcestershire
2 teaspoons paprika
1 can cream of chicken soup
1 can cream of mushroom
  soup
1 (8-ounce) carton sour cream
1 (4-ounce) can chopped ripe
  olives

1 (4-ounce) can sliced
  mushrooms, drained
1 onion, chopped, ½ green
  pepper, chopped, and ½ cup
  celery, chopped and sautéed
  in 2 tablespoons butter
  (optional)
1 pound Cheddar cheese,
  grated and divided in half

Simmer the chicken breasts in water for 1 hour. Remove the chicken breasts from the broth (reserve broth); let them cool. Cut breasts into bite-size pieces. Boil the spaghetti in reserved chicken broth for 10 minutes. Drain spaghetti in a colander. Mix the chicken bites, cooked spaghetti, Worcestershire, paprika, soups, sour cream, olives, and mushrooms together. Sautéed vegetables may be added at this time, if desired. Add half the Cheddar cheese to this mixture and stir.

Spoon into a greased 3-quart baking dish. Cover the chicken mixture with the remaining grated Cheddar cheese. Bake, covered with foil, at 350° for 30 minutes until the cheese melts and the casserole is hot. Serves 8.

Gourmet: The Quick and Easy Way (Oklahoma)

Chicken-Spaghetti Casserole

½ cup diced celery
½ cup chopped onion
¼ cup chopped bell pepper
2 cups chicken broth
1 (14½-ounce) can
   tomatoes

1 (10¾-ounce) can mushroom
   soup
Salt and pepper to taste
2 cups diced, cooked chicken
1 (8-ounce) package thin
   spaghetti, cooked and drained

In large saucepan simmer celery, onion, and bell pepper in chicken broth until tender. Add tomatoes and soup; season to taste; bring to a boil. Remove from heat; fold in chicken and spaghetti; pour into a greased 9x13-inch baking dish; top with cheese. Bake at 400° until cheese melts.

Celebration (Arkansas)

Chicken Marco Polo

This is a festive way to use up leftover chicken, turkey, or ham.

2 slices bacon
½ cup onion, diced
½ cup celery, sliced
1 (2-ounce) jar pimentos,
   chopped
1 can water chestnuts,
   drained and sliced

1 can cream of mushroom soup
6–8 ounces sharp Cheddar
   cheese, cubed
½ cup almonds, slivered
2–3 cups cubed chicken or
   other meat
1 pound fine spaghetti, cooked

Sauté bacon (remove from pan). In bacon drippings, sauté onion and celery for 5 minutes. Add all other ingredients to cooked spaghetti. Toss lightly and carefully with 2 forks. Put in a buttered casserole. Bake at 350° for 45 minutes. If soupy, serve on chow mein noodles.

Treasured Recipes Book 1 (Missouri)

Wild Rice Baron

2 cups raw wild rice	½ cup butter
4 cups water	¼ cup soy sauce
2 teaspoons salt	2 cups sour cream
2 pounds lean ground beef	2 teaspoons salt
1 pound fresh mushrooms	¼ teaspoon pepper
1 cup chopped onion	½ cup slivered almonds
½ cup chopped celery	

Gently cook wild rice in water and 2 teaspoons salt (uncovered) for 45 minutes or until rice is done. Drain, if necessary. Brown ground beef. Rinse mushrooms; slice and sauté with onion and celery in butter for 5–10 minutes.

Combine soy sauce, sour cream or soup (see Note), and remaining salt and pepper. Add cooked wild rice, beef, onions, mushrooms, celery mixture, and almonds. Toss lightly and place in 3-quart buttered casserole. Bake at 350° about 1 hour, uncovered. Add a little water during baking if necessary and stir several times during baking.

Note: May use 2 cans cream of mushroom soup, undiluted, instead of sour cream and fresh mushrooms, or use both.

United Methodist Cookbook 1993 (Oklahoma)

Sausage Pilaf

1 pound hot pork sausage	1 cup cream of mushroom
1 cup chopped celery	soup
½ cup chopped onion	½ cup chopped cashew
½ cup chopped bell pepper	nuts or peanuts (optional)
3 cups cooked rice	

Brown sausage; add celery, onion, and pepper. Cook 3–5 minutes. Stir in rice and soup. Pour into a 1-quart casserole. Cover. Bake 20 minutes at 250°. Remove from oven, sprinkle nuts on top, and return to oven uncovered for 10 minutes longer.

Prairie Harvest (Arkansas)

Shrimp Fried Rice

3 green onions, tops
  included, chopped
1 onion, chopped
½ cup butter
3 cups cold cooked rice
2 eggs, beaten

4 ounces water chestnuts,
  drained and sliced
Soy sauce to taste
1 (7¾-ounce) can tiny
  shrimp, drained and rinsed

Sauté onions in butter in wok or large frying pan over moderately high heat. Stir in rice, mixing until heated and coated with butter. (Add more butter, if necessary.) With wooden spoon, make a path to bottom of pan; pour in eggs and gently scramble. Mix throughout rice. Add water chestnuts and sprinkle liberally with soy sauce to taste. Gently fold in shrimp and heat. Serves 4.

Company's Coming (Missouri)

Fried Rice

It gets better every time it's reheated! I think all of our children or their spouses have called to ask for this recipe.

2 cups rice
4 cups cold water
1 teaspoon salt
5 strips bacon, diced
1 bell pepper, chopped
2 bunches green onions,
  chopped

1 can sliced water chestnuts
Soy sauce and black pepper
  to taste
2 eggs, beaten

Combine rice, water, and salt in a covered pan. Cook until rice is tender. Remove from heat and cool thoroughly. I use a deep Dutch oven iron skillet to cook bacon in, then I add bell pepper, green onions, and water chestnuts, and sauté about 5 minutes. Stir in the rice; add soy sauce and black pepper. Stir as it heats over low heat, then stir in eggs. It won't take long for the eggs to cook.

When ready to serve, if it needs reheating, you can heat it in a covered baking dish in the oven or microwave.

Clabber Creek Farm Cook Book (Arkansas)

Red Beans and Rice

1 pound ground beef
1 large onion, chopped
1 large bell pepper, chopped
1 tablespoon chili powder
2 teaspoons salt

1 (16-ounce) can tomatoes
  or juice
1 cup water
1½ cups uncooked rice
1 can red kidney beans

Brown meat with onion and pepper. Add remaining ingredients except rice and beans, and simmer for 15 minutes. Remove from heat and pour into 9x13-inch pan. Evenly distribute 1½ cups uncooked rice and 1 can red kidney beans in mixture. Cover and bake at 350° for 1 hour. Take out and stir, cover, and return to oven for another 15 minutes.

The Farmer's Daughters (Arkansas)

Rice Almondine

2 cups raw rice
3 envelopes Lipton Chicken
  Noodle Soup
8½ cups boiling water
2 pounds pork sausage

1 bunch celery, chopped
2 medium onions, chopped
1 green bell pepper, chopped
2 medium cans pimentos
1 can chopped almonds

Combine rice, soup mix, and water. Cook for 30 minutes. Fry sausage. Reserve some of the fat to cook celery, onions, and pepper. Cook until soft, then add pimentos and almonds. Combine with rice mixture and bake uncovered at 350° for 30 minutes.

What's Cooking in Okarche? (Oklahoma)

Simply Southwest

This recipe takes less than 15 minutes to get to the table and tastes fantastic!

1 (14½-ounce) can chicken broth
2¼ cups quick-cooking brown rice
2 teaspoons sunflower oil
1 medium onion, chopped
2 garlic cloves, minced
2 cups diced cooked turkey breast

2 cups (2 small) thinly sliced zucchini
1 medium red bell pepper, chopped (use the seeds)
1 teaspoon ground cumin
½ cup picante sauce

Bring broth to a boil; add rice. Cover and simmer on lowest heat 8–10 minutes. While it simmers, sauté onion and garlic in the oil. Add remaining ingredients to the onion/garlic mixture, and cook for just a very few minutes—just till the vegetables are tender-crisp. Serve the turkey mixture on top of the rice. Makes 4 large servings.

Note: This dish can be made extra hot and spicy by the kind of picante sauce you use. Green bell pepper can be substituted for red, but the red pepper makes this a beautiful dish, plus it ups the beta carotene a tremendous amount. Also, you can use leftover cooked chicken or turkey. I like to bake a small turkey just to have meat available for dishes like this. You can also use Louis Rich Oven Roasted Turkey Breast.

Variation: Try thin carrot slices and bite-size pieces of cauliflower. Be creative. Enjoy!

15 Minute, Lowfat Meals (Oklahoma)

Having gained world-wide recognition from Merle Haggard's song, Muskogee, nestled in the rolling hills of Green County on the west bank of the Arkansas River, is one of Oklahoma's most recognized cities. The Five Civilized Tribes Museum, a museum dedicated to preserving the art and culture of the Cherokee, Chickasaw, Choctaw, Muscogee (Creek), and Seminole tribes, is located there.

Jalapeño Rice and Cheese

1 cup uncooked rice
2 cups chicken broth (or 4
   chicken bouillon cubes
   in 2 cups water)
1 cup sour cream (8 ounces)
1½ tablespoons chopped
   jalapeño

1½ tablespoons jalapeño juice
⅓ cup creamy Italian dressing
1 (10-ounce) package
   Monterey Jack cheese

Cook rice in chicken broth until tender; combine all ingredients except cheese. Pour half of rice mixture into buttered 2-quart casserole and cover with half of cheese; add rest of rice and cover with rest of cheese. Bake at 350° for 30 minutes or until bubbly. Serves 4–6.

Betty "Winks" at Cooking (Arkansas)

Broccoli and Ham Quiche

1 (10-inch) unbaked pie crust
1 (10-ounce) package frozen
   chopped broccoli, cooked
   and well drained
2 cups chopped ham
⅓ cup minced onion
½ cup shredded Swiss cheese

½ cup shredded Cheddar
   cheese
4 eggs, slightly beaten
2 cups whipping cream
¾ teaspoon salt
¼ teaspoon sugar

Preheat oven to 425°. Sprinkle broccoli, ham, onion, and cheeses in pie crust. Blend eggs and cream. Add salt and sugar. Pour over mixture in crust. Bake 15 minutes at 425°. Reduce heat to 300° for 35–40 minutes. Let stand for 10 minutes before serving. Serves 6.

Luncheon Favorites (Missouri)

Onion Cheese Pie

Ultra lowfat. One of my favorites.

2 large fat-free flour tortillas
Buttermist nonstick cooking spray
1 teaspoon Molly McButter
1 (16-ounce) carton fat-free cottage cheese
⅓ cup fat-free liquid egg product
2 teaspoons dry onion flakes
1 medium onion, thinly sliced
⅓ cup grated fat-free Parmesan cheese
5 slices fat-free Swiss cheese
⅓ cup grated fat-free Cheddar cheese
1 large ripe tomato, thinly sliced
Garlic salt
Black pepper to taste

Preheat oven to 325°. Place 1 tortilla in large pie plate sprayed with nonstick cooking spray. Spray tortilla lightly with Buttermist and sprinkle with ½ teaspoon Molly McButter. Repeat process with second tortilla on top of the other.

In large bowl, combine cottage cheese, egg product, and onion flakes and mix with spoon. Pour half over tortillas and gently smooth and spread with spoon.

Add layers in this order: half of the sliced onion, all the Parmesan and Swiss cheese, remaining cottage cheese mixture, all the Cheddar cheese, remaining sliced onion, and all the sliced tomato. Sprinkle top with garlic salt and black pepper. Bake at 325° for 1 hour and 20 minutes. Cool slightly before slicing. Makes 8 servings.

Fat Free 2 (Oklahoma)

Wood Chuck

2 cups medium white sauce
1 medium can mushrooms
½ pound grated American or
   Cheddar cheese
1 can cream of mushroom
   soup

1 small jar chopped pimentos
½ green bell pepper, chopped
   (optional)
1½ cups cubed, cooked ham
6 hard-boiled eggs, chopped
2 cans Chinese noodles

Blend together all ingredients except eggs and Chinese noodles.
Simmer over low heat and stir eggs in just before serving. Serve over 2
cans Chinese noodles. Serves 10.

Four Generations of Johnson Family Favorites (Oklahoma)

Meats

COURTESY OF OKLAHOMA TOURISM

Capture pioneer adventure at one of the many working ranches across Oklahoma. Simple and functional in its design, chuck wagons were used during the westward migration and cattle drives. Chuck wagon dining is popular at the ranches and remains the social center and recreational spot—a natural gathering place for recounting the experiences of the day.

Winter Steak
with Tarragon Butter

1 (2-inch thick) sirloin
   steak, second or third cut
Salt and pepper to taste

1½ tablespoons butter
1½ tablespoons oil

Pat steak dry. Salt and pepper steak on both sides. Sear in butter and oil for 2–4 minutes on each side or until dark brown. Transfer meat to large baking dish and bake at 350° for 25 minutes for medium rare. Transfer to a warm platter. Makes 4–6 servings.

Note: Top each serving of beef with a pat of Tarragon Butter and garnish with sprigs of fresh tarragon.

TARRAGON BUTTER:

2 medium shallots
2½ tablespoons chopped
   fresh parsley
4 teaspoons tarragon vinegar
1½ teaspoons fresh tarragon
   or ½ teaspoon dried

½ teaspoon freshly ground
   pepper
½ cup butter, well chilled
   and cut into small pieces

Mince shallots in food processor, using steel blade. Add parsley, vinegar, tarragon, and pepper; process briefly. Add butter and blend well. Transfer to wax paper and form a roll. Refrigerate or freeze until firm.

Beyond Parsley (Missouri)

PAULINE FAHLE

The Great Western Trail Drive in northwest Oklahoma offers an exciting vacation adventure. Seasoned cattlehands ride along with greenhorns and city slickers in an old west cattle drive straight out of the 1800s. The ride begins as riders drive cattle down Vici's Main Street and continues thirty miles over the course of three days.

Roast Peppered Rib Eye of Beef

1 (5- to 6-pound) boneless
  rib eye beef roast
½ cup coarsely cracked
  pepper
½ teaspoon ground
  cardamom seed
1 tablespoon tomato paste

½ teaspoon garlic powder
1 teaspoon paprika
1 cup soy sauce
¾ cup vinegar
1½ tablespoons cornstarch
  (optional)

Have fat trimmed from roast. Marinate by combining cracked pepper and cardamom seed; rub all over beef and press in with heel of hand. Place in shallow baking dish and set aside. Combine tomato paste, garlic powder, and paprika. Pour over roast. Add soy sauce and vinegar. Refrigerate overnight.

Spoon marinade over meat. Remove meat from marinade and let stand at room temperature for one hour. Wrap in foil, place in shallow pan and roast at 300° for 2 hours (medium rare). Open foil, ladle out, and reserve drippings. Brown roast uncovered at 350° while making Gravy.

GRAVY:

1 cup meat juices
1 cup water

Cornstarch mixed with ¼
  cup cold water if needed

Bring meat juices and 1 cup water to boil. If desired, add a little marinade. Serve au jus or thickened with cornstarch mixed with water. Serves 8–10.

Submitted by G.W. "Bill" Swisher, Jr., founder of the CMI Corporation
and third-generation native Oklahoman.

The Oklahoma Celebrity Cookbook (Oklahoma)

Roast Prime Rib of Beef

Feeds a crowd!

6 whole celery stalks
6 whole carrots
6 onions, halved
1 (15-pound) prime rib of beef

Salt and crushed black pepper
2 cups minced fresh parsley
 or 1 cup parsley flakes

Place celery, carrots and onions in bottom of large roasting pan. Place roast on top and cover with the mixture of salt, pepper, and parsley. Cover and bake in a slow oven (250°) 4 hours until well-done on the outside, but rare in the center. Serve thick slices with natural juices poured over. About 3 servings per pound.

Feasts of Eden (Arkansas)

Beef Tips over Rice

1 pound sirloin steak,
 cubed, sprinkled with
 unseasoned tenderizer
1 medium onion, chopped
2 cloves garlic, minced
2 tablespoons olive oil
1 small can mushrooms
 or 8–10 fresh ones
½ cup white wine

2 teaspoons beef base
 seasoning
Salt and freshly ground black
 pepper to taste
1 tablespoon parsley flakes
1 tablespoon cornstarch
½ cup cold water
Hot cooked rice

Brown cubed steak, onion, and garlic in olive oil in a large heavy skillet. Add mushrooms, wine, beef base, salt, pepper, and parsley. Let simmer 15–20 minutes until meat is done, then add the dissolved cornstarch-water mixture and let thicken. Takes just a few minutes.

Serve over hot cooked rice. Baked squash and fresh spinach salad complete this meal. Yields 3–4 servings.

Betty Is Still "Winking" at Cooking (Arkansas)

Swedish Cabbage Casserole

1 pound lean ground beef or
  1 pound ground turkey
½ cup chopped onion
1 (16-ounce) can tomatoes
½ cup instant rice
1 (8-ounce) can tomato
  sauce

½ cup cubed cheese (American
  or Monterey Jack)
1 tablespoon Worcestershire
½ teaspoon salt (optional)
¼ teaspoon garlic powder
3 cups shredded cabbage

Brown beef or turkey and onion until onion is tender; drain. Add tomatoes and rice, stirring to blend tomatoes. Blend thoroughly. Bring to a boil. Cover and turn off heat. Let stand for 10 minutes.

Stir in next 5 ingredients and heat till cheese is melted.

Arrange cabbage in the bottom of an 11x7x2-inch pan. Spread meat mixture over cabbage. Cover. Bake at 350° for 30 minutes. Makes 6 servings.

Blue Ridge Christian Church Cookbook (Missouri)

Margaret Kohler's Goulash

Margaret made this up in a large turkey roaster and took it to the family reunions in the early 1940s. The men thought it was great and Margaret always took home an empty pan.

2 pounds ground beef
½ package Williams Chili
  seasoning
Salt to taste
1 large can tomatoes

2 large potatoes, diced
3 large carrots, diced
1 large onion, diced
3 stalks celery, diced

Brown beef in small amount of oil, then add chili seasoning, salt, and tomatoes. Mix other vegetables and cook until almost tender in a small amount of water. Add to meat and cook in oven at 350° until tender (about 1½ hours). Serve with corn bread.

Kohler Family Kookbook (Missouri)

Western Hash

1 pound ground beef
½ cup chopped onion
½ cup chopped bell pepper
3½ cups canned tomatoes
½ cup uncooked rice

1 teaspoon basil
½ teaspoon salt
Dash of pepper
American cheese slices

Brown beef, onion, and bell pepper in skillet. Drain. Add tomatoes, rice, basil, salt, and pepper. Cover and simmer for 25 minutes, stirring occasionally. Put in casserole dish and top with cheese slices. Heat until cheese is melted and serve hot. Serves 6.

Evening Shade (Arkansas)

Rock Cafe Old Fashioned Hamburger

In Stroud, the Rock Cafe has been a part of Route 66 history since it opened on July 4, 1939.

¼ pound coarsely ground
  beef
½ teaspoon salt, or to taste

¼ teaspoon pepper
1 teaspoon finely chopped
  onion

Mix all ingredients; lightly pat into a burger about ½ inch thick. If you want a juicy burger, don't pack the meat. If the meat is too lean, mix a little ground suet with the patty. Fry patty on grill or in iron skillet for a few minutes; turn and cook a few minutes longer. Overcooking dries out the meat.

  Lightly butter the top and bottom of a bun; place on grill until golden brown. Spread mustard on bottom half; pile with chopped onions, pickles, and meat patty. Spread mayonnaise or mustard on top half of bun. Pat the top of the bun with a spatula loaded with hamburger grease. Provide lettuce, tomato, and ketchup to be used as desired.

The Route 66 Cookbook (Oklahoma)

Silver Dollar City's Meatball Sandwiches

2 eggs, slightly beaten
3 tablespoons milk
½ cup fine, dry bread
   crumbs
¼ teaspoon salt and pepper
1 pound ground beef
½ pound bulk Italian pork
   sausage
½ cup chopped onion
½ cup chopped green bell
   pepper

1 (8-ounce) can tomato sauce
1 (6-ounce) can tomato paste
2 teaspoons sugar
1 teaspoon garlic salt
½ teaspoon crushed dried
   oregano
¼ teaspoon crushed dried
   parsley flakes
1 cup water
8 individual French rolls

Combine eggs, milk, crumbs, salt, and pepper to taste. Add beef and mix well. Form into 24 (1½-inch) meatballs. Brown in hot skillet. Remove meatballs.

In same skillet, combine sausage, onion, and green pepper. Cook until sausage is browned. Drain fat. Stir in tomato sauce, tomato paste, sugar, garlic salt, oregano, parsley, and 1 cup water. Return meatballs to skillet. Cover and simmer for 15 minutes, stirring once or twice. Cut thin slice from tops of rolls and hollow out, leaving ¼-inch wall. Fill each roll with 3 meatballs and some sauce.

Silver Dollar City's Recipes (Missouri)

THEMEPARKREVIEW.COM

What began in 1960 as a cave tour attraction has grown to one of the World's Top Theme Parks. Silver Dollar City, an 1880s-style theme park located near Branson, Missouri, presents six world-class festivals from April through December each year. The 55-acre park has 12 stages, 22 rides, 12 restaurants, and 60 shops, including 100 resident craftsmen. Silver Dollar City is rustic and charming, built on the natural terrain of the Ozark Mountains.

Hamburger Boats

¾ pound ground chuck
¾ pound ground round
½ cup chopped onion
½ cup ketchup
1 egg

2 tablespoons seasoned bread
  crumbs
Salt and pepper to taste
3 French rolls (each 5½ inches
  long)

Combine ground chuck, ground round, chopped onion, ketchup, egg, bread crumbs, salt, and pepper. Mix until ingredients are thoroughly blended.

   Cut rolls in half. Scrape soft bread from centers of each half to make cavity. Spread cavity with either ketchup or mustard or combination of the two. Divide meat mixture into 6 equal parts and mound over cavities of each roll. Bake in 350° oven for 30 minutes uncovered. Easy. Do ahead. Serves 4–5.

Cooking in Clover (Missouri)

Excellent Meatloaf

MEATLOAF:
1½ pounds ground beef
½ can tomato soup
1 cup Pepperidge Farm
  Herb Stuffing
2 ribs celery
1 egg

1 large onion, chopped
½ cup grated American cheese
½ cup chopped bell pepper
1½ teaspoons salt
¼ teaspoon black pepper
Bacon slices

SAUCE:
2 tablespoons butter, melted
2 tablespoons soy sauce
1 (8-ounce) can tomato
  sauce

¼ cup water
¼ cup vinegar
½ cup brown sugar

Mix all meatloaf ingredients; form into loaf and top with bacon slices. Pour Sauce over top and cook at 350° for 1 hour and 15 minutes. Baste with Sauce every 5 minutes.

The Bonneville House Presents (Arkansas)

Blender Quick Cheeseburger Pie

Very much like a quiche, this recipe is super simple!

1 pound ground beef   **1½ cups chopped onions**

Preheat oven to 400°. Grease a 10x1½-inch deep pie plate or an 8½x11-inch baking pan. Brown beef and onions. Drain. Spread in baking dish.

⅔ cup whole-wheat flour   **1½ cups milk**
1 teaspoon baking powder   **2 tablespoons butter or**
½ teaspoon salt   **margarine**
3 eggs

Blend the above ingredients in blender on high for about 15 seconds or with a hand beater about 1 minute. Pour over hamburger. Bake 25 minutes. Add Topping; bake 5 minutes longer.

TOPPING:
2 fresh tomatoes, thinly   **1 cup shredded Cheddar**
** sliced**   **cheese**

After baking 25 minutes, top with tomatoes and cheese; bake about 5 minutes longer until cheese melts. Makes 4–6 servings.

War Eagle Mill Wholegrain and Honey Cookbook (Arkansas)

OKLAHOMAHISTORY.NET

The Meers Store is all that remains of Meers, Oklahoma, a boom town in the turn-of-the-century gold rush in the Wichita Mountains. The store was once a drugstore, doctor's office, newspaper office, post office, and later a general store. Meers population has dwindled from the gold rush peak of 500 to one family of six people, eight cats and a dog. "It's our fault" they boast of the Meers Fault—a 15-mile crack in the earth's crust that scientists believe could produce a major earthquake. Today the prosperous family restaurant is famous for "Meersburgers"—7-inch diameter burgers made exclusively from the Texas Longhorn beef raised on the family's ranch. The beef is free from antibiotics, pesticides, and growth hormones and is lower in cholesterol than chicken.

Indian Tacos

INDIAN FRY BREAD:
2½ pounds self-rising flour   1 quart vegetable oil
Whole milk

Mix flour and whole milk slowly together until you have a wet dough. Pinch off a handful of the dough; pat out using flour or vegetable oil on hands. Place the prepared pieces in hot vegetable oil and deep-fry until golden brown on each side. Drain on paper towels.

TOPPING:
2 pounds ground beef   3 ripe medium tomatoes
6 rounds Indian Fry Bread   1 can diced green chiles
½ pound sharp Cheddar   1 cup chopped green onions
  cheese, grated   Salsa (optional)
1 head iceberg lettuce,
  shredded

Brown ground beef. Divide among the 6 fry breads. Sprinkle with cheese, lettuce, tomatoes, chiles, and green onions. Serve with salsa, if desired. The ground beef may be substituted with 2 cans of beef chili.

Oklahoma Cookin' (Oklahoma)

Once known as Indian Territory, Oklahoma is still home to more American Indians than any other state in the Union. Thirty-nine tribal headquarters and members of at least sixty-five tribes make their home here. Native American art galleries, museums, historic sites, powwows, dances, and festivals are part of life in Oklahoma. The American Indian Cultural Center and Museum in Ponca City, Oklahoma, contains a priceless collection of artifacts representing more than thirty tribes from across the United States.

Hickory-Smoked Brisket

1 whole brisket, 4–6 pounds
Salt
Dampened hickory chips or
   liquid smoke
1½ cups ketchup
¾ cup brown sugar
¾ cup chili sauce
½ cup white wine vinegar
¾ cup water
¼ cup bottled steak sauce
¼ cup prepared mustard
1 tablespoon celery seed
½ cup lemon juice
2 tablespoons Worcestershire
1 clove garlic, minced
Dash of Tabasco
Freshly ground pepper
   to taste

Salt brisket and place on grill away from hot coals. Add dampened hickory chips, or brush meat with liquid smoke and close hood. Barbeque slowly for 4 hours, or until meat is tender. Cool and slice very thin across grain. Line up slices in shallow pan. Combine remaining ingredients and simmer 30 minutes; pour over meat. Heat 1 hour on grill or in 200° oven. Serves 8–12.

Company's Coming (Missouri)

Beef Brisket

1 (5- to 8-pound) beef brisket
2 teaspoons liquid smoke
2 teaspoons Worcestershire
2 tablespoons soy sauce
2 teaspoons garlic salt
1 teaspoon onion salt
2 teaspoons celery salt
2 teaspoons pepper
1½ teaspoons salt

Put brisket on heavy foil. Mix remaining ingredients together for marinade and rub over brisket. Fold up foil and place in refrigerator overnight.

Next morning, place in 250° oven for 6–7 hours. Take out of oven. Cool slightly. Put in freezer for 2 hours. Remove from freezer. Remove all fat from marinade and brisket; drain and reserve sauce and slice brisket. Put in pan; add enough water to sauce to almost cover slices of brisket. Cover with foil or lid. Refrigerate until ready to heat and serve. Heat for 2 hours. Serve with barbecue sauce on side. This can be made the day before.

Spring Creek Club (Oklahoma)

Barbeque Rub

2 cups sugar
¼ cup paprika
2 teaspoons chili powder
½ teaspoon cayenne pepper

½ cup salt
2 teaspoons black pepper
1 teaspoon garlic powder

Combine all ingredients and use as a rub for any barbeque meat. Yields about 3 cups.

The Passion of Barbeque

Best Bar-B-Que

I have never seen this recipe in any recipe book. I have had it for 35 years and enjoy it every time we have a party or have a number of guests.

2 pounds beef roast (no fat, no bone)

2 pounds pork roast (no fat, no bone)

Boil together or in separate containers until very tender. Remove from broth. Let cool. Save broth. Do not cut meat, but tear apart with fingers or forks or both when cool.

In separate pan, mix:

1 medium bottle tomato ketchup
1 medium jar India relish
1 cup finely diced onions

1 cup diced celery
1 cup diced bell pepper
Salt and pepper to taste

Mix ingredients with meat. Simmer (do not boil) for 1½–2 hours. Add some broth, just enough to make moist. (This can be served as sandwiches.) Makes a large amount for about 20 people.

Cooking on the Road (Missouri)

Barbecue Spareribs

4 pounds spareribs
½ cup chopped onion
2 cloves garlic, minced
1½ cups ketchup
2 tablespoons vinegar
1 cup honey

½ teaspoon salt
1 teaspoon prepared mustard
½ teaspoon black pepper
2 tablespoons escoffier
   sauce (or any steak sauce)

Cut spareribs in serving-size portions. Simmer in enough water to cover plus 2 teaspoons salt for ½ hour. Mix the remaining ingredients and cook over low heat for 5–7 minutes. Drain ribs and place in baking pan. Pour sauce over ribs and bake in oven, 400°, for 45 minutes or until tender. Baste every 10 minutes with sauce. Makes 4-6 servings.

The Wonderful World of Honey (Arkansas)

German Sauerkraut & Country Ribs

Just good, plain, fattening food. Do serve with mashed potatoes,' and chew slowly to enjoy every swallow!

3 pounds country pork or
   spare ribs
1 large can or 2 pounds bulk
   kraut
1 teaspoon caraway seeds

1 teaspoon celery seeds
½ cup barley (old-fashioned
   pearl, if you can find it)
Dash of pepper

Wash and cut pork into serving-size pieces. Mix all ingredients together. Do not rinse kraut. Simmer slowly about 2 hours, adding a bit of water as needed. Serves 4--maybe--depends on the size of your appetite.

Treasured Recipes Book (Missouri)

Barbequed Pork Loin Baby Back Ribs

1 slab pork loin baby
  back ribs

MARINADE:
½ cup chicken stock
½ cup soy sauce
¼ cup oil

Dry barbecue seasoning
  (your favorite kind)

¼ cup vinegar
6 tablespoons sugar
2 cloves garlic, minced

Combine Marinade ingredients and marinate ribs in refrigerator for 2 hours to overnight.

Remove ribs from marinade and sprinkle with dry barbeque seasoning. Cook over medium coals (225°) until internal temperature registers 160° on a meat thermometer. Baste with Marinade or sprinkle lightly with dry seasoning every 30 minutes during cooking process. Serves 2–3.

The Passion of Barbeque (Missouri)

Barbecued Pork Burgers

2 pounds ground pork
¼ cup buttermilk
2 teaspoons seasoned salt
1 teaspoon black pepper

¼ teaspoon garlic powder
¼ teaspoon ground oregano
¼ cup minced onion

Combine all ingredients. Mix thoroughly; form into ¼ pound patties.

Sear patties on the grill, then reduce flame and cook over direct heat for about 10 minutes on each side. Serves 4–6.

Kansas City BBQ (Missouri)

Mushroom Stuffed Pork Chops

2 (1¼-inch) pork loin rib
  chops
1 (4-ounce) can chopped
  mushrooms, drained
1 tablespoon snipped parsley
1 tablespoon finely chopped
  onion
¼ teaspoon salt
Dash of pepper

1 slice Swiss cheese, torn up
1 egg, slightly beaten
¼ cup fine dry bread crumbs
1 tablespoon cooking oil
⅓ cup water
¼ cup dry white wine
1 tablespoon cornstarch
1 tablespoon cold water

Trim excess fat from chops; sprinkle meat with a little salt and pepper.
Cut pocket in fat side of each chop. Combine mushrooms, parsley,
onion, salt, and pepper. Place cheese in pockets of chops; stuff with
mushroom mixture. Reserve any leftover mushroom mix for the sauce.
Dip chops in beaten egg, then in bread crumbs.

In an 8-inch skillet, slowly brown chops in hot oil. Add the ⅓ cup
water and the wine. Cover and simmer about 1 hour or until meat is
tender. Place meat on serving platter and keep warm.

For sauce, blend cornstarch and 1 tablespoon cold water. Stir into
wine mixture in skillet. Cook and stir until thickened and bubbly. Stir
in any reserved mushroom mix; beat through. Serve over meat. For
more than 2 servings, double the recipe.

Delicious Reading (Missouri)

 Oklahoma has more man-made lakes than any other state, with over one
million surface acres of water.

Stuffed Pork Chops

6 center-cut pork chops,
   about 1½ inches thick
2 cups cornbread, crumbled
1 cup light bread, crumbled
1 can chicken broth
1 teaspoon sage
½ teaspoon salt
2 eggs
Pepper to taste
½ cup diced celery
½ cup diced onion

Mix stuffing ingredients together and stuff in pork chops. Roll pork chops in flour and brown in skillet. Fasten with toothpicks. Bake in roasting pan covered at 350° for two hours or until done. During the last half hour of cooking time, uncover roasting pan and thicken broth for gravy.

Thirty Years at the Mansion (Arkansas)

One Dish Pork Chop Meal

Everybody likes this, especially men.

Salt and pepper to taste
4 (½-inch thick) pork chops
3 cups uncooked rice (can use
   instant rice and not have to
   precook rice)
2 cups tomato juice
Salt and pepper (sprinkle)
1 teaspoon sugar
1 onion
1 green pepper

Salt and pepper pork chops and sear in slightly greased skillet. Cover skillet tightly; set aside. Cook rice in boiling water until ⅓ done. Drain and pile on each pork chop. Press down slightly. Season tomato juice with salt, pepper, and sugar. Pour over chops, being very careful not to wash rice away. Cut onion and green pepper into thin rings and put over chops and rice. Bake at 350° for 40 minutes in airtight skillet. May need to add water. Good served with baked apples.

Four Generations of Johnson Family Favorites (Oklahoma)

Ham Loaf and Mustard Sauce

1¼ pounds ground
  smoked ham
¾ pound ground veal or
  ground beef
1 cup dry bread crumbs
  soaked in 1 cup milk

2 teaspoons dry mustard
2 tablespoons brown sugar
½ teaspoon pepper
2 eggs, slightly beaten

Mix all ingredients and let stand 1 hour or overnight if possible. Make into 2 loaves; bake 1½ hours at 350°. Good plain or with a sauce such as:

GRAM'S HAM SAUCE WITH MUSTARD:

3 egg yolks
1 tablespoon flour
½ cup canned undiluted
  Campbell's tomato soup

½ cup French's mustard
½ cup white vinegar
½ cup white sugar
½ cup vegetable oil

Whisk egg yolk with flour until smooth. Combine all ingredients in top of a double boiler and whisk, over medium heat, till smooth and thickened. Cool before serving. Keeps well refrigerated.

A Great Taste of Arkansas (Arkansas)

Ham Red Eye Gravy

When you fry ham, leave the "leavings" in the skillet. Take 1 teaspoon salt and sprinkle over the bottom of the skillet (less if ham is salty). A sprinkle of sugar may be added. Brown sugar and salt, then add 1 cup coffee (already made), put lid on so it won't spew on stove. Before adding coffee, make sure the fat and skillet are real hot. Pour off excess fat. Good on hot biscuits.

Seems Like I Done It This A-Way III (Oklahoma)

Crispy Corn Dogs

You will be a hit with your family when you make homemade corn dogs. Use up the remaining batter by dipping onion rings and frying them last—a great combination.

1 cup all-purpose flour
¾ cup yellow cornmeal
2 tablespoons sugar
1 tablespoon dry mustard
2 teaspoons baking powder
1 teaspoon salt
1 cup milk

1 egg, slightly beaten
2 tablespoons shortening, melted
12 hot dogs
12 skewers
Vegetable oil for deep-fat frying

Combine flour, cornmeal, sugar, mustard, baking powder, and salt. Add milk, egg, and shortening. Mix until smooth. Pour mixture into a tall glass. Put hot dogs on skewers and dip, one at a time, in cornmeal batter. Fry until golden brown in vegetable oil heated to 375°. Drain on paper towels. Yields 12 corn dogs.

Variation: To make bite-size corn dogs: cut each hot dog into 10 pieces. Dip hot dog sections into batter, covering completely. (Wooden picks work well for dipping.) Drop in hot oil and cook until golden, turning once; drain on paper towels. Insert party picks and serve immediately. Serve with mustard or ketchup if desired.

From the Ozarks' Oven... (Missouri)

Quick and Spicy Deer Sausage

8 pounds deer burger (ground
 fine with suet)
5 tablespoons Morton's
 Tender Quick
2 tablespoons coarse black
 pepper
2 tablespoons mustard seed

1 tablespoon brown sugar
1 tablespoon garlic powder
2 tablespoons cayenne or
 ground red pepper
1 tablespoon liquid smoke
1 cup dry quick oats
3 cups warm water, divided

Mix deer burger, spices, oats, and 2 cups water thoroughly until combined. Cover, let stand 1 hour at room temperature. Mix in third cup
of water; let stand 30 minutes. Stuff into casings or roll into 2x10-inch
rolls and wrap in aluminum foil. Punch small holes in casings or foil
to allow drainage during cooking.

 Place on rack in foil-lined pan. Bake 70 minutes at 350°, turning
once after 35 minutes. After cooling slightly, wrap in paper towels to
absorb excess liquid. Cool before slicing. Wrap excess rolls in foil.
Place in plastic bags and freeze.

The Sportsman's Dish (Missouri)

Onion Marmalade

Good with roasted meat or poultry.

½ cup butter
6 medium red onions (about
 2½ pounds), sliced
1 bunch scallions, white
 parts only

3 tablespoons sugar
¼ cup red wine vinegar or
 balsamic vinegar
1 cup dry red wine

In a medium skillet, melt butter. Add onions and scallions; cook over
medium-high heat, stirring, 15 minutes or until tender. Add sugar and
cook 1 minute, stirring constantly. Add remaining ingredients and
continue cooking, stirring until liquid is absorbed, about 15 minutes.
Easy. Can do ahead—may freeze. Yields 2½ cups.

Cooking in Clover II (Missouri)

Ranchero Sauce

Ranchero sauce is an important ingredient in Huevos Rancheros, but also hits the bull's eye when served with grilled steaks or pork chops. This recipe makes a large batch, and it freezes well.

¼ cup olive oil
1 medium onion, chopped
1 small stalk celery, chopped
1 medium green bell pepper, seeded and chopped
2 cloves garlic, minced
1 (28-ounce) can chopped tomatoes, undrained
1 (4-ounce) can chopped mild green chiles, drained
2 tablespoons Worcestershire
2 tablespoons chopped fresh parsley
2 teaspoons sweet or hot Hungarian paprika
1 teaspoon dried oregano
¼ teaspoon freshly ground pepper
½ teaspoon hot red pepper sauce, or to taste

In a medium saucepan, heat the oil over medium heat. Add the onion, celery, bell pepper, and garlic, and cook, covered, until the vegetables are lightly browned, about 10 minutes.

Add the tomatoes with their juices, green chiles, Worcestershire, parsley, paprika, oregano, and pepper and bring to a simmer. Reduce the heat to low and simmer, uncovered, until slightly thickened and the tomato juices are almost evaporated, about 30 minutes. Stir in the hot sauce. Serve the sauce hot, warm, or at room temperature. (The sauce can be prepared up to 5 days ahead, cooled, covered, and refrigerated. Reheat gently before serving.)

National Cowboy Hall of Fame Chuck Wagon Cookbook (Oklahoma)

Poultry

MISSOURI DIVISION OF TOURISM

With over 200 fountains, Kansas City is said to be the home of more fountains than any city in the world except Rome. Many of Kansas City's most famous fountains are found on the Country Club Plaza, including the J.C. Nichols Memorial Fountain, the most photographed and well known of all the Kansas City fountains.

Sunday School Chicken

1 pound fresh carrots
4 potatoes, unpeeled
4 onions

1 pound fresh mushrooms
1 whole fryer
Salt and pepper to taste

Scrub vegetables. Place chicken and vegetables in large roaster; salt and pepper to taste and cover. Add no water. Place in cold oven. Turn thermostat to 250° when you leave for Sunday School and enjoy a delicious meal when you return from church. Alter proportions as needed.

Pulaski Heights Baptist Church Cookbook (Arkansas)

Chicken Fricassee with Dumplings

1 (2½- to 3-pound) fryer,
  cut up
1 cup Bisquick Baking Mix
2 teaspoons salt
1 teaspoon paprika

⅛ teaspoon pepper
2 tablespoons shortening
1 tablespoon butter
1 can cream of chicken soup
1½ cups milk

Wash chicken pieces and pat dry. Mix baking mix, salt, paprika, and pepper in paper or plastic bag. Shake 2 or 3 pieces of chicken at a time in bag to coat thoroughly. Melt shortening and butter in large skillet; brown chicken on all sides. Remove chicken. Drain fat from skillet; stir in soup and milk; add chicken. Cover and simmer about 1 hour or until thickest pieces are tender. Twenty minutes before end of cooking time, prepare Dumplings.

DUMPLINGS:

2 cups Bisquick Baking Mix
¼ teaspoon poultry seasoning

½ teaspoon parsley flakes
⅔ cup milk

Mix 2 cups Bisquick, poultry seasoning, and parsley flakes. Add milk until soft dough forms. Drop dough by spoonfuls onto hot chicken. Cook, uncovered, 10 minutes; cover and cook 10 minutes longer. Makes 4 servings.

Feast in Fellowship (Oklahoma)

Chicken Croquettes

2 (1½- to 2-pound) broilers	1 egg, beaten
Boiling, salted water	1½ cups bread crumbs
1 tablespoon minced onion	Pure vegetable oil
¼ cup butter	3 tablespoons butter
⅓ cup flour	3 tablespoons flour
1½ teaspoons salt	½ teaspoon curry powder
¼ teaspoon pepper	¼ teaspoon salt
2 cups milk	1½ cups chicken broth

Cook broilers in water to cover for 45 minutes, or until tender. Reserve broth—you should have 6 cups. Remove chicken from bones; chop.

Sauté onion in ¼ cup butter until soft. Stir in flour, salt and pepper. Cook until bubbly; remove from heat. Stir in milk. Cook on medium, stirring constantly, until thickened and bubbly. Add chicken. Spread in shallow pan; cover and chill several hours.

Divide mixture into 8 portions. Shape each into a round, slightly tapered shape. Dip each croquette into egg, then roll in crumbs to coat evenly. Let dry about 15 minutes.

Fill deep fat fryer or large saucepan ⅔ full of oil. Heat to 375°. Fry croquettes for 2–3 minutes until golden brown; drain.

Melt 3 tablespoons butter in saucepan; add flour, curry powder and salt. Cook 1 minute. Add broth and stir until thickened and bubbly. Serve over warm croquettes. Serves 6.

High Cotton Cookin' (Arkansas)

Arkansas, the Natural State, has over 2½ million acres of national forest lands, 9,700 miles of streams and rivers, and over 500,000 acres of surface water comprising 11 big lakes and hundreds of smaller ones. No wonder there is such great hunting and year-round fishing.

Miss Bonnie's Fried Chicken with Her Original Chicken Fried Biscuits

Mama has made these biscuits for years, and finally she shared her secret. They are wonderful when accompanied with your favorite fried chicken. This is a favorite summer meal with fresh corn on the cob and a good salad. With fresh strawberries and your favorite homemade ice cream—big city guests will be in for a fantastic country dinner!

1 whole fryer, cut into pieces	**Salt**
Buttermilk	**Pepper**
Flour	**Crisco oil**

Wash and dry chicken parts. Marinate in buttermilk 1 hour. Preheat oil in electric skillet, 375°, while preparing chicken. (Tip—heat skillet slightly before pouring in oil.) Put 2 cups flour into large brown bag. Place chicken parts which have been coated in buttermilk into bag and shake well. Place in heated oil and sprinkle with salt and pepper. Cover and cook 20 minutes per side. For crispy chicken, do not cover. Larger pieces can finish cooking in a 325° oven. Cover with foil if you don't wish to have a crisp crust.

Note: Removing skin from chicken does get rid of extra fatty layers and some extra calories as well. This buttermilk method allows for a good crisp crust. If you desire a few extra crunchies, add ¼ cup grits or cracker crumbs to the flour. Salt and pepper the chicken as you begin frying. The salt will help the chicken to bleed and give up some of its own juices—thus making more flavorful biscuits as well as gravy.

BISCUITS:

2 cups flour	**½ teaspoon salt**
1 tablespoon baking powder	**1¼ cups milk**
1 tablespoon sugar	

Remove chicken from frying pan (hold in oven to keep warm). Sift dry ingredients together. Stir in milk. Mixture will be gooey. Drop by teaspoonful into 375° or 400° oil in skillet in which you have just prepared chicken. All the little crunchies will adhere to these biscuits. Turn once. Each side should be golden brown. Make sure oil is correct temperature. These biscuits are light and crisp and they do not absorb oil. Drain on paper towels.

Stir Ups (Oklahoma)

Orange and Chicken Cashew

4 (6-ounce) chicken breasts
¼ cup flour
1 teaspoon salt
1 teaspoon paprika
¼ cup butter
1 cup orange juice
¼ cup toasted cashews
    or almonds

Dust chicken lightly in flour with salt and paprika. Sauté in butter until golden brown (turn only once). Add orange juice; cover and cook over low heat for 20 minutes. Uncover; remove chicken to a serving dish. Reduce liquid to a thickened sauce. Pour over chicken, sprinkle with nuts, and serve at once with rice.

Dixie Cook Book V (Arkansas)

Route 66 Diner Philly Chicken

One of the specials at the Route 66 Diner in Tulsa is the Philly Chicken.

½ cup chopped celery
½ cup chopped onion
¼ medium green pepper,
    chopped
3 tablespoons vegetable oil
½ teaspoon tarragon
¼ teaspoon lemon pepper
2 cloves garlic, minced
1 pint heavy cream
1 (8-ounce) package cream
    cheese, softened
¾ cup milk
1 chicken, cooked, skinned
    and deboned (approximately
    3 cups diced)
¼ cup grated Parmesan cheese
Wild rice or pasta

In a large saucepan, sauté the celery, onion, and pepper in vegetable oil. Add the tarragon, lemon pepper, and garlic. Cook until vegetables are tender. Add cream, cream cheese, milk, and chicken and heat to simmer but do not boil. Sprinkle with Parmesan cheese and serve over wild rice or pasta. Makes 6–8 servings.

The Route 66 Cookbook (Oklahoma)

Route 66 crosses Oklahoma for nearly 400 miles. The "Mother Road" was in fact born in Oklahoma, as the road's architect, Cyrus Avery, lived in Tulsa. Travelers find neon-lit diners, drive-in theatres, mom-and-pop gas stations, and rustic trading posts along the route. You can still "get your kicks on Route 66."

Chicken Camille

A real palate pleaser––decidedly different!

4 chicken breasts
Salt and pepper (about
⅛ teaspoon per chicken
breast)
1 clove garlic, crushed

4 tablespoons butter or
margarine
2 (8-ounce) cartons sour cream
4 ounces crumbled Roquefort
cheese

Sprinkle each chicken breast lightly with salt and pepper. Rub skillet with crushed garlic clove and discard. Melt 4 tablespoons butter over moderately high heat and place chicken breasts in skillet. Brown on both sides in melted butter and remove to baking dish when browned, about 10–12 minutes.

While chicken is browning, preheat oven to 350°. Mix sour cream and Roquefort together. Pour over chicken breasts. Cover baking dish and bake 30 minutes. Do not overcook or sour cream will separate. Place chicken breasts on individual plates, spooning ample amount of sauce over each. Sprinkle with paprika and garnish with parsley. Pass remaining sauce at table. Preparation time: 15 minutes. Cooking time: 30 minutes. Serves 4.

Rush Hour Superchef! (Missouri)

Oven-Fried Chicken

1 cup cornflake crumbs
1 teaspoon paprika
½ teaspoon garlic powder
¼ teaspoon ground thyme

¼ teaspoon red pepper
6 chicken breast halves,
skinned
¼ cup buttermilk

Combine first 5 ingredients in plastic bag. Shake to mix well. Brush both sides of chicken with buttermilk. Place in bag of crumbs and shake to coat. Place chicken on broiler pan that has been sprayed with vegetable spray. Bake at 400° for 45 minutes or until done. Yields 6 servings.

Take It to Heart (Arkansas)

Herb Cheese Chicken Florentine

4 chicken breast halves,
  boned and skinned
1 bunch fresh spinach
8 ounces garlic herb cream
  cheese

½ cup buttermilk dressing
1 cup bread crumbs
¼ cup grated Parmesan cheese

Spray 11x13-inch baking pan with nonstick vegetable oil. Place chicken breast between two sheets of wax paper and pound to flatten.

Wash spinach and remove stems. Steam in microwave for 2 minutes. Drain well. Cover each chicken breast with drained spinach leaves. Portion 2 ounces herb cheese on spinach and roll up. Secure with toothpick if necessary. Dip into buttermilk dressing and roll in bread crumbs mixed with Parmesan cheese. Bake in 350° oven 45 minutes. Serves 4.

The Never Ending Season (Missouri)

Boneless Cheesy Chicken Breasts

6 chicken breasts, boneless
6 (4x4-inch) slices Swiss
  cheese
1 can cream of chicken
  soup, undiluted
½ cup white wine

1 cup Pepperidge Farm
  Herb-Seasoned Stuffing
  Mix, crushed
¼ cup butter or margarine,
  melted

Arrange chicken in a lightly greased 9x13-inch baking dish. Top with cheese slices. Combine soup and wine, stirring well. Spoon sauce evenly over chicken and sprinkle with stuffing mix. Drizzle butter over crumbs. Bake at 350° for 45–55 minutes. Yields 4–6 servings.

Betty Is Still "Winking" at Cooking (Arkansas)

Chicken Sicilian

**4 chicken breasts, boned and
skinned**
¼ cup olive oil
2 tablespoons minced garlic
**2 tablespoons chopped
shallots**
1 cup diced tomatoes
1 cup whole black olives
**2 cups julienned red bell
pepper**

**2 cups julienned green bell
pepper**
**2 tablespoons chopped fresh
thyme**
**2 tablespoons chopped fresh
basil**
¼ cup chicken broth
1 pound linguini, cooked

Grill or broil chicken breasts. While chicken is cooking, heat oil in a
large sauté pan. Add garlic and shallots, and cook until soft. Add diced
tomatoes, black olives, julienned peppers, and herbs, and sauté until
hot but still crisp. Pour vegetables into a bowl and set aside until ready
to serve. In the same pan, pour in chicken broth and add cooked linguini. Heat thoroughly.

Divide linguini equally among 4 plates. Place a chicken breast on top
of pasta, then divide vegetables equally over each breast. Serves 4.
Round out this creation with a salad or side dish.

Recipe by Coyote Grill
Kansas City Cuisine (Missouri)

LIBRARY OF CONGRESS

In 1925, while working for a St. Louis aircraft
corporation, Charles Lindbergh heard that some-
one was offering a prize of $25,000 to the first
pilot to cross the Atlantic nonstop from New
York to Paris. On May 20, 1927, history was
made as he crossed 3,600 miles of the Atlantic in
the "Spirit of St. Louis," a custom-built single-
engine, single-seat monoplane. "Spirit of St.
Louis" was named in honor of Lindbergh's sup-
porters in St. Louis, Missouri, who paid for the
aircraft. Lindbergh's autobiography, *The Spirit of
St. Louis*, recounts his solo trans-Atlantic flight.
The book won the Pulitzer Prize in 1954 and was
made into a film starring James Stewart in 1957.
Today, Lindbergh's Spirit of St. Louis is housed
in the Smithsonian National Air and Space
Museum in Washington, D.C. It is one of the
museum's most popular attractions.

Lemon Chicken for the Grill

2 chickens, cut in pieces
1 cup vegetable oil
1 tablespoon salt
2 teaspoons onion powder
½ teaspoon thyme
½ cup lemon juice
1 teaspoon paprika
2 teaspoons crushed basil
½ teaspoon garlic powder

Place chicken in 9x13-inch glass dish. Combine remaining ingredients, blending well. Pour over meat and cover tightly. Chill 6 hours, turning chicken occasionally. Remove from refrigerator 1 hour before grilling. Cook 20–25 minutes on medium heat on grill, basting often and turning for 20 minutes.

Pulaski Heights Baptist Church Cookbook (Arkansas)

Deb's Lip-Lickin' Chicken

4 chicken breasts
Seasoned salt to taste
Lemon pepper to taste
Minced garlic to taste
½ cup soy sauce
½ cup Worcestershire sauce

Wash chicken breasts and pat dry. Rub with spices and place on the grill, meat side down, searing for 5 minutes. Flip to bone side down and sear for 5 more minutes. Lower firebox to ⅔ down position and, with heat deflector in place, cook for 1 hour and 15 minutes.

Put soy sauce and Worcestershire in a spray bottle and use to baste meat frequently (every 20 minutes). Serves 4–6.

Kansas City BBQ (Missouri)

Ozark Chicken Casserole

2 cups cooked diced chicken
1 cup cooked rice
1 tablespoon lemon juice
1 cup chopped celery
1 medium onion, chopped
½ cup mayonnaise

3 hard-boiled eggs, chopped
1 can cream of chicken soup
Salt and pepper to taste
½ stick butter, melted
2 cups Pepperidge Farm
   Herb-Seasoned Stuffing Mix

Combine chicken, rice, juice, celery, onion, mayonnaise, eggs, soup, and seasoning thoroughly and place in greased casserole. Mix butter and stuffing and sprinkle over top. Bake at 350° for about 30 minutes.

Talk About Good (Missouri)

Stir-Fry Chicken

2 whole boneless chicken
   breasts
3 tablespoons cornstarch
4 tablespoons soy sauce
1 stalk fresh broccoli
1 small onion, thinly sliced,
   separated into rings

2 tablespoons peanut oil
¼ pound mushrooms, sliced
2 cups fresh bean sprouts
1 (8-ounce) can water
   chestnuts, drained, sliced
1 cup chicken broth

Cut chicken into thin slices. In small bowl combine cornstarch and soy sauce; stir in chicken; stir to coat; marinate 15 minutes. Cut off broccoli flowerets; thinly pare stalks; slice inner stalk into thin slices. Heat oil in wok or deep skillet over high heat. Add chicken; stir-fry until browned; remove; set aside. Add broccoli and onion; stir-fry 2 minutes; add mushrooms, bean sprouts, water chestnuts, and chicken. Stir in broth; cover and cook gently 5 minutes or until vegetables are crisp-tender. Serve over hot rice.

Celebration (Arkansas)

Chicken Crêpes

Served regularly in Victorian Sampler Tea Room in Eureka Springs.

2 tablespoons butter
1 tablespoon minced onion
2 tablespoons flour
1½ cups half cream, half milk
1 cup diced chicken

¼ cup sherry or white wine
¼ cup grated Parmesan cheese
¼ cup sliced almonds
6 or 8 Basic Crêpes

Melt butter. Add onion and sauté until yellow. Add flour and cook until thick and smooth. Add milk and cream, stirring until medium thick sauce is made. Add chicken and sherry to half the sauce. Place 2 tablespoons mixture in each crêpe and roll. Place in buttered pan, seam-side-down. Cover with remaining sauce; sprinkle with cheese and almonds. Bake at 450° until brown. Makes 6 crêpes.

Variation: Substitute crab, shrimp, scallops, or combination instead of chicken.

BASIC CRÊPES:

3 eggs
1⅓ cups milk
1 cup Wondra instant
  blending flour

¼ teaspoon salt
Vegetable oil

Combine all ingredients, except oil, using blender. Batter should be smooth. Let stand 30 minutes (important for lighter and tender crêpe). Place a greased crêpe pan or 8-inch skillet over moderately high heat until hot. Brush pan lightly with oil. Pour 2–3 tablespoons crêpe batter in center. Tilt pan and swirl batter to cover and form a thin crêpe. Pour excess back in bowl. Cook crêpe 30–45 seconds until light brown. Turn and cook briefly on other side. Remove to plate and trim any ragged edges. Cool and separate with wax paper until ready to use.
  Very versatile, can be made ahead and frozen.

Victorian Sampler (Arkansas)

Chicken á la King in Toast Cups

1 (4-ounce) can mushrooms,
  drained
¼ cup chopped green bell
  pepper
¼ cup butter
¼ cup flour

1 teaspoon salt
⅛ teaspoon pepper
1 cup chicken broth
1 cup milk
1 cup diced cooked chicken
¼ cup chopped pimento

Sauté mushrooms and green pepper in butter. Blend in flour, salt, and pepper. Let bubble. Slowly stir in chicken broth and milk; bring to boiling over low heat, stirring constantly. Boil 1 minute. Add chicken and pimento; heat through. Serve in Toast Cups. Serves 6.

TOAST CUPS:

Cut crusts from day-old bread; brush lightly with melted butter. Press into muffin pan or custard cups. Toast in oven (350°) for 15–30 minutes.

Talk About Good (Missouri)

Chicken Broccoli

2 carrots, sliced
1 onion, diced
2 stalks celery, diced
½ cup chicken broth
Salt to taste
1 fryer, cooked and diced
2 (8-ounce) cartons sour cream

2 cans cream of mushroom
  soup
2 (10-ounce) packages
  frozen chopped broccoli
Grated Cheddar cheese
Lemon pepper
Slivered almonds

Cook carrots, onion, and celery in chicken broth, adding water if necessary. Add salt and chicken. Combine sour cream and soup in a separate bowl. Layer chicken, broccoli, soup mixture, and cheese in a 2-quart casserole, sprinkling each layer with lemon pepper. Bake at 350° for 45 minutes. Sprinkle almonds on top and bake 10 minutes longer. Serves 6–8.

Favorite Recipes from Associated Women for Harding (Arkansas)

Mexican Chicken

2 pounds chicken, cooked and boned
1 onion, chopped
1 (5¾-ounce) bag nacho cheese Doritos, crushed
1 can cream of chicken soup, undiluted

½ pound grated American cheese
½ can Ro-Tel tomatoes
1 can cream of mushroom soup, undiluted

Layer all ingredients in greased 9x13-inch casserole dish, beginning at top of list. Bake uncovered at 350° for 30 minutes.

Classroom Classics (Arkansas)

Aztec Casserole

1 (10¾-ounce) can cream of mushroom soup
1 (10¾-ounce) can cream of chicken soup
1 (7-ounce) can green salsa sauce or (7-ounce) can chopped green chiles (undrained)
¾ cup milk

12 corn tortillas, cut into 1-inch squares
4 boneless, skinless chicken breasts, cooked and cubed
1 small onion, minced
½ pound Monterey Jack cheese, grated
½ pound Cheddar cheese, grated

In a medium bowl, combine soups, salsa, and milk for sauce and set aside. Spray 9x13-inch baking dish with nonstick vegetable spray. Alternate layers in dish beginning with a small amount of sauce, tortillas, chicken chunks, onion, sauce, and cheeses. Repeat layers, cover and refrigerate overnight to soak and set mixture. Bake in oven preheated to 325° for 1–1½ hours or until bubbly. Yields 8 servings.

Cafe Oklahoma (Oklahoma)

Chinese Egg Rolls

MARINADE:

⅓ cup orange juice
¼ cup teriyaki sauce
1 teaspoon sesame oil
2 teaspoons brown sugar

¼ teaspoon each: cayenne
    pepper, ground ginger, and
    garlic

INSIDES:

1 chicken breast, boned,
    skinned, and diced
    (uncooked)

4 carrots, shredded
3 celery ribs, sliced thin
1 package egg roll wrappers

Marinate the Insides in the Marinade for 30 minutes or overnight.
  Heat a nonstick skillet sprayed with cooking spray over medium heat.
Cook in small batches till chicken is done. Roll in egg roll wrapper,
spray the egg roll with cooking spray, covering all sides, and bake at
400° for 10–12 minutes or till golden. Serves 12.

Eat to Your Heart's Content, Too! (Arkansas)

Peachy Chicken Casserole

This is great for family and entertaining friends.

6 chicken breasts (skinless)
2 teaspoons salt
Pepper to taste
1½ teaspoons paprika
¾ cup flour
½ cup butter
½ cup slivered almonds

1 cup water
2 cans beef consommé
2 tablespoons ketchup
2 cups sour cream
1 large can sliced peaches,
    drained
¼ cup grated Parmesan cheese

Preheat oven to 350°. Dredge chicken with mixture of salt, pepper,
paprika, and flour. Reserve remaining flour mixture. Brown chicken
on all sides in hot butter. Place in 3-quart casserole. Lightly brown
almonds in drippings in skillet. Stir in remaining flour. Gradually stir
in water and consomme. Add ketchup; cook and stir until thickened.
Remove from heat and stir in sour cream. Pour over chicken and bake,
uncovered, for about 1 hour. Arrange sliced peaches on top of chicken.
Sprinkle with cheese and return to oven for 10 minutes. Serves 8–12.

Four Generations of Johnson Family Favorites (Oklahoma)

Sadie's Deep-Dish Chicken Pot Pie

½ cup finely chopped celery
¼ cup finely chopped onion
4 tablespoons butter
4 tablespoons flour

2 cups chicken stock
2 cups cubed, cooked chicken
Salt and pepper

Sauté celery and onion in butter until tender. Add flour and mix well. Gradually add stock, stirring and cook slowly until medium thick. Season to taste and set aside to cool.

PASTRY:

3 cups flour
1½ teaspoons salt

6 heaping tablespoons
 shortening

Mix until dough looks like coarse meal. Sprinkle with ice water (10–12 teaspoons) until dough sticks together. Roll into ball and divide into 2 parts. On floured board, roll 1 part of dough to ¼ inch thick. Line a 2-quart round baking dish with pastry, allowing it to extend a little over the sides. Add chicken and sauce. Roll other part of dough and place over top of baking dish. Handle pastry carefully to avoid holes. Trim any excess crust around edge of dish. Moisten edges of crust with ice water and stick together. Make several slashes in top crust to allow steam to escape while cooking. Bake at 350° for 1 hour.

Southern Accent (Arkansas)

Turkey Pot Pie

1 cup frozen peas
1 cup diced carrots
1 cup diced celery
2 medium potatoes, diced
1 medium onion, diced
4 cups turkey broth

½ cup sifted flour
1 cup milk
Salt and pepper to taste
2 cups diced cooked turkey
Hot Water Pastry (see below)

Cook the vegetables just until tender in the turkey broth. Remove vegetables and measure broth; add water to make 4 cups. Blend flour with the milk and stir until smooth. Stir into the hot broth and cook until thick. Add the vegetables and turkey to the gravy. Season. Pour the mixture into a large (9x13-inch) buttered casserole.

HOT WATER PASTRY:
¾ cup shortening
2 cups flour
¾ teaspoon salt

1 egg, separated
½ cup hot water

Cut the shortening into the flour and salt. Stir in the beaten egg yolk and water blended together, and stir until a soft dough is formed. Roll to ½-inch thickness; cut to fit top of baking dish. Pierce with fork for steam to escape. Brush dough with the beaten egg white. Bake in a 425° oven for about 25 minutes.

Eat Pie First...Life is Uncertain! (Missouri)

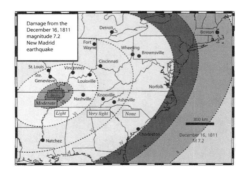

New Madrid, Missouri, is famous for being the site of a series of over 1,000 earthquakes in 1811 and 1812, ranging up to approximately magnitude 8, the most powerful non-subduction zone earthquake recorded in the United States. A few of these earthquakes were so violent that the Mississippi River changed its course. Some sections of the Mississippi River appeared to run backward for a short time, and church bells were reported to ring as far as Boston, Massachusetts.

Turkey Vegetable Pot Pie

PASTRY SHELL:

1 cup whole-wheat pastry
    flour (or unbleached
    all-purpose flour)

½ teaspoon salt
¼ cup vegetable oil
2 tablespoons ice water

In medium bowl combine flour and salt. Blend in oil with fork. Sprinkle water over mixture; mix well. Shape into ball; chill 1 hour.

FILLING:

3 carrots, cut into 1-inch
    pieces
2 large onions, chopped
3 tablespoons light margarine
¼ cup all-purpose flour
½ teaspoon salt
¼ teaspoon crumbled dried
    thyme

¼ teaspoon freshly ground
    pepper
2 cups chicken bouillon
½ cup frozen peas
2 cups chopped, cooked
    turkey or chicken

Cook carrots and onions in water in medium pan until tender-crisp, about 10 minutes. Drain; set aside. In same pan, melt margarine over low heat. Blend in flour, salt, thyme, and pepper; cook 1 minute, stirring. Gradually add bouillon, stirring constantly, until sauce is thick. Set aside.

In 2-quart casserole, combine carrot mixture, sauce, peas, and turkey; mix well.

Roll dough out between 2 pieces of wax paper. Remove top layer of paper; invert pastry over top of casserole. Remove paper; seal pastry around dish. Cut slits in top for steam to escape. Bake 30 minutes at 400° or until pastry is golden brown. Yields 6 servings.

Hint: If prebaked pie shell is needed for another use, bake in preheated 450° oven 10–12 minutes.

Sounds Delicious! (Oklahoma)

Wild Turkey Kiev

Boneless wild turkey breast
1 stick margarine
Chopped chives (fresh or
  dried)
1 cup flour
¾ cup milk

1 egg
1 teaspoon salt
1 teaspoon pepper
Cracker crumbs
Vegetable oil for frying

Cut larger turkey breast portions into ¼-inch slices, smaller pieces into ½-inch slices. Place between 2 sheets wax paper. Flatten to ⅛-inch by pounding lightly with the flat edge of meat cleaver or bottom of a skillet.

Place 1 pat of margarine on edge of turkey breast. Add 1 teaspoon chives and roll, folding in edges to seal margarine. Make a batter by mixing flour, milk, egg, salt, and pepper. Beat until smooth. Dip turkey rolls in batter; coat with cracker crumbs. Deep fry at 365°–370° until golden brown. Drain on a rack.

The Sportsman's Dish (Missouri)

Ozarks Smoked Turkey

1 onion, minced
½ cup butter
3 tablespoons light brown
  sugar
1 (0.4-ounce) package
  Italian salad dressing mix

1 clove garlic, minced
1 teaspoon salt
Freshly ground pepper
  to taste
¾ cup tarragon vinegar
1 (20-pound) turkey

Combine all ingredients except turkey in a small saucepan. Simmer 3–4 minutes. Stuff turkey, if desired, and truss as usual. Brush generously with herb sauce. Cook in smoker according to manufacturer's directions. One hour before cooking is finished, add damp hickory chips to smoker and baste turkey every 20 minutes with the herb sauce. Serves 16–18.

Sassafras! (Missouri)

Turkey-Vegetable Stir-Fry

1 (4-ounce) can sliced
   mushrooms, undrained
1 large onion, coarsely
   chopped
2 small green bell peppers,
   cut into 1-inch strips
1 (8-ounce) can water
   chestnuts, sliced and
   drained
3 cups cooked turkey, cut
   into 1-inch pieces
¼ cup plus 1 tablespoon lite
   soy sauce
2 teaspoons cornstarch
½ teaspoon sugar
⅛ teaspoon red pepper
3 cups cooked rice, unsalted

Drain mushrooms, reserving liquid; set aside. Spray wok or skillet with vegetable spray and allow to heat at medium high (325°) for 1 minute. Add onion and green peppers to wok; stir-fry 3–4 minutes or until vegetables are crisp-tender. Push up to sides of wok and add water chestnuts, turkey, and sliced mushrooms. Heat thoroughly. Combine lite soy sauce, reserved mushroom liquid, cornstarch, sugar, and red pepper and add to wok; mix well.

Reduce heat to low (225°); simmer 2–3 minutes or until slightly thickened. Serve over rice. Yields 6 servings.

Take It to Heart (Arkansas)

Marinated Duck Breasts

4 boneless duck breasts
½ cup Italian dressing
1 tablespoon Worcestershire
Juice of one lemon
¼ teaspoon garlic powder
¼ teaspoon ground cloves
Bacon slices

Soak duck in salt water for 3 hours. Remove from water and drain on paper towel; pat dry and place in shallow pan. Combine all ingredients; pour over duck breasts and marinate for 4 hours. Wrap each breast in bacon and secure with toothpick. Cook on grill over a slow fire 7 minutes per side, or until bacon is done.

The Farmer's Daughters (Arkansas)

Barbeque Sauce for Chicken

½ cup oil
1 cup water
2 tablespoons chopped onion
1 clove garlic, crushed
1½ teaspoons sugar
1 teaspoon salt
1 teaspoon chili powder
1 teaspoon paprika
1 teaspoon pepper

½ teaspoon dry mustard
Dash of cayenne
1 teaspoon Worcestershire
1 teaspoon hot sauce
¼ cup lemon juice
1 cup ketchup
¼ cup steak sauce
½ green bell pepper, chopped
1 tablespoon cider vinegar

Combine all ingredients in a saucepan and simmer for 1 hour. Brush onto grilled chicken pieces. Yields about 3 cups.

The Passion of Barbeque (Missouri)

Sweet 'n' Sour Sauce

½ cup pineapple juice
2 tablespoons lemon juice
1 tablespoon vinegar
2 tablespoons brown sugar
1 tablespoon soy sauce

1 tablespoon cornstarch
¼ teaspoon powdered ginger
¼ green bell pepper, chopped
1 (9-ounce) can pineapple
   tidbits, undrained

Combine all ingredients except for undrained pineapple tidbits and green pepper in a blender. Blend until mixed. Pour mixture into saucepan and add peppers and pineapple. Cook over moderate heat until thick and clear. Serve over roast lean pork or poultry. Serves 6.

Eat to Your Heart's Content, Too! (Arkansas)

Seafood

COURTESY OF ARKANSAS DEPT. OF PARKS & TOURISM

Lake Chicot in southeast Arkansas is a twenty-mile-long, former main channel of the Mississippi River. Formed 600 years ago by the meandering of the Mississippi River, it is the largest oxbow lake in North America and the state's largest natural lake.

Psari Plaki
(Baked Fish and Vegetables)

1 pound cod or orange
  roughy*
Salt and pepper to taste
Juice of ½ lemon
3 onions, chopped
¾ cup olive oil
1½ cups canned tomatoes

½ cup chopped parsley
2 cloves garlic, chopped
2 carrots, sliced
2 ribs celery, sliced
¼ cup raisins (optional)
½ cup water
1 cup white wine

Clean fish thoroughly. Rub with salt and pepper. Sprinkle with lemon juice. Sauté onions in oil until golden brown. Add all remaining ingredients and simmer until vegetables are tender. Bake fish at 350° in greased baking pan until done. Remove fish from baking pan onto serving dish. Cover with vegetable sauce. Serve immediately. Yields 6 servings.

*You may substitute almost any fish of your choice: haddock, bluefish, etc.

The Art of Hellenic Cuisine (Missouri)

Lemon Baked Fish
with Vegetables

2 pounds fish fillets*
3 lemons
1 tablespoon reduced-
  calorie margarine
1 tablespoon polyunsaturated
  oil

2 bell peppers, chopped
3 tomatoes, chopped
1 onion, chopped
¼ teaspoon salt (optional)
Pepper, as desired

Rinse fish in cold water. Soak for 1 hour in ice water with juice of 1 lemon. Drain and pat fillets dry.

In 9x13-inch baking dish, melt margarine and oil. Separately layer tomatoes, peppers, and onions on bottom of baking dish. Sprinkle lightly with salt and pepper. Squeeze 1 lemon over mixture. Place fillets over vegetables. Garnish with lemon slices.

Bake in preheated 500° oven for 20 minutes or until fish flakes easily with a fork. Yields 10 servings.

*Suggested fish: Orange Roughy, Sole, or Cod

Take It to Heart (Arkansas)

Fillet of Fish Parmesan

1 pound (fresh or frozen)
boneless fish fillets (any
mild tasting fish—flounder,
crappie, sole, trout)
3 tablespoons butter
½ teaspoon salt
½ teaspoon coarsely ground
black pepper

1 tablespoon bottled lemon
juice
1 tablespoon dry white wine
¼ cup grated Parmesan cheese
Paprika
Parsley
Lemon wedges

Preheat oven to 400°. Cut 3 tablespoons butter into small cubes and place in shallow baking dish in preheated oven. While butter is melting, sprinkle fillets on both sides with salt and pepper. Remove melted butter from oven and add lemon juice. Place fillets flesh side down in sizzling butter and bake in oven 10 minutes (if fish is thick, cook 15 minutes).

Turn with spatula and baste with juices. Add wine, Parmesan, and sprinkle with paprika. Return to oven; bake until done, approximately 5 minutes. Serves 2.

To serve, garnish with parsley and lemon wedges. Preparation time: 4 minutes; cooking time: 10–15 minutes.

Note: You may run fish under broiler if fillets are not brown enough.

Rush Hour Superchef! (Missouri)

Grouper with Dilled Cucumber Sauce

The Dilled Cucumber Sauce is also an excellent accompaniment to grilled or steamed vegetables.

DILLED CUCUMBER SAUCE:

1 cup peeled, seeded, and diced cucumber	**2 sprigs fresh dill (or 1 teaspoon dried dill weed)**
¼ cup sliced green onions	**½ teaspoon salt**
¼ cup oil	**Freshly ground pepper to**
1 tablespoon lemon juice	**taste**

In an electric blender or food processor, combine all sauce ingredients and purée. Refrigerate.

3 tablespoons butter	**2 sprigs fresh dill**
1 tablespoon lemon juice	**2 (6-ounce) grouper fillets**

Melt butter in a small saucepan and add lemon juice. Set aside.

   Grill fillets over hot coals for 5 minutes per side. Baste while cooking, using sprigs of dill to brush on lemon butter. Serve with Dilled Cucumber Sauce. Serves 2.

Hooked on Fish on the Grill (Missouri)

A port in Oklahoma? That's right. In fact, the Tulsa Port of Catoosa is one of the largest, most inland river ports in the United States. Primarily following the Arkansas River, it offers year-round, ice-free barge service with river flow levels controlled by the U.S. Army Corps of Engineers. Located in a 2,000-acre industrial park and employing more than 2,500 people, products can travel easily and efficiently from America's Heartland to the rest of the globe.

Oven-Poached Rainbow Trout with Cucumber-Dill Cloud

Rainbow trout is one of our guests' all-time favorite entrées. Partly this is because we serve it only when we can get it really fresh-fresh. There are those who still like their trout dipped in milk, rolled in cornmeal and pan-fried, a classic Ozark treatment, but we prefer the sweet and delicate flavor of this oven-poached trout. With white wine for a poaching liquid and a grated cucumber and fresh dill garnish, this recipe fairly sparkles.

CUCUMBER-DILL CLOUD:

½ cup sour cream
¼ cup plain yogurt
1 teaspoon Tamari soy sauce

1 tablespoon minced fresh
  dill (or 1 teaspoon dried)
¼ cup finely grated cucumber

Blend together well, preferably several hours in advance so flavors have a chance to marry.

4 small rainbow trout,
  about 10 ounces each
½ cup white wine

1 cup water
Juice of 2 lemons
Paprika

Preheat oven to 325°. Wash and pat dry the rainbow trout. Place them in a buttered baking dish and pour the wine and water over; sprinkle with lemon juice and paprika.

Bake for 35–40 minutes, or until fish is firm to the touch, and flakes easily with a fork.

Gently spoon Cucumber-Dill Cloud over each trout and serve, garnished with a large sprig of fresh parsley. A tomato provençal and a heap of tiny steamed and buttered new potatoes works very well with this, as with so many fish dishes. Serves 4.

The Dairy Hollow House Cookbook (Arkansas)

Catfish Sesame

Crispy and flavorful

**3 pounds fresh or frozen
catfish fillets or steaks**
3 cups water
¼ cup vinegar
1 cup fine dry bread crumbs
3 tablespoons sesame seeds
**2 tablespoons Greek
seasoning**

⅛ teaspoon white pepper
1 teaspoon salt
¼ cup all-purpose flour
1 egg, beaten
2 tablespoons milk
Vegetable oil
Lemon wedges

Place catfish in a bowl and cover with water and vinegar. Prepare more solution, using same proportions, if needed. Soak for an hour or more.

Place bread crumbs on wax paper and mix in sesame seed, Greek seasoning, pepper, salt, and flour.

Mix egg and milk in a shallow dish. Drain and dry catfish. Dip in egg mixture and coat with bread crumb mixture.

Fry in 1-inch deep hot oil (360°) 4–5 minutes on each side. Drain on paper towels and keep hot in a 200° oven. Garnish with lemon wedges. Makes 8 servings.

Hint: If preferred, bake fish on an oiled cookie sheet 15–20 minutes at 375° only until fish flakes easily with a fork.

Home for the Holidays (Arkansas)

Scallops Dijonnaise

1 pound sea scallops, halved
1½ tablespoons dry white
  wine
3 tablespoons flour
1 teaspoon salt
Freshly ground pepper to
  taste
3 shallots, minced

1 clove garlic, minced
½ cup clarified butter
½ cup dry white wine
½ cup heavy cream
2 tablespoons Dijon mustard
Salt and freshly ground
  pepper to taste
Minced fresh parsley

Place scallops in medium bowl, add 1½ tablespoons wine, cover, and refrigerate for 1 hour. Combine flour, salt, and pepper. Drain scallops and pat dry on paper towels. Dust scallops with flour mixture and shake off excess. Sauté shallots and garlic in butter until fragrant. Add scallops and sauté until golden. Transfer to serving dish.

Over high heat deglaze skillet with wine. Add cream and mustard and reduce sauce until thickened. Add salt and pepper. Pour over scallops and sprinkle with parsley. Serves 3–4.

Cooking for Applause (Missouri)

ARKANSASSTRIPERS.COM

Bayou Bartholomew has the distinction of being the longest bayou in the world. A bayou (pronounced by-oo or by-oh) is a marshy, curving channel filled with slow moving, sometimes stagnant, water. Bartholomew begins its journey northwest of the city of Pine Bluff, Arkansas, and flows approximately 375 miles crossing the Louisiana border joining the Ouachita River. Over 117 species of fish have been found in Bayou Bartholomew.

Lemon-Basil Basted Shrimp

24 jumbo shrimp (about 1¼ pounds), shelled and deveined

MARINADE:

2 teaspoons finely chopped
  garlic
2 teaspoons finely chopped
  shallots
1½ teaspoons Dijon
  mustard

⅓ cup dry white wine
⅓ cup fresh lemon juice
¼ teaspoon black pepper
½ cup olive oil
⅓ cup finely chopped fresh
  basil

Combine Marinade ingredients. Add the shrimp and toss until thoroughly coated. Marinate until coals are ready.

Remove shrimp from Marinade and pour remaining liquid into a saucepan. Arrange shrimp on grill topper, keeping them flat. Cook for about 3 minutes or until shrimp can be lifted from grill without sticking. Then turn over and cook for about 2 more minutes.

Bring pan of Marinade to a boil and simmer for 2 minutes. Arrange shrimp on a platter and spoon Marinade over all. Serve immediately. Serves 4.

Hooked on Fish on the Grill (Missouri)

Easy Shrimp Scampi

1–2 tablespoons sliced
  green onions
2–4 cloves garlic, crushed
½ cup butter
1 pound shrimp, peeled
  and deveined
2 tablespoons dried basil

¼ cup dry white wine
2 tablespoons lemon juice
½ teaspoon grated lemon
  rind (optional)
¼ teaspoon hot sauce
  (Tabasco)
Salt and pepper to taste

Sauté onions and garlic in butter a few minutes; turn heat to low and add shrimp. Cook, stirring frequently, about 3 minutes. Add remaining ingredients and simmer another 2–3 minutes, or until shrimp turn pink. Do not overcook or use high heat or shrimp will be tough.

Serve with French bread split in half brushed with olive oil and sprinkled with Parmesan cheese. Heat under broiler 1–2 minutes. Serves 4.

Tasty Palette (Missouri)

Shrimp Etouffée

ROUX:

6 tablespoons oil   6 tablespoons flour

Make roux, medium brown. Keep stirring until brown, 20 minutes.

2 cups chopped onions
1 cup chopped bell pepper
1 cup chopped celery
5 garlic cloves, crushed
1 small can stewed tomatoes
2 (10½-ounce) cans chicken
  broth
2 cups water
2 bay leaves

1 teaspoon basil
1 teaspoon chili powder
½ teaspoon cayenne
¼ teaspoon black pepper
1 teaspoon Season-All
3–4 pounds peeled shrimp
1 cup chopped green onions
2 tablespoons chopped parsley

Add to roux the onions, bell pepper, celery, and garlic. Add canned tomatoes, mixing well. Add chicken broth and water. While simmering, add spices. Let simmer 1 hour. Now add shrimp, green onions, and parsley. Cook 20 minutes, on very low heat, until shrimp are done. Serve over rice.

Nibbles Cooks Cajun (Arkansas)

Shrimp and Chicken Jambalaya

½ pound smoked sausage, diced
½ pound ham, cubed
½ cup oil
3 chicken breasts, deboned, chopped
1 cup chopped onion
1 cup chopped bell pepper
1 cup chopped celery
1 cup chopped green onions
2 cloves garlic, minced
1 (16-ounce) can tomatoes
1 teaspoon thyme
1 teaspoon black pepper
¼ teaspoon cayenne pepper
1 teaspoon salt
1 cup rice, uncooked
2 tablespoons Worcestershire
1½ cups chicken stock
2 pounds peeled shrimp

Sauté sausage and ham in the oil until lightly browned in big Dutch oven. Remove from oil. Add chicken; sauté till it looks done. Remove from oil.

Sauté onion, bell pepper, celery, green onions, and garlic in meat drippings until tender. Drain tomatoes, saving the juice. Add tomatoes, thyme, pepper, and salt. Cook 5 minutes. Stir in rice.

Mix liquid from tomatoes, Worcestershire, and stock to equal 2½ cups. Add to pot and bring to a boil. Reduce to simmer. Add raw shrimp, ham, sausage, and chicken. Cook, uncovered, stirring occasionally for 30 minutes or until rice and shrimp are done.

Nibbles Cooks Cajun (Arkansas)

ARKANSASEDC.COM

The Buffalo National River, located in northern Arkansas, was the first river in America to receive national park protection (1972). Its beauty is highlighted by towering limestone bluffs, clear rushing waters, and wide gravel bars. The National River designation protects natural rivers from industrial uses, impoundments, and other obstructions that may change the natural character of the river or disrupt the natural habitat for the flora and fauna that live in or near the river.

Herbed Italian Shrimp
with Italian Wine Marinade

1½ tablespoons salt or
   salt substitute
1 tablespoon garlic onion
   magic
1 tablespoon lemon juice,
   plus rind halves

2 bay leaves
5 pounds fresh or frozen shrimp
1 (6-ounce) package shrimp
   and crab boil

Fill an 8-quart kettle half full of water and add all of the above seasonings except the shrimp boil. Bring to a full rolling boil and add the shrimp boil. Bring water to boil again and cook for 10 minutes, or until the shrimp curl and are pink. (Do not overcook!) Drain and rinse in cool water. Peel, if desired. Refrigerate in a large bowl covered with plastic wrap. If in a hurry, chill down in the freezer for at least 1 hour.

MARINADE:

1 (16-ounce) bottle low-
   calorie Italian dressing
½ teaspoon dried, crushed
   sweet basil
½ teaspoon fresh or dried
   crushed thyme

1 teaspoon minced dried garlic
1 tablespoon garlic onion
   magic
½ cup white semisweet wine

Mix all of the above ingredients together in a quart jar. Shake vigorously and pour over chilled shrimp. Marinate, stirring shrimp every 30 minutes, for 2 hours. The shrimp will absorb the flavors. Serve on a chilled platter or large bowl with picks. Serves 6.

A Kaleidoscope of Creative Healthy Cooking (Arkansas)

Seafood Casserole

½ cup chopped bell pepper
½ cup chopped onion
4 cups cooked rice
3 tablespoons butter
2 (6½-ounce) cans crabmeat
1 pound shrimp, cooked
  (may use more)
1 (10¾-ounce) can cream
  of celery soup
1 (8½-ounce) can sliced water
  chestnuts
½ cup Hellmann's mayonnaise
1 egg, beaten
½ pound sharp Cheddar cheese,
  grated
1 tablespoon Worcestershire
2 tablespoons lemon juice
Salt and white pepper to taste
Bread crumbs, buttered

Sauté bell pepper and onion in butter until soft. Combine all ingredients except bread crumbs; mix gently. Put in buttered casserole and top with bread crumbs. Bake at 350° for 30 minutes.

May be made ahead, and baked later; be sure to cover and refrigerate. Increase baking time about 10 minutes if refrigerated. Yields 10–12 servings.

In Good Taste (Arkansas)

Cakes

COURTESY OF OKLAHOMA TOURISM

Muscle Car Ranch in Chickasha, Oklahoma, represents nostalgic Americana featuring thousands of antique automotive signs, muscle cars, vintage motorcycles, a 1900s Dairy Farm, and a fully restored 1940s diner collected by owner Curtis Hart. The ranch hosts the Annual Muscle Car Ranch Swap Meet twice a year on the seventy-acre farm.

Miracle Butter Cake

1 Duncan Hines Yellow Cake Mix	2 eggs 1 stick butter, melted

Mix and spread in bottom of 9x13-inch pan.

TOPPING:

1 (8-ounce) package cream cheese, softened	1 box powdered sugar 2 eggs

Mix Topping ingredients and pour over cake mixture. Bake at 350° for 35–40 minutes only.

Asbury United Methodist Church Cook Book (Arkansas)

Coon Cake

1 package Duncan Hines
  Butter Cake Mix (take out
  ⅔ cup of the cake mix)
	1 stick butter or margarine
	1 egg

Mix well and press in the bottom of a 9x13-inch pan. Bake at 350° for about 15–20 minutes. Do not get too brown.

⅔ cup cake mix	½ cup brown sugar
1 tablespoon flour	1 teaspoon vanilla
3 eggs	2 cups pecans, chopped
1½ cups dark Karo syrup	or whole

Mix well and pour on baked, cooled cake portion. Cook about 30–35 minutes. Start cooking at 350° until it gets hot; then turn the oven down to 325° and continue to cook until center of cake is like a pecan pie. Do not overcook!

Asbury United Methodist Church Cook Book (Arkansas)

Orange Poppy Seed Cake

Ultra lowfat—the best—wonderful.

1 package low-fat white cake
   mix
2 tablespoons poppy seeds
¾ cup fat-free liquid egg
   product
1 cup fat-free sour cream

1 (6-ounce) can frozen orange
   juice concentrate
⅓ cup water
2 teaspoons cinnamon
2 tablespoons sugar

Preheat oven to 350°. In large bowl, combine all ingredients except cinnamon and sugar and beat with electric mixer 2 minutes. Spray Bundt pan with nonstick cooking spray. Combine sugar and cinnamon and sprinkle evenly over inside of pan. Pour in cake batter and bake at 350° for 45 minutes. Makes 12 servings.

Fat Free 2 (Oklahoma)

Harvey Wallbanger Cake

1 package yellow cake mix
1 package vanilla instant
   pudding
½ cup oil

¼ cup vodka
¾ cup orange juice
¼ cup Galliano
4 eggs

Mix all together and beat for 4 minutes. Put in greased and lightly floured Bundt pan. Bake 45–50 minutes at 350°.

GLAZE:

1½ cups powdered sugar
1½ tablespoons vodka

1½ tablespoons Galliano
1½ tablespoons orange juice

Mix together and pour over cake to glaze.

Dine with the Angels (Oklahoma)

Post Office Cake

1 Duncan Hines Butter
  Cake Mix
½ cup oil

2 eggs
1 small can mandarin oranges
  with juice

Mix thoroughly and bake at 350° in 3 layers until toothpick inserted in center comes out clean.

ICING:

1 large carton Cool Whip
1 small box vanilla instant
  pudding mix

2 small cans crushed
  pineapple (drained)

Mix and spread between layers; refrigerate.

Evening Shade (Arkansas)

Surprise Lemon Pudding Under Golden Cake Topping

1 cup sugar
¼ cup sifted enriched flour
Dash of salt
2 tablespoons melted butter
  or margarine

5 tablespoons lemon juice
2 teaspoons grated lemon peel
3 egg yolks, well beaten
1½ cups milk, scalded
3 egg whites, stiffly beaten

Preheat oven to 325°. Combine sugar, flour, salt, and butter; add lemon juice and peel. Combine the beaten egg yolks and milk; add to first mixture. Fold in egg whites and pour into 8 greased 5-ounce custard cups (Pyrex).

Bake in pan of hot water in slow oven (325°) 45 minutes. When baked, each dessert will have custard on the bottom and sponge cake on top. Makes 8 servings.

Covered Bridge Neighbors Cookbook (Missouri)

Philbrook's Italian Cream Cake

Tulsa's beautiful Philbrook Museum reopened its restaurant with a new name and an exciting new creative menu. This delicate cream cake, a creation of their executive chef, Jody Walls, appears often at their Sunday brunch.

1 cup buttermilk	5 eggs, separated
1 teaspoon baking soda	2 cups all-purpose flour, sifted
½ cup butter, softened	1 teaspoon vanilla extract
½ cup shortening	3½ ounces flaked coconut
2 cups sugar	1 cup chopped pecans

Preheat oven to 350°. Grease and flour 3 (9-inch) cake pans. Combine buttermilk and baking soda and set aside. Cream butter, shortening, and sugar. Add egg yolks, one at a time, beating after each addition. Alternately, add buttermilk and flour, small amounts at a time. Add vanilla extract. Beat egg whites to stiff peaks; fold into batter and flour mixture. Stir in coconut and pecans. Bake for 25 minutes. Cool on racks.

ICING:

1 (8-ounce) package cream cheese, softened	1½ cups chopped pecans
1 cup butter, softened	3 teaspoons vanilla extract
8 cups powdered sugar, sifted	

In mixer, cream together cream cheese and butter. Add sugar slowly to spreading consistency. Add pecans and vanilla. Frost cake. Makes 12 servings.

Applause! (Oklahoma)

The Philbrook Museum of Art is truly Tulsa's unique treasure. The legacy of oilman Waite Phillips endures in this stunning Renaissance-style villa and gardens.

Coconut Sour Cream Cake

1 box white cake mix
   (Duncan Hines preferred)
   with no pudding in mix
¼ cup oil

3 eggs
1 (8-ounce) carton sour cream
1 (8.5-ounce) can cream of
   coconut

Mix all ingredients with an electric mixer as per other cake mix elaborations. Bake in greased 9x12-inch pan at 350° for 30 minutes. Cool cake in pan. Cover with Icing.

ICING:

1 box powdered sugar (3.5
   cups
1 (8-ounce) package cream
   cheese, softened

2 tablespoons milk
1 teaspoon vanilla
1 can Angel Flake Coconut

Blend powdered sugar into cream cheese; then work in the milk and vanilla. Ice cake. Sprinkle coconut over the iced cake. Can freeze.

Wanda's Favorite Recipes Book (Missouri)

Pineapple Ice Box Cake

½ cup pineapple juice
1 package lemon gelatin
1½ cups sugar
½ pound butter, softened

4 eggs, separated
1 cup pineapple (drained)
1 cup chopped pecans
¾ pound vanilla wafers

Heat pineapple juice to boiling point. Add gelatin and stir until dissolved. Set aside to cool. Cream sugar and butter; add well-beaten egg yolks, pineapple, gelatin, and nuts. Beat egg whites until stiff and fold in. Roll vanilla wafers on dough board with a rolling pin until they are crumbs. Put half the crumbs in flat pan or glass tray about 8x10 inches. Add fruit mixture. Spread last half of crumbs on top and pat down gently. Leave in ice box 24 hours.

Seems Like I Done It This A-Way I (Oklahoma)

Missouri Upside Down Cake

3 tablespoons butter or
  margarine
¾ cup brown sugar
2 cooking apples, peeled
  and sliced
¼ teaspoon cinnamon
⅓ cup shortening

⅓ cup sugar
2 eggs
1 teaspoon vanilla
1½ cups all-purpose flour
2 teaspoons baking powder
½ teaspoon salt
⅔ cup milk

Melt butter in 9-inch round pan. Add brown sugar and stir until melt-ed. Arrange sliced apples on sugar/butter mixture. Sprinkle cinnamon over apples.

Cream shortening and sugar. Blend in eggs and vanilla, beating thoroughly. Add dry ingredients alternately with milk. Pour over apples in pan. Bake at 350° for 40–45 minutes, or until done. Turn out onto serving plate immediately.

Serve with whipped cream or pistachio ice cream. Yields 6–8 servings.

From the Apple Orchard (Missouri)

Fresh Apple Cake

Wonderful for Christmas brunch.

2 cups sugar
½ cup shortening
2 eggs, beaten
2 cups all-purpose flour
½ teaspoon salt
1 teaspoon baking soda

1 teaspoon cinnamon
1 teaspoon nutmeg
4 cups peeled and finely
  chopped apples
1 cup chopped dates
2 cups chopped nuts

Preheat oven to 300°. Grease and flour 9x13-inch pan. Cream sugar and shortening. Add eggs, mixing well. Sift together flour, salt, baking soda, cinnamon, and nutmeg. Add to creamed ingredients. Stir in apples, dates, and nuts. Pour into prepared pan and bake 50 minutes or until brown. Serve warm with whipped cream. Makes 12–16 servings.

Applause! (Oklahoma)

Rosy Apple Cake

1 cup all-purpose flour
1 teaspoon baking powder
¼ teaspoon salt
3 tablespoons butter or
  margarine
1 egg, beaten with 1 tablespoon
  milk

4–5 medium cooking apples
1 (3-ounce) package strawberry
  gelatin
1–2 tablespoons sugar

Mix first 3 dry ingredients. Cut in butter. Add egg and milk mixture. Mix together thoroughly and press in bottom and up sides of an 8-inch round pan. Peel apples and slice into dough-lined pan. Sprinkle dry gelatin over top of apples. Add 1–2 tablespoons sugar, depending on tartness of apples. Sprinkle Topping over apples.

TOPPING:
¾ stick butter or margarine
¾ cup sugar

¾ cup all-purpose flour

Cut butter into sugar/flour mixture, until crumbly. Sprinkle over top of apples. Bake at 375° for 45 minutes. Yields 6–8 servings.

From the Apple Orchard (Missouri)

Jonathan, Red Delicious, and Golden Delicious are the three most commonly grown apples in Missouri, but the state also grows others like Gala, Fuji, Winesap, and Rome Beauty. A good apple should be bright, crisp, and juicy. Fresh apples need to be stored in a cool place to help keep them fresh—about 32 to 40 degrees F. Be careful not to get below 32 degrees because freezing will deteriorate the apples quickly.

Bavarian Apple Torte

CRUST:

½ cup butter, room
  temperature
⅓ cup sugar

¼ teaspoon vanilla
1 cup all-purpose flour

Cream butter, sugar, and vanilla. Blend in flour. Spread dough on the bottom and 1 inch up the sides of a 9-inch springform pan.

FILLING:

12 ounces cream cheese,
  room temperature
¼ cup sugar

1 egg
1 teaspoon vanilla

Beat together cream cheese and sugar. Blend in egg and vanilla. Pour into pastry-lined pan.

TOPPING:

⅓ cup sugar
½ teaspoon cinnamon
4 cups peeled and sliced
  tart apples

¼ cup slivered almonds
1 cup heavy cream, whipped
Cinnamon

Combine sugar and cinnamon; toss with apples. Arrange apples in concentric circles over cream cheese layer, avoiding spilling apple juice on pastry. Sprinkle with slivered almonds. Bake at 450° for 10 minutes. Reduce heat to 400° and continue baking for 25 minutes. Cool before removing rim of pan.

Serve with a bountiful amount of whipped cream, laced with cinnamon. Makes 8 servings.

Beyond Parsley (Missouri)

Pumpkin Torte

STEP 1:

24 graham cracker squares,
   crushed
⅓ cup brown sugar

½ cup butter
½ cup chopped nuts

Mix and pat into bottom of 9x13-inch pan.

STEP 2:

1 (8-ounce) package cream
   cheese, softened

½ cup sugar
2 eggs

Beat together well and pour over crust; bake 15–20 minutes at 350°
till set.

STEP 3:

1¼ cups pumpkin
3 egg yolks (save whites)
⅓ cup brown sugar
1 teaspoon vanilla
½ cup milk (canned)
½ teaspoon salt

1 teaspoon cinnamon
1 envelope Knox Gelatine
¼ cup warm water
3 egg whites
¼ cup powdered sugar
Cool Whip

Mix first 7 ingredients together and cook, stirring, long enough to cook
eggs. Dissolve Knox Gelatine in warm water. Add to pumpkin mixture
while still warm. Beat egg whites stiff; add powdered sugar. Fold into
pumpkin mixture. Pour over baked layers and refrigerate. Can be made
ahead. When ready to serve, cover with layer of Cool Whip.

Blue Ridge Christian Church Cookbook (Missouri)

Pumpkin Roll

5 eggs
1½ cups sugar
1 cup pumpkin
1 teaspoon lemon juice
1 cup plus 2 tablespoons
  all-purpose flour

1½ teaspoons baking powder
¾ teaspoon salt
¾ teaspoon nutmeg
3 teaspoons cinnamon
1½ teaspoons ginger
Powdered sugar

Beat eggs at high speed for 5 minutes. Add sugar, pumpkin, and lemon juice. Add flour, baking powder, salt, nutmeg, cinnamon, and ginger, adjusting measurements of spices to taste. Spread mixture into a greased and floured 15x10x1-inch pan. Bake for 15–20 minutes at 350°. Roll in a towel with powdered sugar and add powdered sugar on top. Leave rolled until cool. Unroll, spread with Filling, and re-roll.

FILLING:

2 (3-ounce) packages cream
  cheese, softened
1 cup powdered sugar

2 cups chopped pecans
½ teaspoon vanilla
4 tablespoons softened butter

Mix all ingredients together. Unroll cooled pumpkin roll; spread Filling on top and re-roll.

Feast in Fellowship (Oklahoma)

LIBRARY OF CONGRESS

Known as Oklahoma's favorite son, Will Rogers was born November 4, 1879, to a prominent Indian Territory family. Rogers was one of America's brightest media stars during the 1920s and 1930s, a Cherokee cowboy-philosopher who did rope tricks while making pointed—and humorous—political observations. He traveled around the world 3 times, made 71 movies (50 silent films and 21 "talkies"), and wrote more than 4,000 nationally-syndicated newspaper columns. Route 66, dubbed the "Will Rogers Memorial Highway," rolls within a few blocks of the Will Rogers Memorial in Claremore, Oklahoma. The Will Rogers birthplace is in nearby Oologah.

Peanut Butter Sheet Cake

2 cups all-purpose flour
1 teaspoon baking soda
2 cups sugar
½ teaspoon salt
1½ sticks margarine
½ cup Crisco oil

½ cup chunky peanut butter
1 cup water
2 eggs, slightly beaten
1 teaspoon vanilla
½ cup buttermilk

Mix flour, baking soda, sugar, and salt in mixing bowl. Bring margarine, oil, peanut butter, and water to a boil. Pour over dry ingredients and mix well. Add beaten eggs, vanilla, and buttermilk and mix well. Pour into 11x15x1-inch sheet pan; bake 15–18 minutes at 350°.

While cake is baking, make icing. Let cake cool 5 minutes before spreading on icing.

PEANUT BUTTER CAKE ICING:

½ cup Milnot or milk
1 cup sugar
1 teaspoon vanilla
½ cup extra crunchy peanut
  butter

½ cup miniature
  marshmallows
2 tablespoons margarine

Bring Milnot, sugar, and margarine to a boil and cook 2 minutes, stirring gently to keep from scorching. Remove from heat and stir in peanut butter, marshmallows, and vanilla until melted. Wait 5 minutes for cake to cool, then pour over cake and spread to cover.

Thank Heaven for Home Made Cooks (Oklahoma)

LIBRARY OF CONGRESS

Diamond, Missouri, is the birthplace of George Washington Carver, the first black scientist to achieve nationwide prominence. Carver's best-known work was his discovery of over 900 by-products of the peanut, which would become one of the South's most important crops. Carver's presentation to Congress in 1920 in favor of a peanut tariff made him famous, while his intelligence, eloquence, amiability, and courtesy delighted the general public. Three American presidents—Theodore Roosevelt, Calvin Coolidge and Franklin Roosevelt—met with him, and the Crown Prince of Sweden studied with him for three weeks.

Milk Chocolate Candy Bar Cake

CAKE:

2½ cups all-purpose flour
¼ teaspoon salt
2 sticks butter or margarine, softened
2 cups sugar
4 eggs

8 (1.65-ounce) milk chocolate bars
1 cup chocolate syrup
¼ teaspoon baking soda
1 cup buttermilk
2 teaspoons vanilla

Grease and flour tube pan. Sift together the flour and salt. In a mixer bowl cream butter and sugar. Add 4 eggs, one at a time, mixing between each addition. Melt chocolate bars; add chocolate syrup. Mix baking soda and buttermilk and add to butter, sugar, and egg mixture. Blend in flour, then chocolate mixture and add vanilla. Pour into prepared pan and bake 2 hours at 300°.

ICING:

1½ cups sugar
1 cup evaporated milk
¼ stick butter or margarine

4 (1.65-ounce) milk chocolate bars
1 teaspoon vanilla

Put sugar, evaporated milk, and butter in a saucepan over medium heat and bring to a boil. Boil 10 minutes. Add chocolate bars and vanilla. Beat until smooth and well mixed. Spread or pour over cooled cake. Serves 24.

Cookin' in the Spa (Arkansas)

Chocolate Ice Box Cake

1 dozen ladyfingers
½ pound sweet chocolate
3 tablespoons sugar
3 tablespoons water
4 eggs, separated
½ pint whipping cream

Line sides and bottom of mold with ladyfingers. Melt chocolate in double boiler; add sugar and water and well-beaten yolks of eggs. Cook until smooth and thick, stirring constantly. When cool, add stiffly beaten egg whites. Cover ladyfingers with filling; place in refrigerator twelve hours or more before serving. When ready to serve, remove to chop plate and cover with sweetened whipped cream, if desired.

Dixie Cook Book V (Arkansas)

Aunt Susan's Red Earth Cake

This cake is reputed to have been the favorite of the late Sam Walton.

½ cup shortening
1½ cups sugar
1 egg
4 tablespoons cocoa
1 teaspoon red food coloring
2 tablespoons strong hot
  coffee
2 cups cake flour
1 teaspoon salt
1 teaspoon baking soda
1 cup buttermilk
1 teaspoon vanilla

Cream the shortening and sugar until they are light and fluffy. Blend in the egg, which has been beaten until it is light and foamy. Mix the cocoa, coloring, and hot coffee to make a smooth paste. Stir this into the mixture. Sift the flour and measure it, then sift it again with the salt and baking soda. Add a bit of the measured flour to the mixture, then alternately add buttermilk and flour, folding and beating it lightly after each addition. Add the vanilla. Turn into 2 (8-inch) pans, 2 inches deep, lined on the bottom with buttered wax paper. Bake in a moderate oven, 375°, for 30–35 minutes.

Spiced with Wit (Oklahoma)

Burnt Caramel Cake

This was before margarine, so my mother always used fresh-churned butter. This recipe has been in our family since my childhood. I've used it many times and it's always been one of our favorites.

½ cup sugar, burnt until dark
½ cup water
1½ cups sugar
⅔ cup butter or margarine, softened
2 eggs, beaten

1 cup water
Pinch of salt
1 teaspoon vanilla
2 cups flour
2 teaspoons baking powder

In heavy pot or skillet, burn ½ cup sugar until dark. Put ½ cup boiling water in burnt sugar; let boil to a syrup (takes about 7 minutes). Cool but keep warm. Cream sugar and butter or margarine; add the eggs and beat to a creamy batter. Then add water, salt, vanilla, and burnt syrup, leaving 2 tablespoons in the skillet for filling. Add the flour and baking powder; beat for 2 minutes. Bake in 2 greased and floured 9-inch cake pans in preheated 350° oven 25–30 minutes.

FILLING:

2 cups sugar
2 tablespoons burnt sugar
3 tablespoons butter

⅔ cup milk or cream
2 tablespoons white corn syrup

Put 2 cups sugar in skillet with burnt syrup; add butter the size of a small egg, milk or light cream, and white corn syrup. Boil until it forms a soft ball in cold water; then cool and beat. Spread on cake. If icing gets too thick to spread, add a little cream or milk.

Recipes and Remembrances (Oklahoma)

Jam Cake

¾ cup butter	1 teaspoon each: salt,
1 cup sugar	cinnamon, allspice
3 eggs, separated	2 cups all-purpose flour
½ cup buttermilk	1 cup strawberry jam
1 teaspoon baking soda	½ cup chopped pecans

Cream butter and sugar, and add egg yolks, beating after each one. Add buttermilk. Sift baking soda, spices and flour together and add to mixture, mixing well. Fold in jam and pecans. Fold in stiffly beaten egg whites. Bake in a greased 9x13-inch pan at 350° for 30–40 minutes, or until top springs back when tapped. Allow to cool. Ice with Caramel Icing.

CARAMEL ICING:

½ cup sugar	2 tablespoons butter
2½ cups sugar	¾ cup milk
2 eggs	½ teaspoon salt

Brown ½ cup sugar in heavy iron skillet. Mix 2½ cups sugar, 2 whole eggs, and beat well. Add butter, milk, and salt. Add the browned sugar. Cook slowly until it forms soft ball in cold water, stirring all the time. Take from fire and beat until ready to spread on cake. Serves 10.

Feasts of Eden (Arkansas)

Mammy's Strawberry Shortcake

This recipe has been a specialty of the family for seven Southern generations.

1½ tablespoons butter
½ cup sugar
1 egg
3 tablespoons water
1 heaping cup all-purpose flour

⅛ teaspoon baking soda
¼ teaspoon baking powder
2 quarts strawberries
Whipped cream

Melt butter; add sugar, egg, and water. Mix well. Sift flour, baking soda, and baking powder. Add to mixture to make batter the consistency of soft biscuit dough. Bake at 375° in buttered 8-inch square pan for 20 minutes. This recipe may be doubled. To serve, split cake when cool, through the middle. Crush 2 quarts of strawberries and put part between the layers, the remainder on top. Serve with whipped cream, if desired.

Dixie Cookbook IV (Arkansas)

Fresh Raspberry and Peach Shortcake Supreme

Light, pretty, and refreshing summer dessert.

1 (5x9-inch) loaf angel
  food cake, halved lengthwise
⅓ cup naturally sweet
  fruit spread
3 fresh peaches, skinned,
  sliced thin, soaked in
  ½ cup orange juice

1 pint fresh red raspberries
1 (8-ounce) carton whipped
  topping

Place bottom piece of cake on serving platter. Spread with fruit spread. Drain peach slices from orange juice and pat dry using paper towels. Reserve orange juice for another use. Layer half of the peach slices over fruit spread. Place half the raspberries over peach slices. Spread ⅓ cup whipped topping over fruit. Set second (top) layer of cake over fruit, with cut side down. Ice entire assembled cake with whipped topping on the sides and top. Arrange remaining peach slices and raspberries in a row on the top. Serve within 15 minutes of assembling. Cut at the table, so this can be enjoyed. Serves 4–6.

A Kaleidoscope of Creative Healthy Cooking (Arkansas)

Christmas Pound Cake

Make well ahead—keeps in freezer for three months. Keeps well unrefrigerated for a week to ten days.

1 (18.25-ounce) box yellow cake mix (Betty Crocker Super Moist Butter Yellow Cake Mix preferred)
1 (3¾-ounce) box vanilla pudding and pie filling mix
3 eggs
⅓ cup corn oil
1 (5½-ounce) can apricot nectar (⅔ cup)
¼ cup apricot brandy
1½ teaspoons pure orange extract

Preheat oven to 325°. Grease and flour a 10-inch Bundt pan (or any pan of equivalent size). In mixing bowl, combine cake mix, pudding mix, eggs, oil, apricot nectar, apricot brandy, and orange extract. Mix until all ingredients are well blended.

Pour into Bundt pan and bake 1 hour at 325° or until cake tests done. Invert on a cake plate and prick all over before spooning on Glaze.

GLAZE:
4 tablespoons butter
¾ cup sugar
¼ cup water
⅓ cup apricot brandy

Heat butter, sugar, and water in small saucepan until butter is melted and sugar is dissolved. Remove from heat; add apricot brandy, mixing well. Prick cake on top and sides with fork. Spoon Glaze slowly over cake, letting cake absorb liquid before adding additional Glaze. If freezing, wrap in heavy aluminum foil; leave out overnight. Wrap additionally in freezer wrap; tape all open edges closed, and freeze.

To serve: Place on a cake plate, surround with fresh holly; place sprigs of fresh holly on top of cake, and tuck either red maraschino or candied cherries in and among the holly leaves. Serves 18–20.

It's Christmas (Missouri)

Italian Cheesecake

1 pound ricotta cheese,
  room temperature
1 pound cream cheese,
  room temperature
1½ cups sugar
1 teaspoon fresh lemon juice
1 teaspoon grated lemon rind

1 tablespoon pure vanilla
3 tablespoons flour
3 tablespoons cornstarch
1 stick butter, melted
1 pound sour cream
4 large eggs, slightly beaten

Do not preheat oven. Important to add ingredients as instructed. Blend ricotta and cream cheese. Gradually add sugar and blend. Stir in lemon juice and rind, vanilla, and flour mixed with cornstarch. Add butter and blend well by hand. Add sour cream and eggs and mix by hand. Spray 9-inch springform pan with Pam. Fill with mix, place pan on cookie sheet, and set the pan on a flat surface several times to remove air bubbles. Bake at 325° for 1½ hours. Do not open oven door. Turn off heat and leave cake in oven 2 hours.

The Sicilian-American Cookbook (Arkansas)

Chocolate Turtle Cheesecake

2 cups vanilla wafer crumbs
6 tablespoons margarine,
  melted
1 (14-ounce) bag caramels
1 (5-ounce) can evaporated
  milk
1 cup chopped pecans,
  toasted

2 (8-ounce) packages cream
  cheese, softened
½ cup sugar
1 teaspoon vanilla extract
2 eggs
½ cup semisweet chocolate
  chips, melted

Combine crumbs and margarine. Press into bottom of 9-inch spring-form pan. Bake at 350° for 10 minutes. Melt caramels with milk in 1½-quart heavy saucepan over low heat, stirring frequently, until smooth. Pour over crust. Top with pecans.

Combine cream cheese, sugar, and vanilla, mixing at medium speed until well blended. Add eggs, 1 at a time, mixing well after each addition. Blend in chocolate. Mix well. Pour over pecans. Bake at 350° for 40 minutes. Loosen cake from rim of pan. Cool before removing rim completely. Chill. Makes 10–12 servings.

Delicious Reading (Missouri)

Strawberry Sundae Cheesecake

CRUST:

½ stick margarine
  (4 tablespoons)

2 cups crushed graham cracker
  crumbs

Melt margarine in 9x13-inch pan. Add crumbs and mix well. Pat into bottom of pan.

CHEESECAKE:

2 cups water
2 (3-ounce) boxes wild
  strawberry gelatin

2 cups frozen sweetened
  strawberries (crushed) and
  juice

Heat water to boiling; add gelatin and stir till dissolved. Add frozen strawberries with juice to gelatin. Chill till set.

1 (8-ounce) package cream
  cheese, softened

⅔ cup sugar
1 large container Cool Whip

Mix until smooth. Add to gelatin mixture and mix with mixer. Fold in large container of Cool Whip. Pour over Crust. Chill approximately 2 hours or till set.

Spring Creek Club (Oklahoma)

Cookies and Candies

LUCI BRANYAN, MISSOURI DIVISION OF TOURISM

Everyone knows that Branson, Missouri, is home to some of the best shows and entertainment in the world, but it's also home to the World's Largest Toy Museum. Larger-than-life toy soldiers stand guard as you walk through the doors and step back into your childhood.

Snickerdoodles

1 cup butter or shortening
1½ cups sugar
2 eggs, lightly beaten
2¾ cups all-purpose flour
2 teaspoons cream of tartar

1 teaspoon baking soda
½ teaspoon salt
2 tablespoons sugar
2 tablespoons cinnamon

Cream butter and sugar; beat well and add eggs. Sift dry ingredients (except sugar and cinnamon) together and combine. Chill dough several hours or overnight. Mix 2 tablespoons sugar and 2 tablespoons cinnamon. Roll dough to size of walnuts and coat in sugar and cinnamon before baking 10 minutes at 400° on well-greased cookie sheet. Do not overbake. Cookies will puff up and fall after cooling.

Victorian Sample (Arkansas)

Molasses Cookies

Spicy and old fashioned.

3½ cups all-purpose flour
2 teaspoons baking soda
1 teaspoon cinnamon
½ teaspoon salt
1 cup shortening

1 cup molasses
⅔ cup brown sugar, firmly
  packed
1 cup thick, sour milk or
  buttermilk

First grease 1 or 2 baking sheets to have handy. Sift and measure flour; add baking soda, cinnamon, and salt. Sift again and set aside. Cream shortening. Blend in sugar gradually, then the molasses and mix well. Mix in about ⅓ of the flour, then ½ of the buttermilk; repeat; finish blending in the remaining flour. Drop rounded tablespoons on baking sheet about 1½ inches apart. Spread slightly with back of spoon.

Bake in preheated oven until lightly brown. Cool thoroughly before storing in covered container. Baking time, 12–15 minutes. Baking temperature 375°.

Seems Like I Done It This A-Way II (Oklahoma)

Brown Edge Cookies

You can't make enough!

1 cup butter, softened
⅔ cup sugar
2 eggs
1 teaspoon vanilla

1½ cups all-purpose flour
 (sifted)
¼ teaspoon salt

Cream butter and sugar. Add eggs, beating well. Add vanilla. Mix in flour and salt. Drop by teaspoon onto greased cookie sheet. Bake in preheated 350° oven for 10 minutes. Makes about 60 cookies.

Note: Allow space between dropped dough because cookies spread.

The Cook Book (Missouri)

Sour Cream Cashew Drops

The best cookie we've tasted for your Christmas goodies tray.

2 cups sifted all-purpose flour
1 teaspoon baking powder
¾ teaspoon baking soda
¼ teaspoon salt
1 egg

½ cup soft butter
1 cup brown sugar
1 teaspoon vanilla
½ cup sour cream
1½ cups cashew nuts

Sift flour, baking powder, baking soda, and salt together into mixing bowl. Put egg, butter, brown sugar, vanilla, and sour cream in blender container. Cover and run on medium speed until smooth. Stop blender and add nuts. Cover and run on medium speed until nuts are coarsely chopped. Pour into flour mixture and stir to mix. Drop by teaspoonfuls onto lightly greased cookie sheets. Bake at 375° for 10 minutes or until golden brown. Cool and frost with a white butter frosting. Makes 5 dozen.

FROSTING:

4 tablespoons butter
1 teaspoon vanilla

2 cups powdered sugar
2 tablespoons cream

Cream butter and vanilla. Add remaining ingredients and beat until smooth.

Note: Can be frozen—frost before freezing.

Finely Tuned Foods (Missouri)

English Toffee Cookies

½ cup butter
½ cup margarine
1 cup sugar
1 egg yolk
1 teaspoon vanilla

2 cups all-purpose flour
½ teaspoon salt
1 egg white, beaten
2 cups chopped pecans

Blend butter, margarine, and sugar in food processor or electric mixer until creamy. Add egg yolk and vanilla and blend. Add flour and salt and blend. Let dough stand in refrigerator at least 30 minutes. With the palm of your hand, spread very thin on cookie sheet, covering it completely. Lightly brush with beaten egg white. Sprinkle with chopped pecans. Bake at for 375° for 12–15 minutes or until light brown. Let cool about 5 minutes and cut into small rectangles.

Feasts of Eden (Arkansas)

Melt in Your Mouth Chocolate Coconut Macaroons

Everybody's favorite.

1 cup sweetened condensed
  milk
4 cups coconut
⅔ cup mini semisweet
  chocolate bits

1 teaspoon vanilla extract
½ teaspoon almond extract

Preheat oven to 325°. Combine sweetened condensed milk and coconut. Mix well by hand (mixture will be gooey). Add chocolate bits, vanilla, and almond extract. Stir until all ingredients are well blended.

   Lightly spray a "nonstick" (Teflon-coated) cookie sheet with a "no stick" cooking spray. Drop by teaspoonfuls onto cookie sheet, one inch apart. Cook 12 minutes or until lightly brown on top.

   Remove from pan with a Teflon-coated spatula and let cool.

   Store in an airtight container or in Ziploc freezer bags. Freezes well. Yields 50–55 cookies.

It's Christmas! (Missouri)

Old-Fashioned Oatmeal Apple Cookies

¾ cup butter Crisco
1¼ cups packed brown
  sugar
1 egg
¼ cup milk
1½ teaspoons vanilla
3 cups quick-cooking oats
1 cup all-purpose flour

1¼ teaspoons cinnamon
¼ teaspoon nutmeg
½ teaspoon baking soda
½ teaspoon salt
1 cup peeled and diced apples
¾ cup raisins
¾ cup chopped walnuts

Cream Crisco, brown sugar, egg, milk, and vanilla. Combine all dry ingredients and add to creamed mixture. Mix well; add nuts and apples. Stir in oats. Drop by tablespoons on greased cookie sheet. Bake at 375° for 13 minutes.

Home Cookin' (Missouri)

Oatmeal Chews

1 cup butter, softened
1 cup sugar
1 cup brown sugar, firmly
  packed
2 eggs
1 teaspoon pure vanilla
  extract

2 cups all-purpose flour
2 teaspoons baking soda
½ teaspoon baking powder
1½ cups old-fashioned oats
½ cup chopped pecans
½ cup chocolate chips
1½ cups flaked coconut

In large bowl cream butter with both sugars. Add eggs and vanilla; mix well. In small bowl combine flour, baking soda, and baking powder; add to butter mixture. Stir in oats, pecans, and chocolate chips. Refrigerate one hour. Roll into walnut-size balls; roll lightly in coconut. Place on lightly buttered cookie sheet; flatten with fork. Preheat oven to 350°; bake 8 minutes. For best results, bake one sheet of cookies at a time on center rack of oven. Yields 5 dozen.

Hint: For variety, substitute raisins for the chocolate chips.

Sounds Delicious! (Oklahoma)

Potato Chip Cookies

2 cups margarine, softened
1 cup sugar
3½ cups all-purpose flour
1 teaspoon vanilla extract
1 cup crushed potato chips
¼ cup powdered sugar

Cream margarine and sugar in mixer bowl until light and fluffy. Add flour and vanilla; mix well. Add crushed potato chips gradually, mixing well after each addition. Drop by teaspoonfuls onto ungreased cookie sheet. Bake at 350° for 15 minutes or until golden brown. Cool on wire rack. Sprinkle with powdered sugar. Yields 36 servings.

The Pioneer Chef (Oklahoma)

Fruit Cake Cookies

1½ pounds pecans, chopped
½ pound candied cherries, chopped
¾ pound raisins
2½ cups all-purpose flour, divided
1 cup brown sugar
¼ pound butter, softened
4 eggs, beaten well
3 scant teaspoons baking soda
3 tablespoons milk
1 teaspoon each: cloves, nutmeg, and cinnamon
1½ ounces whiskey
½–1 pound jar pineapple preserves

Mix together pecans, cherries, raisins, and 1 cup flour; set aside. Cream brown sugar and butter. Add well-beaten eggs. Dissolve baking soda in milk and add alternately with remaining flour and spices which have been sifted together. Add whiskey and preserves to this mixture, and then add nuts and fruits. Drop onto greased cookie sheets and bake at 350° about 12 minutes. Makes a large batch of cookies that stores well in airtight container.

Around the Bend (Arkansas)

Irish Lace Sandwich Cookies

½ cup (1 stick) butter
1 cup sugar
1 egg
1 teaspoon almond extract

2 tablespoons flour
⅓ teaspoon salt
1 cup quick-cooking oats

Cream softened butter and sugar in a mixing bowl. Add egg and almond extract, mixing well. Add flour, salt, and oats. Line a baking sheet with aluminum foil. Use a melon baller (for more uniform shapes) or drop by ½ teaspoonfuls onto foil. (Use only this small amount; dough will spread to give a lacy effect in the finished cookie.) Place only 6 cookies at a time on an average-size baking sheet.

Bake in a 350° oven for 5–8 minutes, or until light brown. Slide foil off sheet and completely cool cookies before removing from foil. (If they resist at all, they are not completely cool.)

FILLING:

4 ounces bittersweet or
    semisweet chocolate
1 tablespoon butter

2 tablespoons grated orange
    zest
1 tablespoon Grand Marnier

Melt chocolate and butter in the top of a double boiler or in a microwave at MEDIUM power. Stir in orange zest and Grand Marnier. Cool slightly. Spread mixture on flat side of 1 cookie and sandwich with a second. Let cool and serve. Makes 18 sandwich cookies.

Note: Serve these light treats with a scoop of vanilla ice cream or orange sherbet, and a cup of cinnamon-flavored coffee.

Above & Beyond Parsley (Missouri)

THESHEPHERDOFTHEHILLS.COM

In 1907 Harold Bell Wright wrote *The Shepherd of the Hills,* which has become one of the best-selling books of all times. At the Shepherd of the Hills Farm, a reenactment of the story is performed from May to October.

Scrumptious Chocolate Surprises

Make ahead and freeze.

1¼ cups (1½ sticks) butter
  or butter substitute, room
  temperature
2 cups sugar
2 eggs
2 teaspoons vanilla extract

¾ cup unsweetened cocoa
  powder
2 cups all-purpose flour
1 teaspoon baking soda
1 teaspoon salt

Preheat oven to 350°. In a large bowl, cream butter, sugar, eggs, and vanilla. Add cocoa and mix until well blended. Add flour, baking soda, and salt. This mixture will seem very thick. Mix until well blended. Drop by one-half teaspoonfuls on a greased cookie sheet (or use a Teflon, nonstick cookie sheet). Bake 8 minutes at 350°.

TOPPING:

1 (10-ounce) bag large
  marshmallows

1 (6-ounce) bag semisweet
  chocolate chips

While cookies are baking, quarter marshmallows and set aside. (Dip scissors into cold water if they become sticky.) Remove cookies from oven at 8 minutes, top each cookie with one quarter of a marshmallow, and return to oven. Cook 4 minutes. Remove from oven and place one semisweet chocolate chip in center of each marshmallow. Gently press chocolate chip into marshmallow. Heat from cookie will slightly melt bottom of chip and allow chocolate chip to adhere to marshmallow. Let cool completely and store in an airtight container, or freeze up to 2 months. Yields 6 dozen.

It's Christmas! (Missouri)

Horney Toads

½ cup sugar
½ cup brown sugar
1 cup white syrup

Pinch of salt
1 cup peanut butter
3 cups cornflakes

Blend sugars, syrup, and salt. Let come to a boil. Turn to warm and add 1 cup peanut butter. Blend well. Blend in cornflakes and drop by teaspoonfuls onto wax paper.

Note: Good using crunchy or creamy peanut butter.

Asbury United Methodist Church Cook Book (Arkansas)

Cowboy Cookies

1 cup shortening
1 cup white sugar
1 cup brown sugar
2 eggs
2 cups sifted all-purpose flour
½ teaspoon salt

1 teaspoon baking soda
½ teaspoon baking powder
1 teaspoon vanilla
1 package semisweet chocolate
    chips or butterscotch chips
2 cups rolled oats (quick)

Cream shortening and sugars. Add eggs and beat. Sift flour, salt, baking soda, and baking powder together and add to creamed mixture. Add vanilla, chips, and oatmeal. Drop by teaspoon onto cookie sheets. Bake at 350° for 15 minutes.

Company Fare I (Oklahoma)

White Chip Orange Cream Cookies

2¼ cups all-purpose flour
¾ teaspoon baking soda
½ teaspoon salt
1 cup butter or margarine, softened
½ cup packed light brown sugar
½ cup granulated sugar
1 egg
2–3 teaspoons grated orange peel
1 (12-ounce) package Toll House Premier White Morsels

Combine flour, baking soda, and salt in small bowl. Beat butter and sugars in large mixer bowl until creamy. Beat in egg and orange peel. Gradually beat in flour mixture. Stir in morsels. Drop dough by rounded tablespoonfuls onto ungreased baking sheets. Bake in a 350° oven for 10–12 minutes or until edges are light golden brown. Let stand for 2 minutes; remove to wire racks to cool completely.

Country Cooking (Oklahoma)

Black-Eyed Susans

½ cup butter or margarine (softened)
½ cup sugar
½ cup firmly packed brown sugar
1 egg
1½ tablespoons warm water
1 teaspoon vanilla
1 cup creamy peanut butter (not crunchy)
1½ cups all-purpose flour
½ teaspoon salt
½ teaspoon baking soda
½ cup semisweet chocolate chips

Combine butter and sugars, creaming until light and fluffy; add egg, warm water, vanilla, and peanut butter. Beat, mixing well. Combine dry ingredients. Add to creamed mixture, mixing well. Using a cookie press with a flower-shaped disc, press dough onto lightly greased cookie sheet. Place a chocolate chip in the center of each flower. Bake at 350° for 8 minutes or until lightly browned. Remove to wire racks and cool. Chill 30 minutes to firm up centers. Yields about 10 dozen cookies.

Court Clerk's Bar and Grill (Oklahoma)

Pecan Diamonds

Diamonds are still a girl's best friend!

½ cup butter, well chilled
1½ cups all-purpose flour

½ cup ice water

Using pastry blender, cut butter into flour until mixture resembles coarse meal. Add water and toss lightly with fork. Gather dough into ball, wrap in plastic, and refrigerate 1 hour. Grease and flour 9x13-inch baking pan, not a cookie sheet. Roll dough out on lightly floured surface to about 10x14-inch rectangle. Fit into prepared pan; dough will come about halfway up sides. Pierce dough with a fork and chill. Preheat oven to 400°.

FILLING:

1½ cups light brown sugar,
  firmly packed
1 cup butter
½ cup honey

⅓ cup sugar
1 pound chopped pecans or
  pecan pieces
½ cup whipping cream

Bring brown sugar, butter, honey, and sugar to boil in heavy saucepan over medium heat, stirring constantly. Boil until thick and dark, about 4 minutes, continuing to stir. Remove from heat. Stir in pecans. Blend in cream. Pour the mixture over dough in the pan. Bake in the preheated oven until edges of crust are golden, about 25 minutes. Cool completely. Cut into 1-inch strips lengthwise then horizontally to create diamond shapes. Serve at room temperature. Makes 80 diamonds.

Applause! (Oklahoma)

ARKANSAS DEPARTMENT OF PARKS AND TOURISM

The Crater of Diamonds State Park, located near Murfreesboro, Arkansas, contains the only diamond-bearing site in the world that is open to the public. In addition to diamonds, visitors may find semi-precious gems such as amethyst, agate, and jasper. Over 25,000 diamonds have been found in the crater since it became a state park in 1972, the largest in 1975 by W. W. Johnson, the 16.37-carat "Amarillo Starlight" Found in 1924, "The Uncle Sam," is the largest diamond ever found in the park. At 40.23 carats, it is the largest diamond ever discovered in North America.

Chess Squares

1 box butter recipe yellow
  cake mix
½ cup margarine
4 eggs, divided

1 (8-ounce) package cream
  cheese, softened
1 (1-pound) box powdered sugar

Combine cake mix, margarine, and 1 egg; press into a greased and floured 9x13-inch pan. Combine remaining 3 eggs, cream cheese, and powdered sugar; pour over crust. Bake at 350° for 45 minutes. Cool and cut into squares. Yields 2 dozen squares.

Variation: Add 1 cup flaked coconut and ½ cup chopped pecans to cream cheese mixture.

Our Country Cookin' (Oklahoma)

Key Lime Squares

A new twist to an old favorite.

CRUST:

1 cup margarine, softened
½ cup powdered sugar

2 cups all-purpose flour
Pinch of salt

Combine margarine, powdered sugar, flour, and salt with pastry blender or mixer. Pat into a well-greased 9x12x2-inch pan. Bake at 350° for 15–20 minutes.

FILLING:

4 eggs
2 cups sugar
6 tablespoons lime juice

6 tablespoons all-purpose flour
Rind of one lime, grated

Beat eggs and add sugar, lime juice, flour, and lime rind. Put on top of baked pastry and bake for 25 minutes. Sprinkle with powdered sugar while warm. Cut into squares.

Finely Tuned Foods (Missouri)

Apricot Butter Bars

½ cup finely snipped
  apricots, cooked
¾ cup cold butter
1½ cups sifted all-purpose
  flour
1 egg

½ cup brown sugar, firmly
  packed
½ teaspoon vanilla extract
½ cup chopped pecans

Put snipped apricots into a heavy saucepan with a small amount of water, 5–6 tablespoons. Cover and cook over low heat until water is absorbed. If they are still in firm pieces, mash them with a fork or give them a buzz in the food processor. Cool.

Cut butter into flour until particles are the size of a rice kernel. Press evenly into a 9x13-inch baking pan. Bake at 350° for 15 minutes. Beat egg, brown sugar, and vanilla until thick. Stir into mixture of apricots and pecans. Spread evenly over partially baked layer in pan. Return to oven and bake about 20 minutes, or until light brown around the edge. Remove from oven and immediately spread Lemon Glaze over top. Cut when cool.

LEMON GLAZE:

¼ cup powdered sugar
2 tablespoons lemon juice

¼ teaspoon lemon extract

Blend and spread on top of apricot mixture.

Eat Pie First...Life is Uncertain! (Missouri)

Toffee Nut Bars

½ cup butter
½ cup brown sugar
1 cup all-purpose flour, sifted
2 eggs, well beaten
1 cup brown sugar
1 teaspoon vanilla

2 tablespoons flour
1 teaspoon baking powder
½ teaspoon salt
1 cup shredded coconut
1 cup sliced almonds
   or chopped pecans

Cream butter and ½ cup brown sugar. Mix in flour and press into ungreased 9x13-inch baking pan. Bake at 350° for 10 minutes. Cool.

Combine eggs, 1 cup brown sugar, and vanilla. Add flour, baking powder, and salt. Add coconut and almonds, and spread mixture over first layer. Return to 350° oven for 20–25 minutes or until topping is golden brown. Cool and cut into 24 bars.

Company's Coming (Missouri)

Yum Yums

50 light caramels
⅔ cup evaporated milk,
   divided
1 (17½-ounce) package
   German chocolate cake mix

⅔ cup butter or margarine,
   melted
1 cup chopped nuts
1 cup semisweet chocolate
   morsels

Combine caramels and ⅓ cup evaporated milk in top of a double boiler. Cook and stir over boiling water until caramels are melted; set aside.

Combine dry cake mix, butter, remaining ⅓ cup milk, and nuts in a large mixing bowl. Stir until dough holds together. Press half the dough into a greased and floured 9x13-inch pan, reserving remaining dough for topping. Bake at 350° for 6 minutes. Sprinkle chocolate pieces over baked crust. Spread caramel mixture over chocolate pieces; crumble remaining dough over caramel mixture. Return to oven and bake 15–18 minutes longer. Cool slightly, then chill for 30 minutes. Cut into bars. Makes 36 bars.

Gourmet Garden (Missouri)

Rocky Road Fudge Bars

2 (1-ounce) squares
  unsweetened chocolate,
  divided
1 cup margarine, divided
1½ cups granulated sugar,
  divided
1 cup plus 2 tablespoons
  all-purpose flour, divided
1¼ cups chopped walnuts,
  divided

1 teaspoon baking powder
2½ teaspoons vanilla, divided
3 eggs, divided
1 (8-ounce) package cream
  cheese, softened, divided
1 cup semisweet chocolate
  chips
2 cups miniature marshmallows
¼ cup milk
3 cups powdered sugar

Preheat oven to 350°. Spray a 9x13-inch pan with cooking spray. In medium saucepan, over medium heat, melt 1 square of the chocolate and ½ cup margarine. Remove and blend in 1 cup granulated sugar, 1 cup flour, 1 cup nuts, baking powder, 1 teaspoon vanilla, and 2 eggs. Spread in pan.

In a large bowl with mixer on high, blend 6 ounces of the cream cheese (reserve 2 ounces), ½ cup granulated sugar, 2 tablespoons flour, ¼ cup margarine, 1 egg, and ½ teaspoon vanilla. Spread over batter in pan.

Mix together remaining ¼ cup nuts and chocolate chips. Sprinkle over batter. Bake 25 minutes. Remove from oven and sprinkle marshmallows over top. Bake another 2 minutes.

In medium saucepan, over low heat, melt ¼ cup margarine, remaining 1 square chocolate, 2 ounces cream cheese, and milk. Remove from heat and add powdered sugar and remaining 1 teaspoon vanilla. Drizzle over top of marshmallows. Swirl layers together. Chill several hours before cutting.

Kitchen Klatter Keepsakes (Oklahoma)

Killer Brownies

4 eggs, beaten
2 cups sugar
1 cup margarine, melted
1½ cups all-purpose flour

1 teaspoon baking powder
6 tablespoons cocoa
1 teaspoon vanilla

Combine and cream eggs and sugar. Add melted margarine alternately with combined, sifted dry ingredients. Add vanilla. Bake in a greased 9x13-inch cake pan in a 350° oven for 27 minutes. Frost with Cocoa Satin Frosting.

COCOA SATIN ICING:

½ cup margarine
½ cup cocoa
1 pound powdered sugar, sifted
7 tablespoons milk

1 teaspoon vanilla
1 cup chopped nuts (if you're making brownies, it has to be black walnuts)

Melt the shortening in a saucepan; add the cocoa and heat for a minute until they are smooth, stirring constantly. Remove from heat and alternately add sugar and milk, beating to spreading consistency. Blend in vanilla and nuts.

Eat Pie First...Life is Uncertain! (Missouri)

One of Missouri's most popular, yet controversial, historical figures, Jesse James, was never convicted of a crime. Accounts of the events surrounding his life are preserved in the Jesse James Home Museum in St. Joseph, Missouri (the house where he was assassinated by Robert Ford on April 3, 1882), and the James Farm in nearby Kearney, where James was born on September 5, 1847, and is also where he was laid to rest.

LIBRARY OF CONGRESS

German Chocolate Brownies

1 (1-pound) package Kraft
  Caramels
⅔ cup Pet Milk
¾ cup margarine, melted
1 package German
  Chocolate Cake Mix

1 cup chopped nuts
1 (6-ounce) package Nestle's
  Chocolate Chips

Melt Kraft Caramels (about 50) with ⅓ cup Pet Milk. Set aside to cool.
Mix melted margarine and remaining ⅓ cup Pet Milk with cake nix.
Add chopped nuts. Mix well. Put half of cake mixture in greased 9x13-
inch pan. Pat evenly on bottom of pan. Bake 6 minutes at 350°.
Remove from oven and sprinkle with the chocolate chips.

Being very careful, pour caramel mixture over chips. Pat remainder
of cake mixture flat with hands, then place on top of caramel mixture.
Bake 20 minutes at 350°. When you remove from oven, run knife
around edges so caramel won't stick.

Southwest Cookin' (Arkansas)

Hello Dolly

¼ pound butter
1 cup graham cracker or
  vanilla wafer crumbs
1 (6-ounce) package
  chocolate chips

1 (6-ounce) package
  butterscotch chips
1 cup flaked coconut
1 cup chopped English walnuts
1 can Eagle Brand Milk

Melt butter in a 9x12x2-inch pan. Add each ingredient one at a time
and do not stir. Bake at 325° for 20–25 minutes. Cool, cut to desired
size, and place on rack.

Company Fare I (Oklahoma)

Lazy Millionaires

2 (14-ounce) packages
  vanilla caramels
1 tablespoon evaporated
  milk

1 cup semisweet chocolate
  chips
⅓ bar paraffin
8 cups chopped pecans

In a heavy saucepan melt first 4 ingredients; stir in pecans; drop onto greased wax paper; cool.

Celebration (Arkansas)

Spiced Candy Cake Roll

½ pound whole shelled
  Brazil nuts (1 cup)
½ pound pitted dates, uncut
  (1 cup)
1 (⅛-ounce) jar red
  maraschino cherries,
  drained (cut)
½ pound fine crushed
  graham crackers

½ pound marshmallows
1 tablespoon grated orange rind
⅓ cup orange juice
⅛ teaspoon cinnamon
⅛ teaspoon nutmeg
⅛ teaspoon cloves
⅛ teaspoon allspice
⅛ teaspoon ginger
½ cup finely chopped nuts

Mix nuts, dates, cherries, and graham crackers well. Melt marshmallows with orange rind, orange juice, cinnamon, nutmeg, cloves, allspice, and ginger in top of double boiler until melted. Stir into fruit and nut mixture. Divide and shape into 2 rolls. Wrap in aluminum foil. Chill 6–8 hours.

Unwrap and cover each roll in ¼ cup finely chopped nuts. Rewrap and freeze until ready to use. Cut ¼ inch thick. (I never freeze—we eat it throughout the holidays and eat it promptly.)

Cooking on the Road (Missouri)

Microwave Almond Butter Toffee

¼ pound butter (do not use
  margarine)
1 cup sugar
½ teaspoon salt
¼ cup water

1 (4-ounce) package sliced
  or slivered almonds
4 ounces semisweet or milk
  chocolate
Additional butter for greasing

Butter a 2- to 3-quart bowl appropriate for microwave cooking along the top edge. Place ¼ pound butter in the bowl. Pour sugar directly on butter and avoid getting sugar on the sides of the bowl. Add salt and water. Place in microwave and cook on HIGH for 7 minutes. Add time in 30-second intervals until mixture is the color of light brown sugar. Meanwhile place almonds on a greased cookie sheet.

When candy is ready, pour over almonds. Do not scrape bowl; let cool. Melt chocolate in microwave on HIGH for about 1½ minutes. Spread chocolate over candy and let cool. If doing in warm weather, refrigerate.) Break candy into pieces. Easy. Can freeze. Serves 10.

Cooking in Clover II (Missouri)

Almond Crunch

This makes a great homemade gift item!

1 cup blanched slivered
  almonds
½ cup butter

½ cup sugar
1 tablespoon light corn syrup

Line bottom and sides of an 8- or 9-inch cake pan with aluminum foil. Set aside. Combine all ingredients in 10-inch skillet. Bring to a boil over medium heat, stirring constantly. Boil until mixture turns golden brown—about 6 minutes. Quickly spread in prepared pan.

Cool about 15 minutes. Break into bite-size pieces.

Arkansas Favorites Cookbook (Arkansas)

Chocolate Almond Bark Crunch

10–12 ounces chocolate
  almond bark
2 tablespoons peanut butter

1 cup chopped nuts
1 cup marshmallows
1½ cups Rice Krispies

Melt almond bark and peanut butter together in a large bowl. Add nuts, marshmallows, and Rice Krispies. Stir and drop by spoonfuls onto buttered foil.

Country Cooking (Oklahoma)

Pecan Pralines

1 cup buttermilk
2 cups sugar
1 teaspoon baking soda

1 tablespoon butter
1 teaspoon vanilla
2 cups pecan halves

Use large (6- to 8-quart) pot—mixture foams. Place buttermilk, sugar and baking soda in pot and cook over medium heat. Stir constantly while cooking. Cook until soft-ball stage. Test small amounts in cool water until forms soft ball. Remove from heat and add remaining 3 ingredients. Return to stove and heat until mixture becomes glossy and starts to crystallize.

Quickly spoon out candy into 2-inch patties on wax paper or greased baking sheet. Candy hardens when cooled.

Tip for ease of removing patty: If using wax paper, place towel under paper.

Southwest Cookin' (Arkansas)

Wal-Mart Stores, Inc. (branded as Walmart) is an American public corporation that runs a chain of large, discount department stores. It is the world's largest public corporation by revenue, according to the 2008 Fortune Global 500. The company was founded by Sam Walton in 1962, incorporated on October 31, 1969, and listed on the New York Stock Exchange in 1972. Wal-Mart is the largest private employer and the largest grocery retailer in the United States. It also owns and operates the Sam's Club retail warehouses in North America.

Orange Candied Pecans

2 cups sugar
1 cup water
3 teaspoons orange juice

Grated rind of 1 orange
3 cups chopped pecans

Cook sugar and water to soft-ball stage. Add orange juice and rind; beat until it begins to thicken. Add pecans, and stir until sugared. Separate on wax paper. (Don't make on rainy day.)

Crossett Cook Book (Arkansas)

Coconut Macaroons

2 ounces Baker's chocolate
2 cans Baker's coconut (½ pound)

1 can Eagle Brand Milk
1 cup chopped nuts
½ cup flour

Melt chocolate in a double boiler. Add remaining ingredients. Drop from teaspoon onto greased cookie sheet. Bake 20 minutes in 275° oven.

Company Fare II (Oklahoma)

Sam and Helen Walton opened their first variety store in 1945 in Bentonville, Arkansas. Sam Walton's original Walton's Five and Dime is now the Wal-Mart Visitor's Center, a museum tracing the history of this marketing giant.

Peanut Brittle

1 cup sugar
½ cup white corn syrup
1 cup raw peanuts
⅛ teaspoon salt

1 teaspoon butter
1 teaspoon vanilla
1 teaspoon baking soda

In 1½-quart casserole, stir together sugar, syrup, peanuts, and salt. Microwave at HIGH, 4 minutes. Stir. Microwave at HIGH, 3–5 minutes until light brown. Add butter and vanilla, blending well. Microwave at HIGH, 1–2 minutes more. Peanuts will be lightly browned and very hot. Add baking soda and gently stir until light and foamy. Pour mixture onto lightly greased cookie sheet, or unbuttered nonstick coated cookie sheet. Set aside to cool, ½–1 hour. When cool, break into small pieces and store in airtight container. Makes about 1 pound.

What's Cooking in Okarche? (Oklahoma)

Molasses Pull Taffy

"Taffy Pulls" were a popular form of entertainment around the turn of the century.

Combine one cup of molasses, two cups of sugar, one tablespoon of vinegar, and a little butter and vanilla. Boil for 10 minutes, then cool slightly. While still warm, pull the taffy again and again until it is white and thoroughly cooled. Cut into bite-size pieces. The taffy will keep for quite a long time.

á la Rose (Missouri)

Pies and Other Desserts

COURTESY OF ARKANSAS DEPT. OF PARKS & TOURISM

White River National Wildlife Refuge, Arkansas, was established in 1935 for the protection of migratory birds. Approximately two-thirds of the bird species found in Arkansas can be seen at White River NWR. The refuge has the largest concentration of wintering mallard ducks in the Mississippi Flyway (a bird migration route). It also has large concentrations of Snow Geese and Canada Geese.

Oklahoma Pecan Pie

3 eggs, lightly beaten
1 cup sugar
1 cup light corn syrup
1 tablespoon melted butter

1 teaspoon vanilla
1 cup pecan halves or pieces
1 (9-inch) pie shell, unbaked

Beat eggs; add sugar, corn syrup, and butter and mix together until well blended. Stir in vanilla and pecans. Pour mixture into pie shell and bake in a preheated 350° oven for 45–55 minutes or until knife inserted halfway between center and edge comes out clean. Cool well on wire rack. Serve plain or with whipped cream. Makes 6–8 slices.

The Route 66 Cookbook (Oklahoma)

Caramel Apple Pecan Pie

¾ cup sugar
¼ cup flour
1 teaspoon cinnamon
Dash of salt
⅛ teaspoon nutmeg

6 cups peeled and sliced
    Jonathan or Granny Smith
    apples
Pastry for a double crust pie
1 tablespoon butter

Combine sugar, flour, cinnamon, salt, and nutmeg. Toss apples and sugar-flour-cinnamon mixture. Turn into a 9-inch pastry shell. Dot with butter. Cover with top crust. Moisten, seal, and flute edges with fingers or fork. Prick or slit top crust to allow steam to escape. Bake at 450° for 10–15 minutes, then reduce heat to 350° for 40–45 minutes:
    Remove from oven, and cool pie. Top with caramel topping.

CARAMEL-PECAN TOPPING:

8 ounces Kraft caramels
2 tablespoons evaporated
    milk

½ cup chopped pecans

Place caramels and milk in double boiler and heat, or melt in a microwave until smooth. Add ½ cup chopped pecans and spread over top of pie.

Baked with Love (Missouri)

Karo Pecan Pie

1 cup sugar	1¾ cups pecan halves
¾ cup light corn syrup	1 teaspoon vanilla
½ cup butter	⅛ teaspoon salt
3 eggs, beaten	1 (9-inch) pie shell, unbaked

Blend sugar, syrup, and ½ cup butter in saucepan. Cook over medium heat, stirring constantly, until mixture comes to a boil. Blend mixture slowly into eggs. Stir in pecan halves, vanilla, and salt. Pour into pie shell. Bake at 350° for 40 minutes.

High Cotton Cookin' (Arkansas)

Peppermint Pie
with Rice Krispies Crust

CRUST:

1 (4-ounce) bar German Sweet Chocolate	4 tablespoons margarine
	3 cups Rice Krispies

Break chocolate into pieces in saucepan; add margarine; heat until melted. Take off fire and add Rice Krispies. Mix well and press in bottom and sides of a 10-inch pie pan. Refrigerate.

FILLING:

¾ cup crushed peppermint candy	½ gallon vanilla ice cream, softened

Break candy into very small pieces; stir into softened ice cream. Put Filling in Crust and freeze until firm, 3–4 hours. Serves 8.

Southern Accent (Arkansas)

Coffee-Toffee Ice Cream Pie

1 jumbo-size chocolate
  almond bar (½ pound)
¼ cup coffee
1 (9 inch) graham cracker
  crust, baked

1 quart coffee ice cream
  slightly softened
3 Heath candy bars

Melt chocolate almond bar with coffee in double boiler. Spread over crust and cool. Fill chocolate-lined pie crust with coffee ice cream. Top with crushed Heath bars (crush better when frozen). Freeze. Remove 10–15 minutes before serving. Serves 6–8.

Note: The size of Heath candy bars makes no difference. The more the better!

The Cook Book (Missouri)

Butter Brickle Ice Cream Pie

½ cup brown sugar
¼ cup butter
1 tablespoon water

4 cups cornflakes
½ gallon vanilla ice cream

Bring to boil the first 3 ingredients, stirring constantly. Pour the mixture over the cornflakes in a large bowl. Using a 9-inch pie tin or plate, press around two-thirds of the mixture in the bottom and up the sides of the pie plate. Soften the ice cream by setting out for a brief time. Spread the ice cream into the cornflake-lined pie plate. When it is filled, spread the remaining cornflake mixture over the top of the ice cream and return to the freezer. Serves 8.

Cookin' in the Spa (Arkansas)

Raisin Pie

It seemed we always had raisins. Mom thought they were good for our blood! When we had company we always had a raisin pie and a "poor man's pie." Every family in Otter Creek Community ate raisin pies. People got to calling um "funeral pies" because every time there was a funeral, folks took in all kinds of food—especially raisin pie.

1 cup raisins	**1 egg, beaten**
½ cup sugar	**2 tablespoons grated lemon peel**
¼ cup all-purpose flour	**3 tablespoons lemon juice**
¼ teaspoon salt	**(optional)**
2 cups water	**Pastry for 9-inch pie**

Rinse raisins; drain off water. Put in top of a double boiler the sugar, flour, and salt. Add water slowly, stirring constantly. Stir in raisins. Now bring to a boil over direct heat and cook 1 minute, stirring fast. Take off and stir a small amount of hot mixture into the egg—I mean stir vigorously or it will cook it. Then immediately stir egg mixture into this in double boiler. Set over simmering water in bottom pan (double boiler) and cook about 5 minutes, stirring constantly. Remove from heat and stir in lemon peel and lemon juice, if desired. Cool. Pour mixture in a pastry-lined 9-inch pie pan. Cover with narrow pastry strips, crisscrossed. Bake at 450° for 10 minutes. Reduce heat to 350°; bake about 20 minutes longer. Makes 1 (9-inch) pie.

Seems Like I Done It This A-Way II (Oklahoma)

The son of a Baptist minister, James Cash (J.C.) Penney was born in Hamilton, Missouri, in 1875, one of 12 children. In 1902 Penney established his impressive chain of retail stores that remain strong today. Wal-Mart founder Sam Walton was employed by JC Penney in Des Moines, Iowa, for a brief time in 1940. During his employment there, Sam was able to meet James Cash Penney, the department store's founder, during a visit to the store.

Black Forest Pie

1 package Pillsbury
  refrigerated pie crusts
¾ cup sugar
⅓ cup cocoa
2 tablespoons flour
¼ cup margarine
⅓ cup milk

2 eggs, beaten
1 (21-ounce) can cherry pie
  filling
1 (9-ounce) carton Cool Whip
1 (1-ounce) square
  unsweetened chocolate,
  coarsely grated

Prepare 1 pie crust according to directions for filled pie. Heat oven to 350°. In medium saucepan, combine sugar, cocoa, and flour. Add margarine and milk. Cook until mixture begins to boil, stirring constantly. Remove from heat. Add small amount of hot mix to eggs, then slowly stir egg mix into pan. Fold in ½ can pie filling. Reserve the rest of the filling for topping. Pour chocolate mix into pie-crust-lined pan. Bake at 350° for 35–45 minutes or until center is set but still shiny. Cool. Chill 1 hour.

Combine 2 cups Cool Whip and grated chocolate; spread over chilled pie. Top with remaining pie filling and Cool Whip. Chill at least ½ hour before serving.

Thunderbird Cookers of AT&T (Oklahoma)

Chocolate Pie

2½ cups milk
1 cup sugar
6 tablespoons all-purpose
  flour
½ teaspoon salt
2 egg yolks, slightly beaten

1 teaspoon vanilla
2 squares Baker's unsweetened
  chocolate
2 tablespoons butter
Baked pie shell
Whipped cream

Heat milk. Meanwhile, mix together in blender, sugar, flour, salt, yolks, and vanilla. Add just enough milk to make a smooth paste. Stir into milk and cook till thick. Remove from heat and add chocolate and butter. This fills a 9- to 10-inch pie shell. Top with whipped cream.

Here's What's Cookin' at Zion (Oklahoma)

Chocolate Meringue Pie

2½ cups milk
¾ cup sugar
4 tablespoons cornstarch
½ teaspoon salt
4 tablespoons cocoa,
    slightly heaped

3 eggs, separated
1 teaspoon vanilla
Gob of butter (about 2
    tablespoons)
1 (8- or 9-inch) pie shell, baked
6 tablespoons sugar

Heat 2 cups milk over medium heat until scalding. In the meantime blend ½ cup milk, the sugar, cornstarch, salt, cocoa, and egg yolks. Add to warm milk, and cook until thick; remove from heat, add vanilla and butter, and pour in pie shell. Make meringue with 3 egg whites and 6 tablespoons sugar. Beat egg whites on high speed with mixer. When they begin to foam up good, start adding sugar 1 tablespoon at a time. When it stands in a peak, place on top of pie and bake in 350° oven until brown.

VARIATION:

Coconut Cream Pie: Leave out the cocoa and add coconut when you add the vanilla and butter. Top meringue with coconut.

Banana Cream: Leave out the cocoa, place bananas in bottom of crust, fill with about half of the filling, more bananas, and finish filling with filling.

Plain Cream: Leave out the cocoa. Sometimes, I want one cream pie and one chocolate pie, so I double the recipe, leaving out the cocoa. Fill the crust for the cream pie, and add either semisweet chocolate chips or unsweetened chocolate to the remainder to make the chocolate pie.

Peanut Butter: Cream pie filling plus 1 or 2 tablespoons peanut butter until it looks and tastes right.

A Collection of Recipes from the Best Cooks in the Midwest
(Missouri)

Chocolate Decadence
(Fudge Pie Supreme)

We do not think there is a dessert on this earth that can top this one for pure unadulterated enjoyment!

½ stick butter, softened
⅓ cup sugar
1 tablespoon flour
1 cup finely chopped pecans
1 stick butter, softened
1 cup sugar
2 ounces unsweetened chocolate, melted and cooled

⅛ teaspoon salt
¼ cup all-purpose flour
2 eggs, beaten
1 teaspoon vanilla
1 cup Kahlúa or to taste
1 quart vanilla ice cream, softened

Preheat oven to 325°. To make crust, combine first 4 ingredients; press into sides and bottom of 9-inch pie plate.

To make filling, cream butter and sugar; add next 5 ingredients; mix well; pour into pie crust; bake 35–40 minutes or until filling is set. Do not overbake! To make ice cream topping, stir Kahlúa into ice cream; put in plastic container; freeze.

To serve, pie should be warm or room temperature; stir ice cream well; spoon over each slice of pie. Serves 6–8 marvelously!

Southern Flavors' Little Chocolate Book (Arkansas)

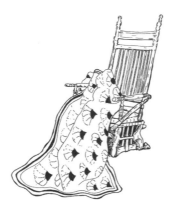

French Silk Pie

CRUST:

1 cup all-purpose flour
1 cup finely chopped pecans
½ cup margarine, melted

Combine flour, nuts, and margarine until crumbly. Press into a large pie plate. Bake for 15 minutes at 375°.

PIE:

1 cup margarine, softened
1½ cups sugar
4 squares unsweetened chocolate, melted and cooled
2 teaspoons vanilla
4 eggs
8 ounces whipped topping
Shaved chocolate for garnish

Beat with mixer the margarine and sugar until fluffy and smooth. Blend in melted chocolate and vanilla. Beat in eggs one at a time, beating 5 minutes after each egg. Turn into cooled pie shell. Chill several hours. Garnish with whipped topping and shaved chocolate, if desired.

Country Cooking (Oklahoma)

Coconut Cream Pie

¼ cup sugar
½ cup cake mix (yellow)
3 egg yolks
1½ cups milk
¼ stick butter
¾ cup flaked coconut
1 pie shell, baked

Mix sugar, cake mix, and egg yolks. Blend in enough milk to mix well. Add remaining milk; cook until thick. Add butter, then coconut, and pour into baked crust.

Evening Shade (Arkansas)

Lemon Angel Pie

4 egg yolks
½ cup sugar
¼ cup fresh lemon juice
1 tablespoon grated lemon
  peel

1 (9-inch) Meringue Pie Shell
  (see below)
Whipped Cream Topping (see
  below)

Beat egg yolks until thick and lemon-colored. Gradually beat in sugar. Stir in lemon juice and grated peel. Cook in double boiler over simmering water, stirring constantly, until mixture is thick, 5–8 minutes. Mixture should mound slightly when dropped from spoon. Cool. Spread into Meringue Pie Shell. Top with Whipped Cream Topping. Chill 12 hours or overnight.

MERINGUE PIE SHELL:

3 egg whites (room
  temperature)
¼ teaspoon cream of tartar

⅛ teaspoon salt
½ teaspoon vanilla
½ cup sugar

Combine egg whites, cream of tartar, salt, and vanilla. Beat until frothy. Gradually add sugar and beat until stiff and glossy peaks form. Spread on bottom and sides of a well-greased 9-inch pie pan. Build up the sides. Bake in a 275° oven for 1 hour. It will be light brown and crisp. Let cool in pan away from drafts. Spoon in the filling and chill. These crusts often collapse in the center and it doesn't make any difference at all.

WHIPPED CREAM TOPPING:

1 cup whipping cream
¼ cup sifted powdered sugar

½ teaspoon vanilla
¼ cup sour cream

Whip the cream and fold in vanilla and sugar. Stir in sour cream. Spread over the pie leaving about a 2-inch circle open in the middle. Garnish with a little lemon zest.

Eat Pie First...Life is Uncertain! (Missouri)

Cheesecake Pie

Easy and Delicious!

1 (8-ounce) package cream
   cheese, softened
¾ cup sugar
1 cup sour cream
2 teaspoons vanilla
1 (8-ounce) carton Cool Whip

1 (9-inch) graham cracker
   pie crust
1 small box frozen sweet
   strawberries, thawed, or
1 can blueberry pie filling,
   or 1 can cherry pie filling

Beat cream cheese until smooth; gradually beat in sugar. Blend in sour cream and vanilla. Fold in Cool Whip, blending well. Spoon into crust (the crust may be bought—makes it even easier). Chill at least 4 hours. Garnish with strawberries or other topping. Yields 6–8 servings.

Betty Is Still "Winking" at Cooking (Arkansas)

Never Fail Meringue

1 tablespoon cornstarch
1½ tablespoons cold water
½ cup boiling water

3 egg whites
6 tablespoons sugar
2 tablespoons vanilla

Dissolve cornstarch in cold water in a small saucepan. Add the boiling water and cook over medium heat. Stir constantly till thick and clear. Set aside to cool.

   Meanwhile, beat the egg whites in a large bowl to soft peaks.

   Beat in the cooled paste. Continue to beat till very firm peaks are formed. Gradually add the sugar, then beat in vanilla. Pile onto pie. Bake at 375° for 6–10 minutes, till peaks are golden.

From Granny, With Love (Missouri)

Fried Pie Crust

5 cups all-purpose flour
1 teaspoon salt
1 teaspoon baking powder
2 teaspoons sugar

1 cup Crisco
1 large can evaporated milk
1 egg

Sift dry ingredients, cut in shortening, and add milk. Mix well. Add egg and gently mix. Put in icebox and chill. Roll and cut dough in saucer-size cutouts. Fill with fruit filling on one side. Fold other side over. Press edges together with fork. Fry in hot grease until brown.

Seems Like I Done It This A-Way II (Oklahoma)

Fried Apple Pies

This recipe comes from the Pioneer Crafts Festival held annually in Rison, Arkansas. It has been a festival secret for over seventy years!

8 ounces dried apples
5 cups water
1 cup sugar

1 teaspoon cinnamon
2½ tablespoons cornstarch
2 tablespoons lemon juice

Cook apples in water for 20 minutes. Combine sugar, cornstarch, and cinnamon. Add to apples. Add lemon juice. Cook until thickened. Cool.

PASTRY:

1 cup plus 2 tablespoons
**   shortening**
3 cups all-purpose flour
1 egg, beaten slightly

7 tablespoons water
1 teaspoon salt
1 teaspoon vinegar

Cut shortening into flour. Combine egg, water, salt, and vinegar. Pour into flour mixture and mix.

Pinch small amount of dough and roll out on floured board.

Cut out, using a saucer as a guide. Put 1 tablespoon apple mixture on dough. Wet edges of dough with iced water. Fold dough over apple mixture and seal by pressing a floured fork around edges. Fry in 1–2 inches of oil in an electric skillet on highest setting. Cook until golden brown, turning only once. Glaze with a mixture of powdered sugar and water. Yields about 24 pies.

A Great Taste of Arkansas (Arkansas)

Arkansas Pastries

Delightful flakiness that comes from both fat and yeast.

1 (¼-ounce) package active
  dry yeast
½ cup warm water
  (115°–120°)
2 sticks pie crust mix
1 tablespoon sugar

1 egg yolk
½ cup strawberry preserves
1 cup powdered sugar, sifted
1 tablespoon milk
1 teaspoon vanilla extract

Dissolve yeast in warm water; set aside. Crumble pie crust mix into bowl; stir in sugar, egg yolk, and dissolved yeast. Mix well. Roll dough into balls the size of a large marble and place on ungreased baking sheet. Make deep indention in the center and shape into shells. Spoon ½ teaspoon preserves into each shell. Let rise in a warm place for one hour. (Pastries do not double in bulk.)

Bake 12–15 minutes at 375°. Cool slightly and remove from baking sheet. Blend powdered sugar, milk, and vanilla for icing. Drizzle or brush over pastries while still warm. Makes 50 bite-sized pastries.

Home for the Holidays (Arkansas)

Banbury Tarts

1 lemon
1 cup raisins
2 soda crackers

1 egg, beaten
1 cup sugar
Pie crust dough

Grind lemon, raisins, and crackers, then mix with egg and sugar. Roll pie crust dough thin, cut in 4-inch squares or in rounds with a cookie cutter. Put a spoonful of the mixture on half of the square, fold over the dough and press edges together. Do the same with the rounds, except use 2 whole rounds, then press together. Puncture a few holes in the top with a fork to let steam escape. Place on a greased pan and bake until golden brown.

Treasured Recipes Book I (Missouri)

Crusty Peach Cobbler

3 cups sliced fresh peaches
¼ cup sugar
1 teaspoon almond extract
1 tablespoon lemon juice
1 teaspoon grated lemon
  peel
1½ cups enriched flour

½ teaspoon salt
3 teaspoons baking powder
1 tablespoon sugar
⅓ cup shortening
½ cup milk
1 egg, well beaten
2 tablespoons sugar

Arrange peaches in greased, 8-inch square baking pan. Sprinkle with mixture of ¼ cup sugar, almond extract, lemon juice, and lemon peel. Heat in oven while preparing shortcake.

Sift together flour, salt, baking powder, and 1 tablespoon sugar; cut in shortening until mixture is like coarse crumbs. Add milk and egg at once; stir just until flour is moistened. Spread dough over hot peaches. Sprinkle with 2 tablespoons sugar. Bake in hot oven (400°) 40 minutes. Serves 6.

Perfectly Delicious (Arkansas)

Applescotch Crisp

4 cups peeled and sliced
  apples (4 medium)
1 tablespoon flour
½ cup water

½ cup firmly packed
  brown sugar
¼ cup milk

Combine in large bowl; mix well. Pour into ungreased 9-inch square baking pan.

⅔ cup flour
½ cup quick oatmeal
½ cup chopped nuts
¼ cup sugar
½ teaspoon salt
1 teaspoon cinnamon

½ cup butter or margarine,
  melted
1 (4-serving size) package
  dry butterscotch or vanilla
  pudding mix (not instant)

Combine in medium bowl; mix until crumbly. Sprinkle over apples. Bake at 350° for 45–50 minutes, until apples are tender and topping is golden brown.

Home Cookin' (Missouri)

Juicy Apple Dessert

1 cup sugar
2 eggs, beaten
4 cups peeled and finely
  chopped apples
¼ cup vegetable oil

2 cups all-purpose flour
1 teaspoon baking powder
1 teaspoon salt
1 teaspoon cinnamon
⅓ cup chopped walnuts

Stir sugar into beaten eggs. Add chopped or grated apples and oil. Stir in sifted dry ingredients. Spread in greased 9x13-inch pan and bake at 350° for 35–40 minutes. When done, poke holes in cake with fork and pour hot Topping over cake. Cover pan with aluminum foil and let cool.

TOPPING:
½ cup granulated sugar
½ cup brown sugar
2 tablespoons flour
¼ teaspoon salt

2 cups water
½ cup (1 stick) butter or
  margarine
1 teaspoon vanilla

Mix the sugars, flour, and salt in 1-quart saucepan. Add water and cook for 3 minutes. Add butter and vanilla. Yields 16–20 servings.

From the Apple Orchard (Missouri)

Red Cinnamon Apple Rings

5 cooking apples
2 cups water
2 cups sugar
½ teaspoon red food
  coloring

2 or 3 sticks cinnamon,
  2½ inches long

Peel and core apples. Slice in ¾-inch rings. Combine water, sugar, food coloring, and cinnamon in large skillet. Stir over low heat until sugar is dissolved. Bring mixture to a boil, stirring often. Reduce heat; simmer 10 minutes. Arrange apple rings in syrup. Cook over low heat, basting often until rings are tender. Makes about 15 rings.

Home Cookin' (Missouri)

Cream Puffs

CREAM PUFFS:

1 cup water	**1 cup flour**
½ cup butter or margarine	**4 eggs**

Heat oven to 400°. Heat water and butter to a rolling boil. Stir in flour. Stir vigorously over low heat for about 1 minute or until mixture forms a ball. Remove from heat. Beat in eggs, all at one time; continue beating until smooth. Drop dough by scant ¼ cupfuls 3 inches apart onto ungreased baking sheet. Bake for 35–40 minutes or until puffed and golden. Cool away from draft. Fill with pudding filling. Dust with powdered sugar.

FILLING:

1½ cups scalded milk	**3 eggs, separated**
¼ cup flour	**2 tablespoons butter**
½ cup sugar	**½ teaspoon vanilla**
¼ teaspoon salt	**6 tablespoons sugar**

Scald milk; mix flour, sugar, and salt. Add milk and cook until thick and smooth. Beat egg yolks; stir in a little of the hot mixture and pour back into pan. Cook for 2 minutes, stirring constantly. Remove from heat and add butter and vanilla. Beat egg whites until stiff and gradually beat in 6 tablespoons sugar. Fold in about one-third of the egg whites into the cooled pudding. Use remainder of whites for another purpose.

Kohler Family Kookbook (Missouri)

Ozark Pudding

This is well remembered as Mrs. Harry S. Truman's simple Missouri pudding during World War II.

1 egg
¾ cup sugar
2 tablespoon all-purpose
   flour
1¼ teaspoons baking powder

⅛ teaspoon salt
½ cup chopped nuts
½ cup chopped apples
1 teaspoon vanilla
Whipped cream or ice cream

Beat egg and sugar until creamy. Add dry ingredients to eggs and sugar. Mix well. Add nuts, apples, and vanilla. Bake in greased 9-inch square glass baking dish at 350° for 35 minutes. Serve warm with whipped cream or ice cream.

Cooking on the Road (Missouri)

Cottage Pudding

This recipe has an unusual name, but the origin is unknown. It was one of my mother's favorite recipes, and was a favorite when I was a child sixty years ago. It's especially good served warm, with the lemon sauce.

⅓ cup butter
1 egg
⅔ cup sugar
1¾ cups all-purpose flour
2 teaspoons baking powder

¼ teaspoon baking soda
¼ teaspoon salt
1 cup sour milk
1 teaspoon vanilla

Cream butter, egg, and sugar together. Sift flour, baking powder, baking soda, and salt together; add to cream mixture alternately with the sour milk. Add vanilla and beat hard. Bake in greased pan at 350° for 25–30 minutes.

LEMON SAUCE:

1 cup sugar
2 tablespoons flour
Dash of salt
1 cup boiling water

2 tablespoons lemon juice or
   extract
2 tablespoons butter

Mix sugar, flour, and salt together. Add boiling water and lemon juice. Add the butter. Cook in double boiler pan until done. Serve hot over the cottage pudding.

Recipes & Stories of Early-Day Settlers (Missouri)

Jo Ann's Banana Pudding

⅔ cup sugar
¼ teaspoon salt
5 tablespoons flour
2½ cups milk
3 eggs, separated
1 tablespoon butter

2 teaspoons vanilla, divided
¼ teaspoon rum flavoring
5–6 small ripe bananas
1 small box vanilla wafers,
  crumbled
¼ cup sugar

Mix first 3 ingredients. Add milk; cook until hot. Add a little of hot mixture to beaten egg yolks, then add egg yolk mixture to milk mixture and cook, stirring constantly, until thick. Add butter, 1 teaspoon vanilla, and rum. Cool. Layer bananas, crumbled wafers, and pudding; repeat.

Beat egg whites until stiff and slowly add ¼ cup sugar and 1 teaspoon vanilla. Spread meringue on top. Bake at 350° until meringue is golden brown.

Note: Do the pudding 1½ times for a 9x13-inch casserole.

MICROWAVE INSTRUCTIONS FOR PUDDING:

Mix dry ingredients. Add milk, cook on MEDIUM-HIGH (#8) for 8 minutes, stirring a couple of times, then add a little of the hot mixture to beaten egg yolks, then add egg mixture to hot milk mixture. Cook an additional 5 minutes on MEDIUM-HIGH, stirring frequently with wire whisk. After removing from micro, add butter and flavorings. Cool.

Betty "Winks" at Cooking (Arkansas)

Date Pecan Pudding

2 eggs
1½ cups milk
1 teaspoon baking powder
1 cup sugar
1 cup chopped pecans

1 cup solidly packed bread
  crumbs
1 cup flaked coconut
1 cup chopped dates
1 tablespoon butter, melted

Beat the first 3 ingredients together. Add the other ingredients except butter. Mix well and add melted butter. Pour mixture in a buttered pan or spoon into individual paper cups. Bake at 350° for 45 minutes, or less for cupcakes. Top with whipped cream or with frosting.

Cookbook of Treasured Recipes (Oklahoma)

German Chocolate Pudding

1 (4-ounce) bar German's
  Sweet Chocolate
¼ pound butter
3 eggs, separated

1 cup powdered sugar, divided
1 teaspoon vanilla
1 pint whipping cream, whipped
1 (10-ounce) box vanilla wafers

Melt chocolate and butter together. Add chocolate mixture to beaten egg yolks; then add ⅔ cup powdered sugar and vanilla. Chill, then fold in whipped cream. Beat egg whites until they begin to stand in peaks. Add remaining ⅓ cup sugar into egg whites and fold into chocolate mixture. Grind vanilla wafers and line 9x9-inch deep dish with part of chocolate mixture over crumbs, then add another layer of crumbs. Repeat until all the mixture is used. Remainder of crumbs go on top. Refrigerate 24 hours.

Court Clerk's Bar and Grill (Oklahoma)

Effie Romberger's Old-Fashioned Rice Pudding

I still hunger for mother's rice pudding!

1 cup uncooked rice
6 eggs
1 cup sugar
1 teaspoon nutmeg

1 teaspoon salt
½ cup milk
1 stick butter (only)

Cook rice. Beat eggs; add sugar, nutmeg, salt, milk, and cooked rice. Pour into 2-quart baking dish in which 1 stick butter has been melted. Bake at 400° about 30 minutes. Do not overcook. Center should be a little shaky.

GRANDMOTHER ROMBERGER'S LEMON SAUCE:

This is good over bread pudding, rice pudding, or leftover crumbled cake.

3 tablespoons cornstarch
½ cup water
¾ cup sugar
⅛ teaspoon salt
⅓ cup lemon juice

1 tablespoon butter
1 egg, beaten
Yellow food coloring (optional)

Mix cornstarch with water. In saucepan, mix sugar, salt, lemon juice, butter, and egg. Add cornstarch mixture. Stir and cook slowly until thick. Makes 1 cup.

Four Generations of Johnson Family Favorites (Oklahoma)

Rice Pudding

5 eggs
1 cup sugar
¼ cup butter or margarine, melted
2 cups milk

1 teaspoon vanilla
¼ teaspoon nutmeg
2 cups rice, cooked
½ cup raisins (optional)

Beat eggs; add sugar, butter, milk, vanilla, and nutmeg. Add rice, and raisins, if desired, and pour into a greased 2-quart casserole. Bake at 350° for 45 minutes.

LEMON SAUCE:

1 cup sugar
1 tablespoon cornstarch
½ teaspoon salt
3 eggs, slightly beaten

Juice of 2 lemons
Rind of 2 lemons, grated
1 cup water
2 tablespoons butter

Mix sugar, cornstarch, and salt. Add eggs, lemon juice, grated rind, and water. Cook in double boiler until thick, stirring constantly. Add butter and let cool.

Thirty Years at the Mansion (Arkansas)

Mousse au Chocolate

4 bars German Sweet Chocolate
¼ pound butter
6 egg yolks
6 tablespoons white corn syrup

1 cup sugar
¼ cup water
6 egg whites
2 cups whipped cream
Shaved chocolate for garnish

Place chocolate and butter in a double boiler and melt slowly. Set aside and cool. Beat egg yolks until thick and creamy. In pan combine corn syrup, sugar, and water until it spins an 8-inch thread, or 232°–234° on a candy thermometer. Pour hot syrup slowly into egg yolks, beating constantly with electric mixer. Add melted chocolate and butter. Fold in stiffly beaten egg whites. Chill 2 hours. Beat furiously. Fold in whipped cream. Chill at least 4 hours before serving. Serve in parfait glasses with shaved chocolate for garnish. Incredible!

Nibbles Ooo La La (Arkansas)

White Chocolate Mousse with Raspberry Sauce

2 pounds white chocolate
10 eggs
1 cup simple syrup (1 cup
   water to ½ cup sugar)

3 cups heavy whipping cream
Semisweet chocolate
   shavings for garnish

Melt white chocolate and set aside to cool. Separate eggs and set whites aside. Slowly whip simple syrup into yolks. Put mixture in double boiler over boiling water and whisk until mixture is warm to the touch. Remove and continue whipping by hand for another 2 minutes until mixture forms a "ribbon" of yolks and sugar. Slowly add melted chocolate to yolk and syrup mixture, and blend well. Continue to whip until smooth. Whip cream until it forms soft peaks, then set aside. Whip egg whites until they form soft peaks and set aside. Fold whipped cream into the chocolate mixture first, then the whipped egg whites. Be careful not to overblend (you don't want to collapse the cream or egg whites by adding too much too fast). Chill mixture at 35° for 8 hours.

Spread a pool of Raspberry Sauce onto dessert plates, followed by a serving of mousse. Garnish each with chocolate shavings. Serves 8–10.

RASPBERRY SAUCE:

10 ounces frozen
   raspberries, thawed and
   drained
2 tablespoons water

3 tablespoons sugar
3 tablespoons fresh lemon
   juice
2 teaspoons light rum

In a saucepan combine raspberries with water and bring to a boil over moderate heat, stirring occasionally. In a food processor fitted with the steel blade or in a blender, purée the raspberry mixture with the sugar, lemon juice, and rum. Force the purée through a fine sieve into a small bowl and cover. Let chill overnight. Makes about 1½ cups.

Kansas City Cuisine (Cafe Allegro) (Missouri)

Strawberry Luscious

2 small packages strawberry
  Jell-O
2 cups boiling water
1 (16-ounce) package
  frozen strawberries

1 (15½-ounce) can crushed
  pineapple
2 large bananas
½ cup sour cream

Dissolve Jell-O in boiling water. Add strawberries and pineapple, undrained. Add whipped bananas. Pour half into 8x12-inch pan; chill until set.

Spread sour cream over top and cover with remaining gelatin. Chill until firm. May use Cool Whip.

Asbury United Methodist Church Cook Book (Arkansas)

Fresh Coconut Bavarian

1½ tablespoons gelatin
¼ cup cold water
1 cup milk
1 cup sugar
2 cups whipping cream,
  whipped

2 cups grated fresh coconut
1 teaspoon vanilla
⅛ teaspoon salt

Soften gelatin in cold water; set aside. Scald milk; add sugar; add softened gelatin. Combine the remaining ingredients. Carefully fold both mixtures together. Refrigerate until firm in large ring mold.

SAUCE:

1 cup brown sugar, packed
1 cup granulated sugar
1 tablespoon flour

1 tablespoon butter
1⅓ cups milk

Combine sugars and flour; add butter and milk. Bring to a boil. Serve hot over the Bavarian. May be made ahead and reheated.

Note: This is an elegant dessert. Bavarian may be poured into champagne glasses or individual peau de crème pots. This is a traditional Christmas dessert in our home.

Prairie Harvest (Arkansas)

Sweet Noodle Kugel

2 (12-ounce) packages
    medium noodles
6 eggs, beaten
1 cup margarine, melted
4 large apples, peeled and
    grated

1⅔ cups sugar
15 ounces golden raisins
2 teaspoons cinnamon

Cook noodles in boiling salted water until tender. Drain and rinse.
Mix eggs, margarine, grated apples, sugar, raisins and cinnamon with
noodles in a large bowl. Pour into a greased 9x13-inch glass baking
dish. Bake at 350° for 45 minutes. Serves 12–14.

From Generation to Generation (Missouri)

Lemon Fluff

A delightful dessert.

1½ cups finely crushed
    graham cracker or vanilla
    wafer crumbs

⅓ cup chopped pecans
6 tablespoons butter

Combine vanilla wafer crumbs, pecans, and butter. Reserve ¼ cup
crumb mixture and press remainder into 10x6x1½-inch baking dish.
Chill.

FILLING:

2 (3-ounce) packages lemon
    gelatin
1¼ cups boiling water
½ cup whipped cream

1 (3¼-ounce) package
    instant lemon pudding mix
1 pint lemon sherbet
Pinch of salt

Dissolve gelatin in boiling water; cool to lukewarm. Whip cream until
soft peaks form. Set aside. Add dry pudding mix to gelatin and mix.
Add softened sherbet and beat at low speed on mixer until thick. Add
pinch of salt. Fold in cream. Turn into baking dish and sprinkle
remaining crumbs on top. Chill at least one hour. This dessert can be
made a day ahead and it keeps nicely in the refrigerator.

Company Fare II (Oklahoma)

Frozen Lemon Crunch

2 tablespoons butter
½ cup crushed cornflakes
3 tablespoons brown sugar
½ cup chopped pecans
3 egg yolks
½ cup sugar

3 tablespoons lemon juice
2 tablespoons grated lemon
  rind
3 egg whites
¼ teaspoon salt
1 cup heavy cream, whipped

Melt butter in skillet; add cornflakes, brown sugar, and pecans. Cook and stir until sugar melts and caramelizes slightly. Set aside.

In small saucepan beat egg yolks and sugar until light and foamy. Cook over low heat until thick. Add lemon juice and rind. Cool.

In large bowl, beat egg whites with salt until stiff. Fold in cooled egg yolk mixture and whipped cream. Place half of cornflakes mixture on bottom of springform pan. Pour in lemon mixture and top with remaining cornflakes mixture. Freeze a minimum of 4 hours. Serves 10.

Company's Coming (Missouri)

Praline Parfait

SAUCE:
2 cups dark corn syrup
⅓ cup sugar

⅓ cup water
2 cups chopped pecans

In medium saucepan heat all Sauce ingredients. Stir to boil. Remove from heat. Cool.

PARFAITS:
Vanilla ice cream
Whipped cream

Chopped pecans

In parfait glass alternate ice cream and Sauce, ending with Sauce. Top with whipped cream and chopped pecans.

Nibbles Cooks Cajun (Arkansas)

Frozen Chocolate Crunch

This is a delicious and impressive dessert. Can be made days in advance.

**8 ounces sweet German
  chocolate or milk chocolate**
⅓ cup light corn syrup
**2 cups whipping cream,
  divided**

**1½ cups crushed chocolate
  Oreo cookies**
**1 cup coarsely chopped
  English walnuts**

In a double boiler pan, combine chocolate and corn syrup. Stir occasionally until chocolate melts. Remove from heat. Stir in ½ cup cream until blended. Refrigerate 25–30 minutes or until cool. Stir in cookies and walnuts.

  In a small bowl, with mixer at medium speed, beat remaining 1½ cups cream until soft peaks form. Gently fold in chocolate mixture just until combined. Spread mixture into a 9-inch glass baking dish and freeze 4–6 hours or until firm. Cut into squares to serve.

Note: You can pour this mixture into 12 individual dessert dishes and freeze. You can garnish with chocolate shaves, nuts, or whipped cream, if desired. This will store, covered, in freezer for up to 1 month. Before serving, let sit at room temperature several minutes.

Shattuck Community Cookbook (Oklahoma)

Twinkie Treat

This is an easy, but delicious dessert. Your friends will think you have spent hours on this luscious treat.

**2 boxes or 24 Twinkies snack
  cakes**
1 large box strawberry Jell-O
**1 large package instant
  vanilla pudding**

1 can strawberry pie filling
**1 medium-size container
  whipped topping**
½ cup chopped pecans

Place all the Twinkies in a 9x13-inch pan (may have to squeeze them to fit). Mix Jell-O according to directions on package. Pour over Twinkies. Prepare pudding mix as directed on package. Pour over Jell-O. Spread pie filling over pudding. Top with whipped topping and sprinkle nuts over all. Chill at least 2 hours before serving. Even better to refrigerate overnight.

Centennial Cookbook (Oklahoma)

Contributing Cookbooks

Bison roam free on the 39,000-acre Tallgrass Prairie Preserve in northern Oklahoma. Once spanning portions of 14 states, the preserve is now the largest protected remnant of tallgrass prairie left on earth. As its name suggests, the most obvious features of this native North American ecosystem are tall grasses that average five- to six-feet tall.

CONTRIBUTING COOKBOOKS

Listed below are the cookbooks that have contributed recipes to this book, along with copyright, author, publisher, city, and state.

Á la Rose ©1998 by Kay Cameron, Point Lookout, MO

Above & Beyond Parsley ©1992 Junior League of Kansas City, MO

Adventures in Greek Cooking ©1982 St. Nicholas Philoptochos Society, St. Louise, MO

Applause! ©1995 Oklahoma City Orchestra League, Oklahoma City, OK

Apples, Apples, Apples ©1991 by Ann Clark, Marionville, MO

Arkansas Celebration Cookbook ©1990 by Zoe Medlin Caywood, Rogers, AR

Arkansas Favorites Cookbook ©1991 J and J Collections, Hot Springs, AR

Around the Bend, Around the Bend Arts & Crafts Assn., Marshall, AR

The Art of Hellenic Cuisine ©1988 Assumption Philoptochos Ladies Society, Town & Country, MO

Asbury United Methodist Church Cook Book, Magnolia, AR

Baked with Love ©1989 Blue Owl Restaurant & Bakery, Kimmswick, MO

Betty "Winks" at Cooking, by Betty J. Winkler, Little Rock, AR

Betty Is Still "Winking" at Cooking, by Betty J. Winkler, Little Rock, AR

Beyond Parsley ©1984 Junior League of Kansas City, MO

Blue Ridge Christian Church Cookbook, Christian Women's Fellowship, Independence, MO

The Bonneville House Presents ©1990 The Bonneville House Assn., Fort Smith, AR

Bouquet Garni ©1989 Independence Regional Health Center Aux., Independence, MO

Breakfast Ozark Style ©1986 by Kay Cameron, Point Lookout, MO

Café Oklahoma ©1994 Junior Service League of Midwest City, OK

Celebration ©1985 Sevier County, Lockesburg, AR

Centennial Cookbook, First Christian Church CWF, Seiling, OK

Clabber Creek Farm Cook Book ©1991 by Bill and Betty Rotramel, Berryville, AR

Classroom Classics, Trinity Episcopal School, Pine Bluff, AR

A Collection of Recipes from the Best Cooks in the Midwest, by Nellie Ogan, Richmond, MO

Come Grow with Us, United Methodist Women, Sayre, OK

Company Fare I & II, Presbyterian Women First Presbyterian Church, Bartlesville, OK

Company's Coming ©1988 Junior League of Kansas City, MO, Belton, MO

The Cook Book ©1979 National Council of Jewish Women, Shawnee, MO

Cookin' Along the Cotton Belt, Stephens Chamber of Commerce, Stephens, AR

Cookin' in the Spa, Hot Springs Junior Auxiliary, Hot Springs, AR

Cooking on the Road, by Montana Whitfield, Steele, MO

Cooking in Clover II ©1986 Jewish Hospital Auxiliary, St. Louis, MO

Cooking A+ Recipes, St. Mary's Catholic School, Ponca City, OK

Cooking for Applause ©1981 Repertory Theatre of St. Louis Backer Board, St. Louis, MO

Cooking for Good Measure, Hughes High School Mu Alpha Theta, Hughes, AR

Cooking to Your Heart's Content ©1990 The University of Arkansas Press, Fayetteville, AR

Country Cooking, Port Country Cousins, Sentinel, OK

Court Clerk's Bar and Grill, Tulsa County Court Clerk's Office, Tulsa, OK

Covered Bridge Neighbors Cookbook, Covered Bridge Neighbors, St. Peters, MO

Crossett Cook Book, Presidents' Council and Executive Board of Adopt-a-School, Crossett, AR

The Dairy Hollow House Cookbook ©1986 by Crescent Dragonwagon, Eureka Springs, AR

Delicious Reading, Friends of the St. Charles City/County Library, St. Peters, MO

Dine with the Angels, St. Michael's Catholic Youth, Henryetta, OK

Discover Oklahoma Cookin' © 1993 Oklahoma 4-H Foundation, Inc. Stillwater, OK

Dixie Cook Book IV & V ©1972 First Presbyterian Church, Fort Smith, AR

Eat Pie First...Life is Uncertain! ©1990
by Joan Jefferson, Freeman, MO

Eat to Your Heart's Content!, by
Woody and Betty Armour, Hot
Springs, AR

Eating Healthy in the Fast Lane
©1989 by Cindy Arsaga and
Ginny Masullo, Fayetteville, AR

Enjoying the Art of Southern Hospitality
©1990 August House Publishers,
Little Rock, AR

Evening Shade Cookbook ©1991
Evening Shade School
Foundation, Evening Shade, AR

The Farmer's Daughters ©1987 by
Flora R. Sisemore, Martha R.
Merritt and Mary R. Mayfield,
DeWitt, AR

Fat Free & Ultra Lowfat Recipes
©1995 by Doris Cross, Prima
Publishing, Rocklin, CA

Fat Free 2 ©1996 by Doris Cross,
Prima Publishing, Rocklin, CA

*Favorite Recipes from Associated
Women for Harding, Station*, Searcy,
AR

Feast in Fellowship, First United
Methodist Women, Altus, OK

Feasts of Eden ©1990 August House
Publishers, Little Rock, AR

Feeding Our Flock, Fort Supply
United Methodist Church, Fort
Supply, OK

15 Minute, Lowfat Meals, by Jayne
Benkendorf, Ludwig Publishing,
Edmond, OK

Finely Tuned Foods ©1987 Symphony
League of Kansas City, Leawood,
KS

*Four Generations of Johnson Family
Favorites*, by Ruth Johnson,
Oklahoma City, OK

From Generation to Generation ©1989
B'nai Amoona Women's League,
St. Louis, MO

From Granny, With Love ©1991 by
Pat Neaves, Kansas City, MO

From the Apple Orchard ©1984 by Lee
Jackson, Maryville, MO

From the Ozarks' Oven... ©1989
College of the Ozarks, Point
Lookout, MO

Gateways ©1990 Twigs–Friends of
St. Louis Children's Hospital, St.
Louis, MO

Gourmet Garden ©1981 Menorah
Medical Center Auxiliary, Kansas
City, MO

Gourmet Our Way ©1995 Cascia Hall
Preparatory School, Tulsa, OK

Gourmet: The Quick and Easy Way, by
Diana Allen, Enid, OK

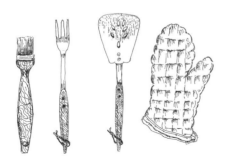

Grandma's Ozark Legacy, by Kay Cameron, Point Lookout, MO

A Great Taste of Arkansas ©1986 Southern Flavors, Inc., Pine Bluff, AR

Healthy America, by Mimi Rippee, Enid, OK

Heavenly Delights, Mothers and Daughters of Zion, Independence, MO

Helen's Southwest Specialties, by Helen L. Krause, Kellyville, OK

Here's What's Cookin' at Zion, Zion Amish Mennonite Church, Thomas, OK

High Cotton Cookin' ©1978 Marvell Academy Mothers' Assn. Marvell, AR

Home Cookin': Apple Recipes from Missouri Apple Growers, Wellington, MO

Home for the Holidays ©1991 The University of Arkansas Press, Fayetteville, AR

The Homeplace Cookbook, Homeplace, Stillwater, OK

Hooked on Fish on the Grill ©1992 Pig Out Publications, Inc., Kansas City, MO

In Good Taste ©1980 El Dorado Service League, Inc., El Dorado, AR

It's Christmas! ©1989 by Dianne Stafford Mayes and Dorothy Davenport Stafford, Carthage, MO

Kaleidoscope of Creative-Healthy-Cooking ©1990 by Janet M. Boyce, R.N., Little Rock, AR

Kansas City Cuisine ©1990 Two Lane Press, Inc., Kansas City, MO

Kitchen Prescriptions, American Academy of Family Physicians, Kansas City, MO

Kohler Family Kookbook, by the descendants of John and Margaret Watkins Kohler, Harrisonville, MO

Lavender and Lace, Arlington United Methodist Women, Bridgeton, MO

Long Lost Recipes of Aunt Susan ©1989 M-PRESS, Hot Springs Village, AR

Luncheon Favorites, The Blue Owl Restaurant & Bakery, Kimmswick, MO

Mary's Recipe Box ©1996 by Mary Gubser, Council Oak Books, Tulsa, OK

National Cowboy Hall of Fame Chuck Wagon Cookbook ©1995 by B. Byron Price, Oklahoma City, OK

The Never Ending Season, Missouri 4-H Foundation, Columbia, MO

Nibbles Cooks Cajun ©1983 by Suzie Stephens, Fayetteville, AR

Nibbles Ooo La La ©1984 by Suzie Stephens, Fayetteville, AR

The Oklahoma Celebrity Cookbook ©1991 Neighbors Executive Coffee, Oklahoma City, OK

Oklahoma Cookin' ©1995 Barnard Elementary School, Tecumseh, OK

Old and New, Abell F.C.E. Club, by Betty Abell, Guthrie, OK

100 Years of Cooking, Oologah United Methodist Church, Oologah, OK

Our Country Cookin', Junior Social Workers of Chickasha, OK

The Passion of Barbeque ©1992 The Kansas City Barbeque Society, Hyperion, New York, NY

Past & Repast ©1983 Missouri Mansion Preservation, Inc., Jefferson City, MO

Perfectly Delicious ©1990 by Cornelia Pryor Lindsey and Elinor Pryor, Little Rock, AR

The Pink Lady...in the Kitchen, Medical Center of South Arkansas Auxiliary, El Dorado, AR

The Pioneer Chef ©1991 Oklahoma Pioneers of America, Bethany, OK

Pow Wow Chow ©1984 The Five Civilized Tribes Museum, Muskogee, OK

Prairie Harvest ©1981 St. Peter's Episcopal Churchwomen, Hazen, AR

Pulaski Heights Baptist Church Cookbook, Members and Friends of the Congregation, Little Rock, AR

Quick Breads, Soups & Stews ©1991 by Mary Gubser, Council Oak Books, Tulsa, OK

Recipes and Remembrances ©1994 Northfork Electric Cooperative, Inc., Sayre, OK

Recipes from Missouri...with Love ©1980 by Sandy Buege, New Boundry Designs, Inc., Chanhassen, MN

The Route 66 Cookbook ©1993 by Marian Clark, Council Oak Books, Tulsa, OK

Rush Hour Superchef! ©1983 by Dianne Stafford Mayes and Dorothy Davenport Stafford, Carthage, MO

Sassafras! ©1985 Junior League of Springfield, MO

Seasoned with Love, Faith United Methodist Women, Woodward, OK

Seems Like I Done It This A-Way I, II, III, by Cleo Stiles Bryan, Tahlequah, OK

Shattuck Community Cookbook, Shattuck Chamber of Commerce, Shattuck, OK

The Sicilian-American Cookbook ©1990 August House, Little Rock, AR

Silver Dollar City's Recipes ©1988 Silver Dollar City, Inc., Branson, MO

Sing for Your Supper ©1989 The River Blenders, O'Fallon, MO

Sisters Two and Family Too, by Nancy Barth and Sue Hergert, Ashland, KA

Sooner Sampler ©1987 Junior League of Norman, OK

Sounds Delicious! ©1986 Volunteer Council of the Tulsa Philharmonic Society, Inc., Tulsa, OK

Southern Accent ©1976 Junior League of Pine Bluff, AR

Southern Flavors' Little Chocolate Book ©1991 Southern Flavors, Inc., Pine Bluff, AR

Southwest Cookin', Southwest Hospital Auxiliary, Little Rock, AR

Spiced with Wit ©1992 M-PRESS Hot Springs Village, AR

The Sportsman's Dish, by Jack Caraway, Hamilton, MO

Spring Creek Club, by Patty Moore, Deer Creek, OK

St. Ambrose "On the Hill" Cookbook, St. Ambrose Church, St. Louise, MO

Stir-Ups, Junior Welfare League of Enid, OK

Sunday Go To Eatin' Cook Book ©1988 by Nita Sappington, Decatur, AR

Take It to Heart ©1989 Stanley E. Evans Heart Institute of AR, Fort Smith, AR

Talk About Good, Forsyth Library Friends, Forsyth, MO

Thank Heaven for Home Made Cooks, Dover Christian Women's Fellowship, Dover, OK

Thirty Years at the Mansion ©1985 August House Publishers, Little Rock, AR

Thunderbird Cookers of AT&T ©1986 Telephone Pioneers-Thunderbird Chapter 94, Oklahoma City, OK

Treasured Recipes Book I & II, Tanneyhills Library Club, Branson, MO

United Methodist Cookbook 1993, United Methodist Women, Elk City, OK

USO's Salute to the Troops Cookbook, James S. McDonnell USO, St. Louis, MO

Victorian Sampler ©1986 by Ruth & Jim Spears, Eureka Springs, AR

Wanda's Favorite Recipes Book, by Wanda Brown, Cass Medical Center Foundation, Harrisonville, MO

War Eagle Mill Wholegrain and Honey Cookbook ©1986 by Zoe Medlin Caywood, Rogers, AR

Watonga Cheese Festival Cookbook 17th Edition, Watonga Cheese Festival, Watonga, OK

What's Cooking in Okarche?, Apron Annies F. C. E., Okarche, OK

When a Man's Fancy Turns to Cooking ©1996 by G. Wesley Rice, PecanQuest Publications, Ponca City, OK

With Hands & Heart Cookbook ©1990 Bethesda Hospital, St. Louis, MO

The Wonderful World of Honey ©1977 by Joe M. Parkhill, Berryville, AR

Index

Led by Meriwether Lewis and William Clark, the Corps of Discovery departed from St. Charles, Missouri, on May 21, 1804. The expedition laid much of the groundwork for the westward expansion of the United States. A monument to the men and their dog, Seaman, stands in Frontier Park. Replicas of a keelboat and pirogues used in the expedition can be seen at the nearby Boathouse and Nature Center.

INDEX